Deborah Kellaway was born in Australia. She came to Oxford in the late 1940s to read English, and spent the rest of her working life teaching English Literature, first at Melbourne University, later at Camden School for Girls in North London. Gardening took firm hold after she and her husband bought a thatched cottage in Norfolk where they created an ambitious garden from a rough field. After twenty years of toiling she wrote a book about it – *The Making of an English Country Garden* (1988). She has been writing about gardens and flowers ever since. Her latest books are about a family of flowers: *Clematis and the Ranuculaceae* (1994), and about the flower paintings of Elizabeth Blackadder – *Favourite Flowers* (1994). Deborah Kellaway lives in London and Norfolk.

THE VIRAGO BOOK OF

WOMEN GARDENERS

EDITED BY
DEBORAH KELLAWAY

A *Virago* Book

Published by VIRAGO PRESS 1996

First published in hardback by VIRAGO PRESS 1995

A CIP catalogue record for this book
is available from the British Library.

ISBN 1 86049 153 7

Printed in England by Clays Ltd, St Ives plc

Companies, institutions and other organizations wishing
to make bulk purchases of this or any other books
published by Little, Brown, should contact their local
bookshop or the special sales department at the address below.
Tel 0171 911 8000. Fax 0171 911 8100.

Virago
A Division of
Little, Brown and Company (UK)
Brettenham House
Lancaster Place
London WC2E 7EN

to
Ruth Petrie
who set me to work

Contents

Introduction

YOU CANNOT make an anthology out of women gardeners unless they sometimes lay down the trowel and take up the pen. So, strictly speaking, this is a collection of women garden *writers*, though most of them have spent hours – years – planting and weeding as well. One or two of them are simply observers. In the seventeenth century Celia Fiennes rode on horseback through England and described any garden that she thought remarkable as she went along. In the eighteenth century Lady Luxborough looked critically at her own newly-acquired garden and wrote letters to William Shenstone about its proposed improvement. But it would not have occurred to her to handle garden tools herself, let alone to write a book about her garden; she was born at least a century too soon. It is significant that most of the entries in this anthology were written within the last hundred years.

The final decade of the nineteenth century had arrived when the Hon. Alicia Amherst undertook to finish a small book on garden history that someone else (a young botanist called Percy Newberry) had begun. She was a highly intelligent, industrious and well-read young woman of twenty-four; she understood Latin and could read fourteenth-century handwriting; her father had a large library of rare herbals and early garden books which she had loved and absorbed since childhood. She warmed to her task and soon began scouring early monastic accounts of Norwich Priory and manuscripts held in the library of Trinity College, Cambridge. She finished the book, re-wrote Percy Newberry's beginning and composed an apologetic preface. *A History of Gardening in England* by Alicia Amherst duly appeared in 1895.

Her own narrative voice was unobtrusive and relied heavily on well-researched quotations from the works of others: Gerard, Parkinson, Lyte, Bacon, Evelyn, Gilpin, Bridgeman, Capability Brown, Repton, Shirley Hibberd and Robinson. Her authors were all men, for the good reason that before 1895 no important garden manuals had been written by women. True, Mrs Horatia Ewing had published *Letters from a Little Garden* in 1886, in which she pleaded the superiority of natural hardy plants over the artificiality of carpet-bedding. But she was a children's author, and was guiding her young readers not only in gardening but in moral behaviour: though you should not have carpet-bedding in your own garden, you should not be beastly about other people's unfortunate gardening taste. Perhaps Alicia Amherst thought this sort of thing did not quite belong in her *History*; nor did she mention the apparently insignificant fact that two women, Frances Hope and the Hon. Mrs E. V. Boyle, had recently become contributors to the newly launched *Gardeners' Chronicle*. She only names one woman gardener in her *History*: she is Mrs Jane Loudon, the clever and devoted wife of the horticultural journalist, John Claudius Loudon, herself a professional writer who switched from horror novels to horticulture under the influence of her husband and, when he died in 1843, continued to edit his *Gardener's Magazine* as well as writing a series of books on gardening for 'Ladies'. Yet it was from John Loudon, not Jane, that Alicia Amherst quoted. The only other women to feature in her history were queens for whom kings made gardens, Celia Fiennes, and Gertrude Jekyll – named in a footnote to the caption of the last photograph in the book.

Apart from her own shining example, Alicia Amherst's book did little to displace women from the plinths where, in literature, men had habitually placed them; they were garden icons, decorative ornaments seen along grassy walks on summer evenings, with whom men fell in love as they stooped to touch the flowers. But the year 1895 is a watershed. In the same year that *A History of Gardening in England* was published, a wealthy young American woman, Beatrix Farrand, set up her first office as a garden designer at the top of her parents' New York house. Two years later, three other women were sitting down to write books about gardening: two of them in Surrey, one in Pomerania, and all of them destined to be stars.

The Pomeranian author was Elizabeth von Arnim, who was thirty-one in 1897, and found herself enraptured by the grounds of her husband's vast estate. She bought every gardening book she saw reviewed and soon embarked on writing one herself. She presented herself as an enthusiastic ignoramus, an impetuous chooser of plants who had to watch while incompetent employees planted them. Her themes were infatuation with natural beauty, a romantic desire to be left alone in her garden undisturbed by household duties, and frustration at having to employ gardeners instead of being allowed to work in the soil herself:

> I sometimes literally ache with envy as I watch the men going about their pleasant work in the sunshine, turning up the luscious damp earth, raking, weeding, watering, planting, cutting the grass, pruning the trees – not a thing that they do from the first uncovering of the roses in the spring to the November bonfires but fills my soul with longing to be up and doing too.

Elizabeth and her German Garden was published by Macmillan in 1898 and proved an instant and sensational bestseller. Its sequel, *The Solitary Summer*, followed in 1899 and the mysteriously anonymous 'Elizabeth' was famous.

So, too, was the very unmysterious Mrs Theresa Earle, author of another runaway bestseller, *Pot Pourri from a Surrey Garden*, which she published in 1897 despite the fact that her husband is said to have offered her a hundred pounds *not* to publish it. It was so popular that it ran into eleven reprints in the first year. At the age of sixty-one Mrs Earle found herself, like Elizabeth, seduced by the ease with which she could turn out winners. She wrote *More Pot Pourri*, *A Third Pot Pourri*, and *Pot Pourri Mixed by Two*. Together her books were rumoured to have made her publishers, Smith Elder and Co., £30,000.

The pot pourris were not sweet-scented, petal-strewn effusions. They were, literally, mixtures. Mrs Earle felt herself free to write about anything on which she had views. She was deeply interested in gardening and knowledgeable about it; the visual world was important to her. She had attended the South Kensington School of Art as a girl and was confident in her own taste. She could break off her gardening advice at will to give her views on the Italian painting she had just seen in Oxford, or in Florence. But beyond the aesthetic, she had robust opinions on politics and social problems; her sympathies were with women (her niece, Lady Constance Lyttleton, became a famous sufragette) but she urged them to improve themselves:

> I cannot explain too much that the object of my book is to try to make everyone think for him or herself, and at the same time to profit by the instruction which in these days is so easy to get, and is all around us. Women are still behind the other sex in the power

of thinking at all, much more so in the power of thinking of several things at once. I hope the coming women may see the great advantage of training their minds early in life to be a practical denial of Swift's cynical assertion that mankind are as unfit for flying as for thinking. Nothing can be done well without thought – certainly not gardening.

Mrs Earle helpfully lists the gardening books on her own shelves and gives Alicia Amherst an accolade:

This is by far the most interesting and remarkable book that, I believe, has ever been written on the subject, and far surpasses in every way Mr. Johnson's 'History of Gardening' . . . The book is full of information, drawn from patient and most diligent research, and will be of real utility to students of the literature and history of gardening and to the owners of large places. It contains little that will practically help people who live in cottages and small villas.

Mrs Loudon is likewise commended for the clarity and simplicity of her expositions, though marked down for 'that early Victorian taste now thought so execrable'. She also reviews the book of a Surrey neighbour:

I feel sure that all Miss Jekyll's books will be referred to again and again long after the mass of present garden literature is of no more value than autumn leaves.

Miss Jekyll was, of course, the third woman who sat down to write a gardening book in the last years of the nineteenth century. *Wood and Garden* was published in 1899 when she was fifty-six years old. It was recognised by the gardening *cognoscenti* as important: a distinctive, authoritative voice was speaking, but it did not, at first, follow the sensational success of the other two books. It went into a mere six imprints in its first year. Elizabeth and Mrs Earle were women who clearly enjoyed writing even more than they enjoyed gardening; they were communicators and each, in her own way, had style and charm and the gift of establishing a bond with her readers. Mrs Earle was a clear-headed adviser working through an unusual combination of imagination and common sense. Elizabeth was more light-weight, but a flatteringly frank and amusing confidante.

Miss Jekyll did not set out to humour her readers. Rather she seemed to assume that they had got the wrong end of the stick and should be helped to get things right. She was a born teacher but her interest was less in her readers than in her subject: her vision of garden beauty. She was single-minded, highly gifted, deeply creative, and she had something new and important to say. The good gardener, she argued, is an artist, the garden a three-dimensional picture which must be 'right' from all points, and in all lights:

> For planting ground is painting a landscape with living things and I hold that good gardening takes rank within the bounds of the fine arts, so I hold that to plant well needs an artist of no mean capacity. (*Wood and Garden*)

Gertrude Jekyll herself was an artist, a phenomenon, a dumpy little woman who towers over the other garden writers of the twentieth century. So great was her energy that, according to her biographer, Sally Festing, she wrote ten books in nine years, fifteen full length books altogether, and a total of two thousand articles for periodicals. She took her own garden photographs and processed them herself. Unsurprisingly, her writing is uneven: sometimes graceful and polished, sometimes pedestrian, but always effortlessly trenchant and unselfconscious. Though her eyesight was notoriously weak, she had a capacity for detailed, concentrated observation which enabled her to distinguish between the different sorts of white on the bark of a birch stem in winter, or to liken the scent of a lupin to 'very good and delicate pepper'.

But she was by no means an armchair gardener. She loved her tools and knew how to use them. She is holding her spade in the jacket photograph of Sally Festing's biography. In her *Children and Gardens* she explains to her young readers how to rake and weed. If she needed a tool for a particular garden job and no such implement was to be had, she made it herself, for she was a skilled metal worker as well as silversmith, gilder, embroiderer and painter (having trained at the same South Kensington School of Art as Mrs Earle). When she decided that the flower vases of her day came in unsatisfactory shapes, she designed satisfactory ones – 'Munstead glasses'. She describes herself in middle age sitting on a stool in her primrose garden in late spring and supervising her gardeners in the division and replanting of the primrose crowns. They brought them to her and she did the dividing herself with a swift blow from a plasterer's hammer, her 'rubber' in a bucket beside her, ready to sharpen her blade. And besides all this she designed, or advised on, about one hundred and fifty gardens for other people, sometimes supplying the recommended plants from her own nursery stock (cheaper that way, she would tell them) and often giving her advice by post. She did not like leaving her garden.

And yet, though she had strong opinions on everything (her voice is dominant in almost every section of this anthology) Gertrude Jekyll had no inflated opinion of herself; she assumed that her friend, Ellen Willmott, was her superior in the art of gardening. In her *Children and Gardens*, Jekyll included the photograph of a woman in front of a thatched cottage deep in vegetation, with the fanciful caption:

> The pretty lady in this picture is a German Princess. She has brought out her work to the old play-house, and is trying to think of herself as a child again. The picture was done by my friend Miss Willmott, the greatest of living women gardeners.

The 'pretty lady' was in fact Elizabeth von Arnim, in a pale dress and a wide hat. Ellen Willmott had travelled to Pomerania to meet her and take her photograph for she, like Miss Jekyll, was an enthusiastic photographer with a large plate camera and her own darkroom (as well as her own workshop for she was also a worker in wood and metal, uncannily like Miss Jekyll, besotted with tools). Her first book was called *Warley Place in Spring and Summer* and was composed entirely of her photographs, black and white pictures of a ravishing paradise garden with paths winding amongst plants, undulating glades, a flower-dotted orchard, a luscious lily pool. Gertrude Jekyll was perhaps half right: Miss Willmott was, if not the greatest of women gardeners, the greatest plantswoman of her day. Most enthusiastic gardeners today are still likely to grow a plant with 'Willmottiae' or 'Warleysii' in its name. But she was not a natural writer; in her spare time she would rather sing or play the violin. Her monumental work, *The Genus Rosa*, was almost stillborn, over-ambitious and under-researched; its long gestation period a publisher's nightmare. Ellen Willmott was too rich, by turns wildly extravagant and eccentrically mean, impossibly selfish and quite unreal in her dealings with other people. Not satisfied with fifty acres in Essex, she bought a château in France and a villa on the Italian Riviera and made inspired gardens in each of them. When she was at home in England, she rose early, donned her sabots and apron and went out to weed (though she is said to have employed over eighty gardeners). And when she was away in Italy or France she persecuted her head gardeners by requiring them to report repeatedly and in detail on everything that was happening in their bit of the garden (see *Miss Willmott of Warley Place* by Audrey le Lièvre). In the end, she overspent herself and became an almost tragic figure, living alone in a huge, cold, empty house with an under-staffed garden reproaching her from beyond the windows, where once not a single weed had been allowed to grow.

As early as 1897 Ellen Willmott and Gertrude Jekyll were both awarded the Royal Horticultural Society's prestigious Victoria Medal of Honour, the first women ever to win it. Typically, Miss Willmott was absent – abroad – when the medals were conferred, but reliable Miss Jekyll was there to represent both of them.

A few years later, in 1902, their names were linked again, along with Mrs Earle's, as patrons of the young Viscountess Wolseley's new Glynde School for Lady Gardeners. Frances Wolseley was a viscountess in her own right, the daughter of a Field Marshall in the Boer War. A diminutive figure with great drive and conviction, she wanted the young gentlewomen of her acquaintance to show more 'grit'. She ran her school rather like an army battalion: the students' uniforms must be immaculate, they must rise early, there must be absolute obedience to rules; good behaviour was rewarded with medals.

> I feel sure that much of the difficulty we have had up to now in introducing garden craft as a profession for women has been, as it still is, that we do not get the right women. If only the daughters of country squires, Army and Navy men and others, many of whom have but limited income and are obliged to earn their living, would come to us for a training, good remuneration in an intensely interesting life would be theirs after two years of study.

Miss Willmott took a cynical view of all this and discredited the lady gardeners who came her way. Miss Jekyll made a point of employing them; and, in theory at least, Mrs Earle must whole-heartedly have approved the venture, having declared, in her first book:

> It is extraordinary, the objection there still seems to be, especially in the suburbs, against women doing the work in the garden.

In fact, garden training had been available to women since 1891, when Swanley Horticultural College began to admit women students. But in the early years of this century the Glynde college attracted wide attention; soon its students were being offered posts even before they had finished the two-year course. Frances Wolseley campaigned for fair pay for women, for the revival of rural industries, for agricultural reform. She was a crusader. After a few years of intensive teaching and lecturing, she felt able to leave the everyday running of her college to a deputy and settle down to write books: books about the college, books about agriculture, and finally, in 1919, her book about gardening, *Gardens, Their Form and Design*.

Frances Wolseley, Ellen Willmott and Gertrude Jekyll were Edwardians, daughters of the Arts and Crafts Movement, unmarried women from upper-class backgrounds who put their exceptional energies, their hearts, minds and souls into their obsession. But they far outlived the Edwardian age. Gertrude Jekyll's work was still a dominant force in the 1920's and when she died Beatrix Farrand bought at auction all her papers, her notes and drawings, and took them across the Atlantic where they are now housed in the University of California at Berkeley. (Jekyll had been an acknowledged influence in North America as early as 1901, when another Mrs Earle, Alice Morse, referred wryly to her strictures on colour in a book called *Old Time Gardens*, and Mrs Helena Rutherfurd Ely popularised the mixed border of hardy perennial plants in *A Woman's Hardy Garden*, 1903.) Miss Jekyll died in 1933. Ellen Willmott stood by her moss-lined grave as the gardeners filled it with earth; a year later, she herself was gone, dropping dead one morning in her bedroom. In the following year, Frances Wolseley died too, at the relatively young age of sixty-two.

But other gardening women were beginning to publish in the first decades of the twentieth century. Each had one book to write: the story of her own garden. Ever since the example of Elizabeth and Mrs Earle had made such books seem possible they were eagerly taking the chance, and there is a sense of the release of pent-up passion felt almost simultaneously in England (*A Garden in the Suburbs*, Mrs Leslie Williams, 1901; *An Artist's Garden*, Anna Lea Merritt, 1908) in the United States (*The Garden of a Commuter's Wife*, Barbara Campbell, 1911) and in India (*My Garden in the Wilderness*, Kathleen Murray, 1913). The authors were largely unknown and at least one of them wanted to remain so – below the title of Barbara Campbell's book came the simple words: '*by a*

Gardener'. Opinionated yet humble, they share an underlying happiness; they describe the satisfaction they feel after a day of weeding, or digging, and they all make plans for the future. Some of them have literary aspirations; they tend to intersperse their observations with quotations from the poets.

Though they have no pretentions to speak for anybody but themselves, they turn out to have surprisingly similar tastes, and even more surprisingly, they are largely the tastes that are still expressed freshly today. They don't like the regimentation of plants in rows; they like herbaceous perennials planted in groups; they enjoy the challenge of vivid colour; they want their plants to cover the ground; they don't want the soil to show. They ask for all-the-year-round planting, they like wild gardens, and they have a sense of appropriate style: they want their gardens to suit their surroundings.

World War One silenced their voices, but when the twenties came there were two clever and prolific professional garden writers on the scene – Marion Cran and Eleanour Sinclair Rohde. These two journalists neatly illustrate the two poles of garden writers: the poets and the pedagogues. Mrs Cran aspired towards poetry – emotional, confessional, impressionistic, sometimes embarrassing but compulsively readable. She was a traveller, an early broadcaster, with the sort of energy that made it hard for her to stop writing books. She lived with her daughters in an untidy and sandy woodland garden in Surrey, and flowers were named after her.

Eleanour Sinclair Rohde was a tireless researcher, a scholarly pedagogue with a moralising turn of mind, who taught her readers about herbs and vegetables and diet, and the early garden saints, and Shakespeare's wild flowers, and indeed the whole history of gardening. She started writing books from her parents' house in Reigate in the twenties, and she was still there, writing *The War-Time Vegetable Garden* in 1940.

Meanwhile, during the thirties, various grand and gifted ladies made beautiful and important gardens: Sybil Burnet at Craithes Castle, Heather Muir at Kiftsgate, Phyllis Reiss at Tintinhull, Dorothy Elmhirst – guided by Beatrix Farrand – at Dartington Hall, Norah Lindsay at Blickling and Trent Park, but they did not write books about what they were doing. Norah Lindsay, in particular, who had begun to work on her own garden at Sutton Courtney as a young bride in 1893, was a charismatic presence rather than a recorded voice. Only once did she write an account of her garden, published in *Country Life* in 1931. Her other writing consisted of ephemeral, pencilled notes and plant lists left behind after whirlwind consultative visits to the great houses and gardens of the day. The urge to write and the urge to garden do not necessarily go hand in hand.

But since World War Two a gardening/writing phenomenon has been taking place. Perhaps it started with Vita Sackville-West in the early fifties. After her achievement in turning the flat, ruined fields around Sissinghurst Castle into one of the loveliest gardens in England she began to write a weekly column in the *Observer*, disarmingly modest but also poetic. One Sunday morning in 1956 she reviewed a book:

> It is a book written by a woman who, with her husband, created out of nothing the sort of garden we should all like to have, a cottage garden on a slightly larger scale . . . I defy any amateur gardener not to find pleasure, encouragement and profit from *We Made a Garden*, by Margery Fish.

Mrs Fish was famous, and she deserved to be. Behind the unpretentious, practical tone of her book lay a deep commitment and degree of knowledge that was to change the sort of plants that people grew. Then, in the sixties, Beth Chatto made a garden around her new house in Essex. Soon she started a nursery and began to write books about what she was doing. Though she, too, wrote in a friendly and unassuming tone, she had the authority and depth of knowledge of a true professional and the eye of an artist.

These were strong new voices, one looking back to half-forgotten cottage flowers of the past, the other looking forward with a modern ecological awareness that seldom spoke of a plant in isolation from the place where it should grow. And everywhere, the increasing crowds of gardeners who read them were inspired to fill their gardens full, and to fill them differently, to value leaves as well as flowers, and to do what Mrs Earle had urged in 1897: to *think* about their gardens.

From then on, there was no stopping the writing of gardening books and the reading of them. Rosemary Verey and Alvilde Lees-Milne, themselves celebrated gardeners, persuaded thirty-five upper-crust owners of deliciously photogenic gardens to describe their endeavours in *The Englishwoman's Garden*, 1980, and again, in answer to steady sales, twenty-eight more in *The New Englishwoman's Garden*, 1987. But the enthusiasm crossed all class divides; the Royal Horticultural Society published articles in its magazine about the garden made by a level crossing keeper's wife on an untidy bit of ground along the Cambridge-London railway line, and another by a woman who lived in a London council flat and made a windy garden on the flat roof of a tower block twenty-three floors above the ground. There was interest in everything to do with gardening, and women were writing books to meet every need: books on planting, books on planning, books on colour, books on town gardens, on cottage gardens, on water gardens, on dry gardens and, increasingly, books that look back nostalgically to the gardens of the past. Alicia Amherst's ground was being traversed again.

Alicia Amherst finished her *History* by looking forward confidently to the future. She believed that 'this is an age of progress in gardening', and she was right. In the hundred years since 1895, gardening has had its greatest century, and if she had been writing her book in 1995, women would have stood beside the men in her series of quotations, just as they now stand beside them in the gardening columns of the press and on the gardening shelves of bookshops.

Yet the tempting generalisations do not work. Women are not better gardeners than men, though Frances Wolseley thought they were. Nor are they more sensitive to plant combinations, nor yet less sensitive to design. (Brenda Colvin and Sylvia Crowe, each originally a student at Swanley Horticultural College, are two of the most renowned landscape architects of twentieth-century Britain.) There is no one sort of woman who takes to gardening, nor any one age-group to which they all belong. Though Mrs Earle declared that 'the maintaining of a garden and the tending of a greenhouse is work particularly suited to women of a certain age', not all women wait until their children are grown-up before flinging themselves into the garden; some young women find strenuous gardening a refreshing respite from clamouring children. The only generalisation to emerge from this anthology is that, before 1895, few women *wrote* much about gardens (except in novels) and now, a hundred years later, many do.

How much they actually *gardened* before 1895 is another matter. It partly depends on what you mean by gardening. If you mean caring about the garden, walking in it and taking an interest in the plants, then women have been gardeners since Roman times. Medieval women were expected to concern themselves with flowers and with the harvesting of herbs. By the sixteenth and seventeenth centuries, men were writing simple instruction books for them, guiding them in their responsibilities.

But, of course, in the end it all depended on how rich they were. The well-off had gardeners to do the work for them, and their worrisome duty was to supervise stubborn gardeners. Though Georgian and Victorian ladies may have snipped and dead-headed in their gardens and tended the 'stove-plants', their hobby was likely to be botany rather than horticulture, and botanic art was an approved accomplishment. The Victorian artist Marianne North, rich and adventurous, packed up her paints and travelled all over the world to record exotic plants. Anne Pratt, a well-to-do whole-sale grocer's daughter, stayed at home and produced an ambitious three volumed work called *The Flowering Plants, Grasses, Sedges and Ferns of Great Britain* (1889) with her own water-colour illustrations.

Less well-off gentlewomen, like Dorothy Wordsworth at Grasmere, watered, hoed and sometimes sowed a row of beans. Clearly, by the mid-nineteenth century there was a large readership of women who could not afford a gardener and were eager for the practical gardening advice which Mrs Loudon's books set out to give.

And what about the really poor? They had no gardens, but they had always gardened. In the early middle ages they were there with their baskets, working in other people's flower-beds for a few pence a year. In the seventeenth century Celia Fiennes marvelled at an effigy of one of them in the gardens of Woburn Abbey. They were still there in the nineteenth century, and Mrs Ewing describes a certain woman in a hood, remembered from her childhood: 'She is not very old but she looks so, because she has lost her teeth, and is bent nearly double.' She was bent double because she spent her working life stooped over the soil. She was, simply, a 'weeder woman'.

This anthology is divided, for convenience, into ten different topics, and begins with weeders. But when a particular writer appears in a particular section, it does not mean that she herself is being typified, only that the chosen extract from her work fits best there. The book aims to be useful, to inspire or amuse. But another editor, even given these three aims, might well have made an entirely different selection. A decision was taken at the outset to resist the vivid, imagined gardens of fiction and stick to fact, that is, to an author's first-hand experience, but a few poems have been included – in particular those of Molly Holden, who gardened until multiple sclerosis overtook her, and thereafter watched her garden from her wheelchair, eager 'to put down truly . . . the small cold characters of plants'.

And there are two exceptions to the ban on fiction: Ruth Draper's impression of a lady showing her garden to a visitor may have been imaginary, but garden owners know it to be true; and Frances Hodgson Burnett's *The Secret Garden* must have given countless readers their first taste of the joy that weeding choked plants can bring, and so it supplies the very first extract in this book.

Note: the date at the end of each entry is a key to the work cited. For the full list of books and articles, see page 247. In the following ten chapters writers are referred to by the names they use or used professionally. For the full names with titles, see *Biographical Notes*.

WEEDERS AND DIGGERS

'She did not know anything about gardening . . .'

'I WONDER if they are all quite dead,' she said. 'Is it all a quite dead garden? I wish it wasn't.'

If she had been Ben Weatherstaff she could have told whether the wood was alive by looking at it, but she could only see that there were only grey or brown sprays and branches and none showed any signs of even a tiny leaf-bud anywhere.

But she was *inside* the wonderful garden and she could come through the door under the ivy any time, and she felt as if she had found a world all her own.

The sun was shining inside the four walls and the high arch of blue sky over this particular piece of Misselthwaite seemed even more brilliant and soft than it was over the moor. The robin flew down from his tree-top and hopped about or flew after her from one bush to another. He chirped a good deal and had a very busy air, as if he were showing her things. Everything was strange and silent and she seemed to be hundreds of miles away from any one, but somehow she did not feel lonely at all. All that troubled her was her wish that she knew whether all the roses were dead, or if perhaps some of them had lived and might put out leaves and buds as the weather got warmer. She did not want it to be a quite dead garden. If it were a quite alive garden, how wonderful it would be, and what thousands of roses would grow on every side!

Her skipping-rope had hung over her arm when she came in, and after she had walked about for a while she thought she would skip round the whole garden, stopping when she wanted to look at things. There seemed to have been grass paths here and there, and in one or two corners there were alcoves of evergreen with stone seats or tall moss-covered flower urns in them.

As she came near the second of these alcoves she stopped skipping. There had once been a flower-bed in it, and she thought she saw something sticking out of the black earth – some sharp little pale green points. She remembered what Ben Weatherstaff had said and she knelt down to look at them.

'Yes, they are tiny growing things and they *might* be crocuses or snowdrops or daffodils,' she whispered.

She bent very close to them and sniffed the fresh scent of the damp earth. She liked it very much.

'Perhaps there are some other ones coming up in other places,' she said. 'I will go all over the garden and look.'

She did not skip, but walked. She went slowly and kept her eyes on the ground. She looked in the old border beds and among the grass, and after she had gone round, trying to miss nothing, she had found ever so many more sharp, pale green points, and she had become quite excited again.

'It isn't a quite dead garden,' she cried out softly to herself. 'Even if the roses are dead, there are other things alive.'

She did not know anything about gardening, but the grass seemed so thick in some of the places where the green points were pushing their way through that she thought they did not seem to have room enough to grow. She searched about until she found a rather sharp piece of wood and knelt down and dug and weeded out the weeds and grass until she made nice little clear places around them.

'Now they look as if they could breathe,' she said, after she had finished with the first ones. 'I am going to do ever so many more. I'll do all I can see. If I haven't time to-day I can come tomorrow.'

Frances Hodgson Burnett, 1911

... perhaps the chiefest attraction of a garden is that occupation can always be found there. No idle people are happy, but with mind and fingers busy cares are soonest forgotten.

Alicia Amherst, 1902

Weeding for children

By the time March comes you should look out for weeds. Of course you must learn to know your weeds, just as you must learn to know your flowers, and you must know them, too, in quite a young state. Like garden flowers, weeds are either annual, biennial, or perennial. The word 'annual', applied to a plant, means one whose whole lifetime is begun and finished within one year. Biennial means one that grows one year and flowers the next, like Sweetwilliam and Foxglove and Canterbury Bell. Perennials are the plants that will go on for ever if they are divided every few years. Some are the better for being divided every year. These are the ones whose roots spread out quickly, like Michaelmas Daisies and some of the Sunflowers. Any of you who have learnt a little Latin will see from the word itself what annual, biennial, and perennial mean; and will see that the words themselves describe, as I have just done, the length of the plant's lifetime. Those who have not learnt Latin must take my word for it . . .

There are three troublesome weeds, one annual, the others perennial, that show quite early in spring. They are up in February, though, if you don't want to do much gardening in February, it will not matter if you don't look out for them till March. They are a little Cress, Dock, and Dandelion; we will take the Cress first. The little plants come up early and look neat and harmless. It is the Hairy Bitter Cress. The botanical name is *Cardamine hirsuta* – hirsuta means hairy. You think the plant is quite smooth; but if you look at the full-grown leaf quite close you will see tiny hairs upon the surface and at the edges . . .

In March it comes into flower, and then is the time to look out for it, unless you have trained your eyes to see it sooner. But it shows up brightly when the little flower is out. You must not miss a single one, for this is what happens. Directly the flower is over the stem elongates; each seed-pod lengthens, and the little seeds inside swell and ripen . . .

Then look out! for as soon as the seed is quite ripe, at the least touch the outer covering of the long pod curls itself up and acts like a catapult, scattering the seeds about quite a long way and filling the garden again with weed-seeds. And you must remember that this crafty little plant has a sly trick of turning a dark bronzy colour that makes it difficult to see. But if you are careful, and get hold of it when it is full-grown, but has not yet thrown up the flower-stem, you can have a glorious revenge. You know the old story of some savage tribes who kill and eat their enemies, and who believe that when they have swallowed some doughty warrior they become imbued with his best qualities. You can do the same with *Cardamine hirsuta*. You pull it up and cut off the little root, and, if it is not perfectly clean you wash it, and dry it in a clean cloth, and you eat it for nursery tea. Put between two bits of bread and butter it is delicious; just as good as Watercress. And if it transmits to you its fine quality of perseverance, why, you will be none the worse.

The other worst early weed is Dandelion. It is a perennial. There can be no doubt about that when you look at its root . . . And it is no use just to pull off the top. When you are weeding you should always use a little blunt knife; there is a good sort of short strong knife with a smooth horn handle that costs sevenpence. It should be one of your regular tools. If you cannot get the Dandelion root right up you should scratch away some of the top soil and cut the root as far down as you can reach with the blade of the knife.

Gertrude Jekyll, 1908

Dandelions

What a wealth to country children are the dandelions with their hollow stalks, linked into chains day after day, with untiring eagerness, and with the white downy balls,

'The schoolboy's clock in every town,'

which come as the flowers fall away, and which sometimes whiten the meadow by their profusion, till a strong gust arises, and scatters them far and wide! Away they float, each white plume bearing onwards the seed at its base, so beautifully balanced, that its motion is most graceful, and its destined place in the soil most surely reached.

Anne Pratt, 1889

Weeding for gardeners

Weeds have a peculiar fascination for us. They are endlessly interesting, like an enemy who occupies our thoughts and schemes so much more than any friend and who (though we would never admit it) we should miss if he suddenly moved away. I know the weeds in my garden better than most of my flowers and, without them, my victories would be insipid affairs. Weeds provide the challenge that most gardeners require. They may sometimes appear to us as ineradicable as Original Sin, but we would be sorry to have to admit that, like sin, we were not conscious of a strong urge to overcome them.

I can find it in me even to enjoy the first weeds of the year. By that I do not just mean eating dandelion leaves in spring salads but, with the soil moist and friable, the ease with which weeds may be removed from flowerbeds. Even the thick creamy roots of ground elder please me for they have not been cemented into the baked summer earth, from which they must be prised by careful fork-work. Nor, in the spring, is there the disappointment that comes later in the summer when I feel the bitter-cress shooting out its seed as I brush against it. In the spring, I still feel confident that I will conquer them *this* year.

They come in an unalterable, even decorous, procession, like a formal dance measure of long ago. First the speedwell in its long trails; the goosegrass, whorled and easy to remove while it is not too sticky; the ground elder with its fresh-green palmate leaves; the hairy bitter cress and the nettles. There is the constant background theme of shepherd's purse and groundsel which, in mild winters, never seem to cease growing. Later, in late April, the first leaves of bindweed will make their entrance, usually after the first mulch is applied so that it can grow unseen and unchecked for some time. As speedwell is the spring's weed, so sowthistle belongs to the early summer; even half an hour's pleasant labour in June will yield a barrow-load of weeds.

How well we know weeds. Even in childhood, some hard-pressed grown-up, jealous of our idleness on summer days, may send us out to weed the path with a broken kitchen-knife. Throughout our lives they are a recurring theme and, in old age, their rankness mocks our failing powers. Even the convinced wild-flower gardener has little time for weeds, and wishes to pretend that wild flowers are pretty and timid like ragged robin and cowslip, not strapping and aggressive like creeping buttercup or ground elder.

No one who calls himself a gardener, or who would wish to do so, can avoid weeding. It is best to enjoy it, for it is a constant which will never go away, unless the scientists invent the infallible, toxic only to weeds, selective weedkiller. Most people grow to savour the way they have to slow down their pace to weed and the freedom it gives for untrammelled reflection. All that is only possible, however, if we feel we are ultimately getting somewhere rather than desperately fighting against stacked odds.

Fortunately there are ways of making weeding more enjoyable. I allot myself a small area, smaller than I am likely to have the energy for, and stake it out in my mind's eye. I have learned not to go out imagining that, if the weather holds, I shall have the whole garden 'done' by teatime. I choose, if I can, that part of the garden in the sun, especially in the late winter when I need to feel the warmth of it on my back. I take out a trug basket and a 'donkey', the one for perennial and flowering or seeding annual weeds, the other for leafy annual weeds. I must say, with all the authority that I can muster, that putting perennial weeds on a compost heap is like sowing tares deliberately amongst wheat. The heat of the compost heap will never kill those roots so they must be burned on the fireheap or incinerator. I get pleasure from such perfectionism although I have been known, in a fit of absent-mindedness, to throw the string, secateurs, knife, and all the other contents of the trug onto the fireheap as well. A bucket will do equally as well as a trug.

That is all very well but how does one know a perennial weed from an annual weed? After all, are there not two sorts of nettle, annual and perennial? (There are indeed: *Urtica urens* and *Urtica dioica*.) Broadly speaking, you can tell from the roots, until you learn to know your weeds as well as your own children. Annual weeds have no well-developed root systems, whereas the perennial nightmares, like ground elder, couch grass, creeping buttercup, bindweed and nettle, do have good roots because they must survive through a succession of winters. Nettle roots are thin, stringy, yellow and tear quite easily; those of ground elder are thick, fleshy, off-white and hairy and they lie not far below the surface so can be got at by digging; those of bindweed are grey-white and tubular, grow both along and down towards the earth's core and snap with distressing ease; couch grass has white 'stolons' with pointed tips; the perennial sowthistle grows enormously fast, plump and juicy. If the earth is mercifully damp after some soft refreshing rain, the sowthistle can be drawn up easily, cleanly, and without the snap which one begins to dread, when one is left with sap on one's hands, and half a rosette of leaves. All these perennials seed and they must be prohibited from doing so. Any of these perennials' roots can reproduce a new plant although, if regularly hoed or picked off, they weaken eventually to the point when they die out. That takes time and determined effort, however.

The annual weeds are legion but we feel we do not properly have to bother much with them till they start to flower. This may be short-sighted; the cabbage-aphid, for example, will live on shepherd's purse, and lettuce aphid on sowthistle. I use a hand-fork and kneelers for removing annual weeds and sometimes, in idleness, a border fork if I do not feel like bending. I always remove annual weeds; this is partly because I know that, in moist weather, weeds may root again and partly because I desire that satisfaction which results from the presence of a great deal of clean brown earth. I have given up the hoe, except in the vegetable garden where seeds are sown in straight rows, for I consider it now a thoroughly offensive weapon. I have too often hoed off precious self-sown seedlings on the first fine spring day. When I go out to weed I always take a rubber rake with me, to sweep up any soil or weed which has dropped onto the lawn. It is the work of the moment, but is one of those little tasks (like cutting the lawn edges after mowing) which make a disproportionately large impact on the appearance of the garden and, therefore, on one's attitude to it. These little things should never be neglected on the grounds that they are so small that any time (except the present) seems the fitting moment to do them.

I cannot overstate the importance of being able to identify the common weeds. If you have not been brought up to gardening and do not know, or have not absorbed, their names unconsciously by a kind of horticultural osmosis, then ask your mother to take you round her garden, and point out to you speedwell, annual and perennial nettle, bindweed and creeping buttercup. (However keen a gardener she is, she will be able to find some for you!) It is a great disappointment for any new gardener to find that he has

carefully nurtured some plant all through the spring, and scrupu-
lously avoided hoeing it off, only to find it turn overnight into a
rampaging weed which flowers and seeds all over the garden.

Ursula Buchan, 1987

Gardening gloves

June 2nd. – It must be admitted that one of the great drawbacks
to gardening and weeding is the state into which the hands and
fingers get. Unfortunately, one's hands belong not only to oneself,
but to the family, who do not scruple to tell the gardening amateur
that her appearance is 'revolting'. Constant washing and always
keeping them smooth and soft by a never-failing use of vaseline –
or, still better, a mixture of glycerine and starch, kept ready on the
washstand to use after washing and before drying the hands – are
the best remedies I know. Old dog-skin or old kid gloves are better
for weeding than the so-called gardening gloves; and for many
purposes the wash-leather housemaid's glove, sold at any village
shop, is invaluable.

Mrs C. W. Earle, 1897

The ideal outfit

While about the subject of outfit, I think that for a great part of the
year an ideal gardening dress for women is a short tweed skirt, made
very wide, so that one can step across plants without injuring them,
a loose jumper made of khaki or brown flannel (for half an hour in
wet weather will take the shine off a romantically becoming jumper
in pale colours), a gardening apron all pockets, a pair of thick shoes
or boots, and a light scarf tied over one's hair. Hats are dreadfully in
the way, and if quite uncovered and unshingled, our hair catches in
every twig, like Absolom's, and the result is very painful and untidy.

Lady Seton, 1927

Dock

The nastiest of all weeds is that sycophant – Dock, called also Herb Patience. When you grasp the strong-seeming stalk it has no fibre, it melts away in a soft squash, leaving its root in the ground; even Nettles are pleasanter to touch.

Anna Lea Merritt, 1908

Nettles

In the afternoon I went with Philip and cut nettles. They stung my bare legs (for in the summer I didn't wear stockings), and hurt me acutely. It was an odd, irritating, burning sensation, but I love the aromatic smell of cut nettles.

Lady Ottoline Morrell, 1918

Couch grass

In an area badly infested with couch we sowed turnip seed thickly, as we were advised. We now have no couch. You may not want turnips (and, sown so lavishly, you will not get very large ones anyway), but you certainly don't want couch. We have since heard lupins and tomatoes recommended for the same purpose, but have had no need to try them.

Maureen and Bridget Boland, 1976

Enchanter's nightshade

I have got a new weed in my garden – enchanter's nightshade (*Circaea lutetiana*). You can almost fool plant snobs with it. It has the minimalist flowers beloved of the most refined gardeners and if you call it by its proper name, it sounds suitably well-bred and obscure.

It's not more than about a foot high with round-stalked, ovate leaves, deeply veined and slightly washed over with red at the margins. Below ground it is a monster. Each stem that you pull up has at least five thick juicy white running roots, as brittle as rice paper. It seems to favour damp, shady places and had completely crowded out a colony of variegated gingermint, no mean street fighter itself.

A determined weeding session liberated a bed about 30 ft/10 m long by 10 ft/3 m wide. There is a fragile truce now, but I can almost hear those snapped off bits of underground root plotting insurrection.

Underground runners are the sneakiest of weeds, and the most difficult to get rid of. Miraculously, the garden did not have ground elder in it when we first arrived, but it's here now, brought in, I would imagine, on the roots of herbaceous perennials such as golden rod and michaelmas daisy that people always seem to have available to give away in suspiciously large quantities.

Anna Pavord, 1992

Creeping thistle

The path verge is about the only place in the garden where I dare let the self-seeded creeping thistle (a species banned by the Ministry of Agriculture) grow and flower. There is no doubt it is greatly loved by butterflies, perhaps because of its delicious scent, and is sometimes in bloom when all other nectar sources seem to have failed.

Miriam Rothschild, 1983

Chickweed

The Chickweed grows everywhere on rich cultivated land. Now we find it springing up in the garden, after a spring rain, making the beds green with its young shoots, and even in winter having the light tint of the spring leaf. In the fields it calls for the weeder's care; and under the hedge-bank its white flowers bloom all the year long, save when the snows have covered every green thing. It is a very valuable plant to birds; nor is it one of the worst of those herbs which men have sometimes boiled for their food. We need hardly describe its small flower, for it may always be seen, like a little star among its leaves, when the sun is shining. It is a good indicator of the changes of weather; and we would warn the traveller to wrap his cloak about him if the flower is quite closed, for rain, if not come, is coming soon, when this is the case. But if the Chickweed flower is fully expanded, he may walk gaily on, with a pretty good assurance that for hours at least he may be safe from rain; though if half closed, it would be well to take timely warning that the leaf may soon be wet with the passing shower.

Anne Pratt, 1889

Welsh Poppy

One of the prettiest weeds that we have in our modern gardens, and which alternates between being our greatest joy and our greatest torment, is the Welsh Poppy. It succeeds so well in this dry soil that it sows itself everywhere; but when it stands up, with its profusion of yellow flowers well above its bed of bright green leaves, in some fortunate situation where it can not only be spared, but encouraged and admired, it is a real pleasure.

Mrs C. W. Earle, 1897

Star of Bethlehem

I recognise of course that some weeds have got to go, those in the lawn especially, though I wouldn't count buttercups, clover or oxeye daisies among them; and my worst lawn enemy doesn't appear on weed lists. Star of Bethlehem (*Ornithogalum umbellatum*) is a pretty little item in bulb catalogues, who sometimes offer it as a bonus on a large order. Don't touch it. It will invade every part of the garden, choking out everything in its path, and like many undesirables is cunningly constructed to thwart easy extraction – the slippery foliage when tugged instantly separates from the bulblets, leaving them snugly far below ground.

Eleanor Perényi, 1981

'Clover'

Clever small clover
that lets glide over
the blades of cutter
and mower and scythe,
then raises just slightly
her blonde heads, like commas,
to see fallen about her
those sisters more lithe
than she, and more golden, but taller
and, so, subject to knives.

Grow, clover, as always – low, low, low –
and live many more lives.

Molly Holden, 1975

Bindweed

The bank all round the orchard was in a deplorable condition, with brambles, docks, nettles and thorns. Nobody had worried about it for many years. With our neat little beech hedge at the top it looked even worse than it was. We both agreed that if we could expose the wall at the end and clean up the bank, level it and plant it with valerian, it would look very nice. The problem, of course, was labour. Walter and the garden boy had other big jobs on hand, and it was considered too much of an undertaking for me.

But in the end I got it done. One of my sisters providentially came for a holiday and helped me clear the weeds from the bank. We had a magnificent time clearing the ground, because there was a lot of bindweed there, as well as the easier weeds. We both agreed that there is no sport in the world that compares with clearing ground of bindweed. It is far more exciting than golf or fishing. Tracing this tenacious creeping Judas of a weed to its source and getting it out without leaving any small broken pieces behind requires skill and patience, and the reward is a barrowload of the obscene twisting white roots and the joy of burning them.

Margery Fish, 1956

The victorious weeder

A really long day of weeding is a restful experience, and quite changes the current of thought. For some people it is more efficient than a rest cure. It is pleasantest to take a nine-hour day of such work when the earth is wet, or even in rain, because weeds come up more easily, root and branch, from wet earth. I never want an hour at noon for dinner, like the hired man, but would prefer to lunch like horses from a nosebag. It would save time, and especially the necessity of cleaning oneself. After such a day my fingers are bleeding, knees tottering, back bent, dress muddy and soaking, and shoes an offence to my tidy maid; but I have attained the most profound inward peace, and the blessed belief of having uprooted all my enemies.

Anna Lea Merritt, 1908

Circles of soil

All the gardeners I have talked to, professionals and amateurs, have stressed the importance of leaving a generous circle of cultivated soil round shrubs, roses or fruit trees planted in grass for at least two years after planting. One nursery will not consider replacing dead plants unless a circle at least four feet in diameter has been left for trees and at least three feet for small shrubs. In gardens celebrated for their shrub roses, I always observed round every rose a good circle of cultivated soil accessible to air, rain and supplies of food.

Anne Scott-James, 1971

Planting trees

I have no patience with slovenly planting. I like to have the ground prepared some months in advance, and when the proper time comes, to do the actual planting as well as possible. The hole in the already prepared ground is taken out so that the tree shall stand exactly right for depth, though in this dry soil it is well to make the hole an inch or two deeper, in order to leave the tree standing in the centre of a shallow depression, to allow of a good watering now and then during the following summer. The hole must be made wide enough to give easy space for the most outward-reaching of the roots; they must be spread out on all sides, carefully combing them out with the fingers, so that they all lay out to the best advantage. Any roots that have been bruised, or have broken or jagged ends, are cut off with a sharp knife on the homeward side of the injury. Most gardeners when they plant, after the first spadeful or two has been thrown over the root, shake the bush with an up and down joggling movement. This is useful in the case of plants with a good lot of bushy root, such as Berberis, helping to get the grains of earth well in among the root; but in tree planting, where the roots are laid out flat, it is of course useless. In our light soil, the closer and firmer the earth is made round the newly-planted tree the better, and strong staking is most important, in order to save the newly-placed root from disturbance by dragging.

Some trees and shrubs one can only get from nurseries in pots. This is usually the case with Ilex, Escallonia, and Cydonia. Such plants are sure to have the roots badly matted and twisted. The main root curls painfully round and round inside the imprisoning pot, but if it is a clever root it works its way out through the hole in the bottom, and even makes quite nice roots in the bed of ashes it has stood on. In this case, as these are probably its best roots, we do not attempt to pull it back through the hole, but break the pot to release it without hurt. If it is possible to straighten the pot-curled root, it is best to do so; in any case, the small fibrous ones can be laid out. Often the potful of roots is so hard and tight that it cannot be disentangled by the hand; then the only way is to soften it by gentle bumping on the bench, and then to disengage

the roots by little careful digs all round with a blunt-pointed stick.
If this is not done, and the plant is put in in its pot-bound state, it
never gets on; it would be just as well to throw it away at once.

Gertrude Jekyll, 1899

Longing to dig

If I could only dig and plant myself! How much easier, besides
being so fascinating, to make your own holes exactly where you
want them and put in your plants exactly as you choose instead of
giving orders that can only be half understood from the moment
you depart from the lines laid down by that long piece of string! In
the first ecstasy of having a garden all my own, and in my burning
impatience to make the waste places blossom like a rose; I did one
warm Sunday in last year's April during the servants' dinner hour,
doubly secure from the gardener by the day and the dinner, slink
out with a spade and a rake and feverishly dig a little piece of ground
and break it up and sow surreptitious ipomæa and run back very
hot and guilty into the house and get into a chair and behind a book
and look languid just in time to save my reputation.

Elizabeth von Arnim, 1898

Digging for ladies

It must be confessed that digging appears at first sight, a very
laborious employment, and one peculiarly unfitted to small and
delicately formed hands and feet; but, by a little attention to the
principles of mechanics and the laws of motion, the labour may be
much simplified and rendered comparatively easy. The operation
of digging, as performed by a gardener, consists in thrusting the
iron part of the spade, which acts as a wedge, perpendicularly into
the ground by the application of the foot, and then using the long

handle as a lever, to raise up the loosened earth and turn it over. The quantity of earth thus raised is called a spitful, and the gardener, when he has turned it, chops it to break the clods, with the sharp edge of his spade, and levels it with the back. During the whole operation, the gardener holds the cross part of the handle of the spade in his right-hand, while he grasps the smooth round lower part of the handle in his left, to assist him in raising the earth and turning it, sliding his left hand backwards and forwards along the handle, as he may find it necessary . . .

The first point to be attended to, in order to render the operation of digging less laborious, is to provide a suitable spade; that is, one which shall be as light as is consistent with strength, and which will penetrate the ground with the least possible trouble. For this purpose, the blade of what is called a lady's spade is made of not more than half the usual breadth, say not wider than five or six inches, and of smooth polished iron, and it is surmounted, at the part where it joins the handle, by a piece of iron rather broader than itself, which is called the tread, to serve as a rest for the foot of the operator while digging. The handle is about the usual length, but quite smooth and sufficiently slender for a lady's hand to grasp, and it is made of willow, a close, smooth, and elastic wood, which is tough and tolerably strong, though much lighter than ash, the wood generally used for the handles to gardener's spades. The lady should also be provided with clogs, the soles of which are not jointed, to put over her shoes; or if she should dislike these, and prefer strong shoes, she should be provided with what gardeners call a tramp, that is, a small plate of iron to go under the sole of the shoe, and which is fastened round the foot with a leathern strap and buckle. She should also have a pair of stiff thick leathern gloves, or gauntlets, to protect her hands, not only from the handle of the spade, but from the stones, weeds, &c., which she may turn over with the earth, and which ought to be picked out and thrown into a small, light wheelbarrow, which may easily be moved from place to place.

Mrs Jane Loudon, 1841

The only way to learn is to DO the actual work.

Beatrix Havergal, 1939

Behind the scenes at Sissinghurst

In early autumn we do a quick glean all round to get the garden free of weeds. This makes a great difference when forking later on . . . Once the pruning is done we work round the rest of the garden clearing off the borders as we fork, lifting and dividing herbaceous plants where necessary. Except in the case of prolific seeders, cutting down is not done in advance. Some may find this untidy but dead stalks give valuable protection. Another advantage is that the bulk is much reduced. Light rubbish is carried away in a cloth – we use a six foot square of hessian – finding it far quicker than negotiating a barrow up steps and through narrow entrances.

Pamela Schwerdt and Sibylle Kreutzberger, 1978

White handles

And what a good, if strenuous, month November is in the vegetable garden. We make a great effort to have all the digging finished before the month is out. This is especially important on our heavy soil. The ground should be 'laid up', as they say, in big, fat, upstanding clods, for the frost and rain to get into it and break it down, so that when the time comes for spring sowing it can be raked into a fine tilth. This means manual spade work, as you can never get the same results with any kind of machine. I love digging, with my thirty-year-old stainless steel spade (perhaps it is even older than that, I cannot quite remember). It warms me up when I have a cold job to do, like tying climbers to the walls. The wooden part of my spade is painted white and so are the handles of all our tools. If a tool gets mislaid in a garden like ours it can easily be lost, but a white handle shows it up.

Valerie Finnis, 1980

May I assure the gentleman who writes to me (quite often) from a Priory in Sussex that I am not the armchair, library-fireside gardener he evidently suspects, 'never having performed any single act of gardening' myself, and that for the last forty years of my life I have broken my back, my finger-nails, and sometimes my heart, in the practical pursuit of my favourite occupation?

V. Sackville-West, 1958

ADVISERS AND DESIGNERS

I CANNOT lay too great stress upon the neatness in which a lady's garden should be kept. If it is not beautifully neat, it is nothing. For this reason, keep every plant distinct in the flower-beds; let every tall flower be well staked, that the wind may not blow it prostrate; rake away dead leaves from the beds, and trim every flower-root from discoloured leaves, weeds, &c.; remove all weeds and stones the moment they appear, and clear away decaying stems, which are so littering and offensive to the eye. There is always some employment of this kind for every week in the year.

Marie E. Jackson, 1822

Do not try to fill your borders so full of blossoms that you cannot distinguish one from the other. It is not at all a matter for congratulation when you say that not a square inch can be found in your border, or above it, without a flower. Nor fall into the opposite error of seeing each plant and stake rising from neat brown earth.

A. M. Martineau, 1923

Advice to beginners

Many people who love flowers and wish to do some practical gardening are at their wit's end to know what to do and how to begin. Like a person who is on skates for the first time, they feel that, what with the bright steel runners, and the slippery surface, and the sense of helplessness, there are more ways of tumbling about than of progressing safely in any one direction. And in gardening the beginner must feel this kind of perplexity and helplessness, and indeed there is a great deal to learn, only it is pleasant

instead of perilous, and the many tumbles by the way only teach
and do not hurt. The first few steps are perhaps the most difficult,
and it is only when we know something of the subject and an
eager beginner comes with questions that one sees how very many
are the things that want knowing. And the more ignorant the
questioner, the more difficult it is to answer helpfully. When one
knows, one cannot help presupposing some sort of knowledge on
the part of the querist, and where this is absent the answer we can
give is of no use. The ignorance, when fairly complete, is of such
a nature that the questioner does not know what to ask, and the
answer, even if it can be given, falls upon barren ground. I think in
such cases it is better to try and teach one simple thing at a time,
and not to attempt to answer a number of useless questions. It is
disheartening when one has tried to give a careful answer to have
it received with an Oh! of boredom or disappointment, as much as
to say, You can't expect me to take all that trouble; and there is the
still more unsatisfactory sort of applicant, who plies a string of
questions and will not wait for the answers! The real way is to try
and learn a little from everybody and from every place. There is no
royal road.

Gertrude Jekyll, 1899

Unity

Through all the variations, due tò climate, country, history and the
natural idiosyncrasy of man, which have appeared in the evolution
of the garden through successive civilisations, certain principles
remain constant however much their application may change.
Perhaps the greatest of these, and the one most lacking in the
average garden to-day, is a sense of unity. It is a quality found in all
great landscapes, based on the rhythm of natural land-form, the
domination of one type of vegetation and the fact that human use
and buildings have kept in sympathy with their surroundings.
When we say that a landscape has been spoilt we mean that it has
lost this unity . . .

The lack of unity, which has disrupted the majority of gardens

of the last century and a half, is due to the same causes which have
made chaos of our landscape; too many new things, ill-digested;
new plants which we have not yet learnt to use; materials, such as
Westmoreland rock and crazy paving, which are transported to all
parts of the country and used in positions to which they are
unsuited; foreign influences, copied without being assimilated or
understood. But, above all, there is a lack of decision as to what
each man really wants in his garden . . .

There are, however, two types of pattern which may be considered typical of this century. One is the composition of free forms,
floating over each other and interlocking in different planes to form
the rhythmic pattern of the abstract garden . . . The other is the
cellular, honeycomb design which has been developed to a high
degree in Scandinavia. It is a true expression of the age because
it allows diverse and small-scale uses to be welded into a unified
composition, thus solving the modern problem of maintaining
individual values within a world of crowd-organisation.

This cellular construction also allows for that variety within the
design which has always gone hand in hand with unity, for if lack
of unity brings discord, lack of variety brings boredom. All the
greatest gardens have shown that the two are not incompatible.
Vaux shows endless invention in the design of the lateral gardens
leading off the main axis while at Stowe the proportion and
character of each view is different, the architecture of each arch
and temple individual and distinct.

Surprise and hidden depths are part of the attribute of variety,
whether it is the magnificently conceived hidden canal at Vaux
or merely a curving path disappearing into the shadow of trees
in a small private garden. A garden without mystery is not one
to live with, although it may serve as a setting to some great
building, to be seen purely as part of a view and not felt as an
environment . . .

More often the modern garden has to be in-looking rather
than out-looking and must supply the main interest within its
own boundaries. In a small garden a fine tree or piece of sculpture
may be enough to form the focal point to which all else is
subordinate . . .

One of the simplest forms of garden, especially suitable for long,
narrow sites, is the main walk with a strong terminal feature and
subsidiary interest on each side. It is the final simplification of the

Le Nôtre tradition, the strong axial design. The usual failure in translating it into small gardens is that the subsidiary interest is allowed to be too strong in relation to the main axis. It is true that at Vaux the cross axes reveal gardens of a size and richness which are marvels in themselves, but the main axis is some 1200 yards long, and can hold its own. Hidcote, the skeleton of whose plan is based on axis and cross axes, never allows lateral interest to compete with whichever main axis one is looking down.

Equally satisfying, but perhaps harder to achieve, is the design based on the central open space. Basically this is the form of many small gardens whose chief function is to be open-air rooms. They are similar in intention to the Spanish patio, but instead of being circled by the building and shaded from the sun, they are pushed out from the house to get as much sun as possible.

While in the axial garden the eye is led along to the far end, in the patio garden it is brought to rest in the central space. The features are used as furnishing for the room. There may be a view beyond, but one should not feel impelled to get up and immediately walk to it, but rather be content to sit and admire or, at the most, to wander on after a due rest. This difference in design between the static room and the long walk is a fundamental one, and although in a large garden both moods will occur in different places, there should be no doubt when looking at a particular view, whether the design is static or progressive. Repetition of objects along the line of vision impels the eye forward, as the serried tree trunks do down the lime walk at Sissinghurst, Kent . . . or the urns along the terrace at the Villa Lante. But repetitive objects arranged in an apse, like the caryatids at the end of the exhedra at Chiswick House, Middlesex, suggest finality.

Sylvia Crowe, 1951

Off-centre

A couple of brick steps not set at the right angle to the paths leading to them, or a path of bricks to a garden tank that has not been set in line with the house wall near, are fearful eyesores. One garden, carefully designed at great expense by a well-known architect, is a source of great irritation to its owners. A centre had been arranged with a sundial and an enclosed space, with vistas through yew arches to tall specimen trees at both ends and on each hand. Something was wrong, and it was only discovered after some years, and when the yews had grown into fine hedges, that the line of the *house* ran slightly off the straight; and though all the rest is quite correct in measurement, this one fatal mistake can never be put right.

A garden planned on formal lines needs to be very accurate and correct.

A. M. Martineau, 1923

In starting a garden, the first question, of course, is where to plant. If you are a beginner in the art, and the place is new and large, go to a good landscape gardener and let him give advice and make you a plan. But don't follow it; at least not at once, nor all at one time. Live there for a while, until you yourself begin to feel what you want, and where you want it.

Mrs Helena Rutherfurd Ely, 1903

Making a plan

No one should feel bashful about launching into the field of design. After all, every garden owner is an expert on his plot and his needs, and he can look forward to the satisfaction of creating a garden that is an expression of his own personality and is therefore unique. It may contain traces of ideas gathered from different sources, but these will have been transformed by the needs of the site into something more than a straight copy.

It is obviously impossible to condense into a few paragraphs the wisdom that a professional designer gains in years of training and experience. Nevertheless, here are a few general guide-lines.

Keep the broad lines of the design as simple as possible, or you may end up with oddly shaped spaces that are difficult to maintain and have no real use. Complicated details that are difficult to carry out may look amateurish and are probably best left alone. Plants and people will in any case provide plenty of interest.

In dividing the total area into compartments for different kinds of use, try not to make them equal in size, or your design will be indeterminate and confused as to its purpose. Taking a more positive line (which is also more restful), a garden with roughly one third devoted to a sitting area and the rest to planting is clearly a green garden with somewhere to sit, whereas a very small garden almost entirely taken up by the sitting space is predominantly a paved garden with some plants.

A very long narrow garden might be broken up into three or four compartments of varying lengths, according to the purpose for which they are intended. Similar principles about proportion should be applied to any decision about the ground pattern . . .

A pathway is the backbone of the design of all but the smallest *formal* gardens and should be integrated with the sitting area and other elements which it links. In large gardens, paths are usually wide enough for two people to walk side by side; in a small garden the width required by a person with a wheelbarrow is more in keeping with the scale of the garden. If the path has to cross from one side of the plot to the other, it should do so without cutting across any of the spaces at random . . . A path is a very strong feature in a garden and if it cannot be related to the basic design of spaces it should pass through them as inconspicuously as possible. Examples of 'muted' paths are: stepping-stones, paths slightly sunk below grass level or hard-surface paths that have been made green by grass or moss growing between the joints. A path that winds for no apparent reason may become irritating in time; a tree or large shrub planted inside the bend will make the curve seem inevitable.

In semi-wild *informal* gardens, paths play a less prominent part in the design and should be minimal: perhaps large stepping-stones set into the grass with four to five inches between, to allow the grass to flow through. They may even be dispensed with altogether if the grass is wide enough to vary the route to the end of the garden. A more solid path of closely set stones or bricks can be made to cross a lawn almost invisibly if it is sunk slightly below the level of the turf. In this case, it is better to leave the joints unmortared, to allow rainwater to seep away.

In planning a garden, many gardeners rely a good deal, and rightly, on their intuition. But it can be helpful to clarify one's ideas by drawing a plan on paper, particularly if it is to be carried out in stages. Work at a scale of ⅛ inch to a foot (i.e. 1 in. represents 8 ft) for most gardens, or ¼ inch to a foot for very small gardens.

If the plot is not too complicated by irregular boundaries, changes of level, oddly placed trees, etc., you can make your own rough survey, using the following procedure: (a) make a rough sketch of the outline of the plot in a notebook; (b) mark what measurements are essential; (c) pace these as accurately as possible, which you can do after determining the length of your stride, or use a tape-measure; (d) re-draw the site plan to scale. In a small rectangular garden the whole operation should take less than an hour.

Having now got the outline of the plot on paper it is possible to superimpose tracing paper on which suggestions can be roughed in; if not satisfactory, the tracing paper can be put on one side and a fresh piece substituted. When the design seems about to jell, you can block out in appropriate colours the different areas – grass, planting beds, sitting space, paths, etc. Another method is to cut out pieces of paper, coloured and shaped to represent the various elements, and pin them to the outline drawing, moving them round until a satisfactory arrangement is reached. Finally, turn the completed plan upside down and look at it as a piece of abstract design. If the shape still pleases you, mark it out on the ground with pegs and see if it works in practice and if adjustments are needed.

Irregularly shaped plots are more difficult to handle. It may be best simply to mark out paths, paved areas, etc., on the ground with wooden pegs. On a triangular site . . . blocks of planting should be planned to create spaces that are a more convenient shape and pleasant to sit in.

Susan Jellicoe, 1977

No garden, great or small, should be seen all at one glance; barriers of some kind must be maintained or introduced to give some elements of surprise and secrecy to a garden tour. Each part, however, should lead naturally to another and this can be done by the repetition of a planting scheme or simply by paths of gravel or stone, or better, by extending a narrow section of lawn into another area.

Penelope Hobhouse, 1976

Writing out-of-doors

Who has not been tried by small annoyances, such as excessive heat from the sun, stinging gnats, or blustering winds that send papers hopelessly scattered across the lawn?

All these little troubles tend to make a morning's writing out-of-doors seem like an eternity of hindrances. We tolerate them in the open country, where we have perhaps no more than the deep, warm, protecting heather into which we can fling ourselves for safety; but in a garden, where the careful thoughts of many have been brought to bear upon all creature-comforts, we are more exacting.

All gardens, therefore, should have some hedged-in, completely sheltered part. It should be so shaped that shadow can be had at every moment in the day, while sunshine and protection from wind can both also be gained, when wanted upon cold stormy days.

Viscountess Wolseley, 1919

The garden has always been considered as, and always must be, an adjunct of the house, and therefore must accord with it, if it is to look well. No one would put an Elizabethan garden in front of an Italian house, or vice versa, and an old-fashioned formal garden would not look well in front of a new looking suburban villa, but no hard and fast rules of style can be laid down, as the selection depends on the architecture, scenery, climate and many other things.

Alicia Amherst, 1895

Letter to William Shenstone

Sir,   May-day, 1749.

I have no more than time to let you know that I had your book first and your letter after, very safe; and to thank you for your little sketch of alterations in my Shrubbery. In order to follow it, I have begun by taking down the styles, that no foot-road may prevent the execution of what we propose; and am ungravelling the lime-walk and laying mold on it; which is the whole that can be done till the planting season. In the mean time, I have finished my lower garden, by turning the seven grass-plats that were in the shape of Lord Mayor's Custards, into one large one; and have widened the gravel-walk round from five feet and a half to twelve feet and a half broad. As to the court, the pallisades are removed, the end-walls built, the turf taken away, the slopes made more gentle, the pillars removed to the extremities of the pallisades, and the sun-dial is set in the middle, and the court levelled, raised, and gravelled; the two gates are making. The upper garden is ungravelled, and is making into a bowling-green; the pavillion will be set up next, and the white pales taken away from the wall-side to the stable-court to enlarge that in autumn: the way to the Coppice will be altered according to your directions; and I hope then you will be so kind as to assist me; for it is impossible for you at a distance to judge so well as on the place. – I do not know if you would have the little gates left or no at each end of the Service Walk, though they are to be hid with shrubs. I propose coming into the Coppice from the Service-Walk at the farther end between the Chairs that overlook the Pit, and the farther corner of the Wood beyond what answers to the top of the Hermitage Pit.

Lady Luxborough, 1749

A very high art

Thus all who possess an acre or more of ground think that they alone are fitted to plan out and arrange their gardens, just as they do their drawing-rooms and the interior of their houses. They do not bear in mind that garden design as it is studied by the one nation which really understands it – the Japanese – takes many years of serious application to reach perfection. It is a very high art; as Maurice Hewlett aptly makes one of his characters say: 'Horticulture is next to music the most sensitive of the fine arts. Properly allied to Architecture, garden-making is as near as a man may get to the Divine function' . . .

Our best English gardens are lovely with colour-scheme herbaceous borders filled with well-grown flowers. We have, too, what no other nation possesses, beautiful fresh grass-lawns and wide-branching trees. One thing, however, we still lack, and that is skill in garden design, in the proper selection and arrangement of architectural features, tree-planting, and the right treatment of the lie of the land. We should be nearer perfection did we possess some of that sense of restraint which keeps the Japanese from growing flowers merely for their own sake and restricts their choice to those only which fit in best with a general wide scheme of arrangement.

Viscountess Wolseley, 1919

The parterre

The common, or Mingled Flower-Garden should be situated so as to form an ornamental appendage to the house; and where the plan of ground will admit, placed before windows exposed to a southern or south-east aspect; and, although to this position there may appear the objection of the flowers turning their petals to the sun, and consequently from the windows, this predilection in the tribe of Flora for the rays of that bright luminary, will produce the same effect in whatever place our flowers may be situated, when in the vicinity of a building, as they invariably expose the front of their corols to the light, from which both the petals of flowers and the leaves of plants are believed to derive some material essential to their existence.

The compass of ground appropriated to flowers must vary according to the size of the place of which that ground forms a part, and should in no case be of great extent. The principle on which the parterre should be laid out, ought to be that of exhibiting a variety of colour and form so nicely blended as to present one whole. In a flower-garden viewed from the windows of a house, this effect, as has been observed above, is best produced by straight borders laid sideways of each other, and to the windows from whence they are seen, as by that position the colours shew themselves in one mass, whereas, if placed end-way, the alleys, which are necessary for the purpose of going amongst the flowers, divide the whole, and occasion an appearance of poverty. Should an inter-mixture of turf with the flower borders be preferred, then the borders should be of various forms . . . or they may be laid out in a plain Etruscan pattern . . .

It is more difficult than may at first appear, to plan, even upon a small scale, such a piece of ground; nor perhaps, would any but an experienced scientific eye be aware of the difficulties to be encoun-tered in the disposal of a few shaped borders interspersed with turf. The nicety consists in arranging the different parts so as to form a connected glow of colour: to effect which it will be necessary to place the borders in such a manner that when viewed from the windows of the house, or from the principal entrance into the garden, one border shall not intercept the beauties of another; but in avoiding this error, a still greater must be guarded against, that of vacancies betwixt the borders, forming small avenues, by which the whole is separated into broken parts, and the general effect lost.

Another point to be attended to is the just proportion of green turf, which, without nice observation, will be too much or too little for the colour with which it is blended; and lastly, the breadth of the flower borders should not be greater than what will place the roots within reach of the gardener's arm without the necessity of treading upon the soil, the mark of footsteps being a deformity wherever it appears amongst our flowers. If the form of ground where a parterre is to be situated is sloping, the size should be larger than when a flat surface, and the borders of various shapes and on a bolder scale, and intermingled with grass; but such a flower-garden partakes more of the nature of pleasure-ground than of the common parterre, and will admit of a judicious introduction of flowering shrubs.

Although, in general, a flower-garden should not be upon a large scale, it frequently occurs in the ground allotted for that purpose near small villas, that the appearance of more space than what can be procured on a confined flat surface may be desirable: this I have seen ingeniously effected by removing the earth until a hollow was produced, about the size of a common marl-pit, with hill and dale, the outer part of which, being planted with shrubs, formed one side of a shady walk leading to the valley, the inside of which was laid out in rockery. On rising out of the valley, the eye was agreeably deceived into the belief of entering upon ground not entirely of a flat surface, as by the skilful management of elevated banks, raised by earth taken from the hollow, an appearance was given of greater extent and inequality than actually existed, and the idea suggested of walks winding through shrubberies; while at the same time, these banks screened from the sight, and protected from the wind, a portion of ground appropriated to culinary purposes, and sheltered on two sides a small gay parterre, which lay before the parlour windows.

This ingenious plan had yet the farther merit of having been formed upon the basis of utility. The site of the house and gardens being upon high ground of a wholly flat surface, and close to public roads, afforded shelter neither from weather, nor from the view of passengers; but in the artificial little valley a retreat was secured, completely secluded from the public eye, and between the banks there was placed a rustic seat formed of dried branches of trees, entwined by honeysuckles, and other sweet and ornamental climbers, well calculated for the retirement of a solitary student, and sufficiently spacious for the accommodation of a social party, who might equally wish to escape the observation of the idle or inquisitive traveller.

Marie E. Jackson, 1822

I cannot imagine anything worse than planting everything in the same sized spaces. I once saw a long herbaceous border in a college garden where everything was planted in squares at the back of the border and two parallel lines of dwarf plants running the full length of the border in the front . . .

Beatrix Havergal, 1963

Victorian gardens

Enrichment. That word is the key to much that now happened in gardens. Not only were they to be made more comfortable and usable by means of well-sheltered level ground with gravel walks and good seats, solid walls and steps instead of open grassy slopes, but also there must be enrichment of architectural detail and, above all, of colour.

The landscape garden of the eighteenth century had been limited in its colour effects to varying tones of green and to the soft russets, browns and greys of nature. But exotic plants from sunnier climates had been introduced and cultivated in greenhouses and were capable of giving the brilliant parterres which are often supposed to be the main charm of Italian gardens. In this country they could be raised under glass only, and bedded out in the garden for temporary effects, requiring frequent replacement: but this would add all the more to the 'enrichment' of the garden, and they could never be confused with common flowers.

In the large gardens of the preceding century, garden flowers had been relegated to a place where they would least be seen, and even wild flowers had held little importance. Now the pendulum swung to the opposite extreme, and exotic flowers in the crudest of primary colours found first favour, and were massed trimly in full view of the house. Scarlet geraniums, Reckitt's-blue lobelia, and strong yellow calceolarias in concentric circles, set off by the hardest whites available, were to be accommodated near the buildings. Shrubs as shelter and background could be planted on the slopes so carefully modelled by Kent, Brown and Repton; and flower-beds could be carved out of the lawn. It was, of course, necessary to have gravel paths, wide and solid, meandering lengthily around them to ensure their proper appreciation at close range, and seats for comfort. By the time a few urns and sundials had been added and the former naturalistic composition completely broken up and obliterated, the desired effect was often felt to have been achieved, and so many remained until quite recently as monuments of incongruity. But thinking out new shapes for the beds had evidently taxed the imagination, and when the circle, the half-circle, the crescent, square, diamond, and star had been exploited there was nothing to do but to repeat them.

More co-ordinated results could be had by employing an architect such as Sir Charles Barry, Sir Joseph Paxton or Nesfield to design an 'Italian' garden as was done at Bowood House, Blickling Hall, Eaton Hall, Longford Castle and many others; but these scarcely affected the main treatment of the estates, which, for the rest, remained as their eighteenth-century designers had made them. New formal terraces and parterres of elaborate geometrical design, enclosed by walls and hedges, were laid out in close relation to the buildings, but unrelated to the park or landscape beyond. They remain in parentheses, interpolated into the wider conception of an earlier age. These gardens usually depend for their background, skyline and general setting on the results of eighteenth-century planning, without which many of them would be almost wholly two-dimensional. But they are often found in direct competition with a fine view, and since no concessions are made to the subtler indications of the surrounding land forms, the sense of conflict is aggravated and the beauty of the eighteenth-century surrounding is, as far as possible, nullified.

The formal garden of this period was not freed from the dictum that 'Nature abhors a straight line', but paid tribute to it by means of a lavish use of geometrical curves – one of the hallmarks by which it may always be recognised. Curves were 'in': some of them could scarcely be attributed either to nature or to geometry, but only, as was pointed out by a French critic, to alcoholic intoxication.

Gravel paths had always worried the landscape-gardeners of the eighteenth century because they never looked natural and, when curved, tended to be ungainly: they had used them as little as possible. But now, twisting paths, winding through shrubberies and doubling back on their tracks, were found to be capable of making a place seem larger in extent than it really was. Every device capable of enlarging the apparent size of the private garden was tried, and skill in this matter was regarded as the garden-designer's main function.

Many of the garden developments of the middle and end of the century came as the result of attempting on comparatively small sites effects previously designed for large estates. False perspective had been introduced in a broad way by Kent and his successors as the natural result of the picturesque attitude. But now, applied on a smaller scale, it became nonsense. The ha-ha, which can be effective only under certain limited conditions and which needs very careful handling, was now adopted in the hope of making the place seem larger, in many an inappropriate position.

Foreign conifers were being introduced from America, and were in great favour for their exotic and rich appearance. The monkey-puzzle appears to have been first favourite, a horticultural expert having expressed the view that no gentlemen's demesne could be complete without it. Newly introduced trees, such as *Sequoias* and *Cupressus* first planted on the great estates, became status symbols; and to some extent they can be regarded in this light to the present day. Their unmistakable spiky outlines are visible from afar, marking private estates and gardens well maintained for at least a century. Their introduction coinciding generally with the nineteenth-century Gothic revival led to their frequent association with pointed gables whose forms they echo. Repton had favoured contrast, and not harmony, between the forms of architecture and plants, saying that rounded tree forms were the best foil to Gothic architecture. If that was true of the Strawberry Hill Gothic of his day, it was even truer of the Ruskin Gothic, but his warning had been forgotten and no new voice was raised in protest. The pointed trees and pointed gables still remain in association in countless places to prove that on this Repton's judgment was not at fault.

The heavy furniture of the nineteenth century and all the knick-knacks and ornaments overcrowding the rooms found counterparts in the garden as the century wore on. Heavy shrub planting, much of which was redundant, was monotonous and dull. Often it obtruded too near the buildings and encircled too closely small open spaces, making a stagnant and claustrophobic effect. 'Objects' were never lacking, and the clarity and simplicity of open spaces were overlaid. The objects might be raised flower-beds representing vast baskets with the sides and a gigantic arch forming the handle made of wire trellis, draped in ivy. The baskets would be planted with brilliant hothouse flowers in concentric rings. Other devices were clocks and sundials (figured in carpet-bedding) on a gigantic scale. It was as if machinery, not nature, was the model to be idealised in gardens. The art of topiary was revived in both its sculptural and architectural form, but it was the former which gave the greatest scope for the display of originality and which, when originality flagged, drew the heaviest censure. The habit of clipping bushes, once contracted, easily becomes a vice, and the results could be seen in the serried ranks of green, gold and variegated plants, neatly trimmed to standardised shapes, but often cut to within an inch of death, which appeared not only in private gardens but in parks, railway stations and other public places. To clip groups of shrubs such as these into single specimens ruins their value as shelter or background, and brings them into restless competition for the limelight in the centre of the stage. The practice is an attempt to substitute skill for design, by individuals blind to the need for good design.

Brenda Colvin, 1970

It is with real sorrow that we see so many survivals of an era of not particularly good taste, in the shape of iron benches. It is their undoubted durability which has preserved them, and we who try to rest upon them are the sufferers, not only for their unpleasing appearance, but from the ill-chosen formation of the back . . . they are shaped so that neither by stooping forward nor by reclining absolutely at full length can comfort be obtained. Let us stretch our limbs again in freedom . . .

Viscountess Wolseley, 1919

'All is fine that is fit'

Dear Little Friend,

When, with the touching confidence of youth that your elders have made-up as well as grown-up minds on all subjects, you asked my opinion on Ribbon-gardening, the above proverb came into my head, to the relief of its natural tendency to see an inconvenient number of sides to every question. The more I reflect upon it, the more I am convinced it is a comfortably compact confession of my faith on all matters decorative, and thence on the decoration of gardens.

I take some credit to myself for having the courage of my moderation, since you obviously expect a more sweeping reply. The bedding-out system is in bad odour just now; and you ask, 'Wasn't it hideous?' and 'Wasn't it hateful?' and 'Will it ever come into fashion again, to the re-extermination of the dear old-fashioned flowers which we are now slowly, and with pains, recalling from banishment?'

To discover one's own deliberate opinion upon a subject is not always easy – prophetic opinions one must refuse to offer. But I feel no doubt whatever that the good lady who shall coddle this little garden at some distant date after me will be quite as fond of her borders as I am of mine; and I suspect that these will be about as like each other as our respective best bonnets . . .

'All is fine that is fit.' And is the 'bedding-out' system – Ribbon-gardening – ever fit, and therefore ever fine? My little friend, I am inclined to think that it sometimes is. For long straight borders in parks and public promenades, for some terrace gardens on a large scale, viewed perhaps from windows at a considerable distance, and, in a general way, for pleasure grounds ordered by professional skill, and not by an *amateur* gardener (which, mark you, being interpreted, is gardener *for love*!), the bedding-out style *is* good for general effect, and I think it is capable of prettier ingenuities than one often sees employed in its use. I think that, if I ever gardened in this expensive and mechanical style, I should make 'arrangements', à la Whistler, with flowers of various shades of the same colour. But harmony and gradation of colour always give me more pleasure than contrast.

Then, besides the fitness of the gardening to the garden, there is the fitness of the garden to its owner; and the owner must be considered from two points of view, his taste and his means. Indeed, I think it would be fair to add a third, his leisure.

Now, there are owners of big gardens and little gardens, who like to have a garden (what Englishman does not?), and like to see it gay and tidy, but who don't know one flower from the rest. On the other hand, some scientists are acquainted with botany and learned in horticulture. They know every plant and its value, but they care little about tidiness. Cut flowers are feminine frivolities in their eyes, and they count nosegays as childish gauds, like daisy chains and cowslips balls. They are not curious in colours, and do not know which flowers are fragrant and which are scentless. For them every garden is a botanical garden. Then, many persons fully appreciate the beauty and the scent of flowers, and enjoy selecting and arranging them for a room, who can't abide to handle a fork or meddle with mother earth. Others again, amongst whom I number myself, love not only the lore of flowers, and the sight of them, and the fragrance of them, and the growing of them, and the picking of them, and the arranging of them, but also inherit from Father Adam a natural relish for tilling the ground from whence they were taken and to which they shall return.

With little persons in little gardens, having also little strength and little leisure, this husbandry may not exceed the small uses of fork and trowel, but the earth-love is there, all the same. I remember once, coming among some family papers, upon an old letter from my grandmother to my grandfather. She was a clever girl (she did not outlive youth), and the letter was natural and full of energy and point. My grandfather seems to have apologised to his bride for the disorderly state of the garden to which she was about to go home, and in reply she quaintly and vehemently congratulates herself upon this unpromising fact. For – 'I do so dearly love *grubbing*.' This touches another point. She was a botanist, and painted a little. So were most of the lady gardeners of her youth. The education of women was, as a rule, poor enough in those days; but a study of 'the Linnean system' was among the elegant accomplishments held to 'become a young woman'; and one may feel pretty sure that even a smattering of botanical knowledge, and the observation needed for third- or fourth-rate flower-painting, would tend to a love of variety in beds and borders which Ribbon-gardening would by no means satisfy. *Lobelia erinus speciosa* does make a wonderfully smooth blue stripe in sufficient quantities, but that would not console any one who knew or had painted *Lobelia cardinalis*, and *fulgens* for the banishment of these from the garden.

I think we may dismiss Ribbon-gardening as unfit for a botanist, or for any one who happens to like *grubbing*, or tending his flowers. Is it ever 'fit' in a little garden?

Well, if the owner has either no taste for gardening, or no time, it may be the shortest and brightest plan to get some nurseryman near to fill the little beds and borders with spring bedding plants for spring (and let me note that this *spring bedding*, which is of later date than the first rage for ribbon-borders, had to draw its supplies very largely from 'herbaceous stuff' *myosotis*, *viola*, *aubretia*, *iberis*, &c., and may have paved the way for the return of hardy perennials into favour), and with Tom Thumb Geranium, Blue Lobelia, and Yellow Calceolaria for the summer and autumn. These latter are most charming plants. They are very gay and persistent whilst they last, and it is not their fault that they cannot stand our winters. They are no invalids till frost comes. With my personal predilections, I like even 'bedding stuff' best in variety. The varieties of what we call geraniums are many and most beautiful. I should always prefer a group of individual specimens to a band of one. And never have I seen the canary yellow of calceolarias to such advantage as in an 'old-fashioned' rectory-garden in Yorkshire, where they were cunningly used as points of brilliancy at corners of beds mostly filled with 'hardy herbaceous stuff'.

But there, again, one begins to spend time and taste! Let us admit that, if a little garden must be made gay by the neighbouring nurseryman, it will look very bright, on the 'ribbon' system, at a minimum cost of time and trouble – *but not of money*!

Even for a little garden, bedding plants are very expensive. For you must either use plenty, or leave it alone. A ragged ribbon-border can have no admirers.

If time and money are both lacking, and horticulture is not a hobby, divide what sum you are prepared to spend on your little garden in two. Lay out half in making good soil, and spend the rest on a limited range of hardy plants. If mother earth is well fed, and if you have got her *deep down*, and not a surface layer of half a foot on a substratum of builder's rubbish, she will take care of every plant you commit to her hold. I should give up the back of the borders (if the aspect is east or south) to a few very good 'perpetual' roses to cut from; dwarfs, not standards; and for the line of colour in front it will be no great trouble to arrange roughly to have red, white, blue, and yellow alternately.

One of the best cheap bedders is Pink Catchfly (*Silene pendula*). Its rosy cushions are as neat and as lasting as Blue Lobelia. It is a hardy annual, but the plants should be autumn sown of the year before. It flowers early and long, and its place might be taken for the autumn by scarlet dwarf nasturtiums, or clumps of geranium. Pink Catchfly, Blue Forget-me-not, White Arabis, and Yellow Viola would make gay any spring border. Then to show, to last, and to cut from, few flowers rival the self-coloured pansies (Viola class). Blue, white, purple, and yellow alternately, they are charming, and if in good soil, well-watered in drought, and constantly cut from, they bloom the whole summer long. And some of them are very fragrant. The secret of success with these is never to leave a flower to go to seed. They are not cut off by autumnal frosts. On the contrary, you can take them up, and divide, and reset, and send a portion to other little gardens where they are lacking.

All mine (and they have been very gay this year and very sweet) I owe to the bounty of friends who garden *non sibi sed toti*.

Lastly, if there is even a very little taste and time to spare, surely nothing can be so satisfactory as a garden full of such flowers as (in the words of John Parkinson) 'our English ayre will permitt to be noursed up'. Bearing in mind these counsels:

Make a wise selection of hardy plants. Grow only good sorts, and of these choose what suit your soil and climate. Give them space and good feeding. Disturb the roots as little as possible, and cut the flowers constantly. Then they will be fine as well as fit.

Good-bye, Little Friend,

Yours, &c.

Mrs Ewing, 1886

I know one successful front garden with a central path to the front door where the rectangular panels on either side are simple box hedges enclosing mown grass.

Penelope Hobhouse, 1981

The Dutch garden

In the old days of bedding-out, lawns used to be cut up into beds and patterns. Now the fashion has changed, and bedding-out has become so generally condemned that most people have levelled and turfed-over the rounds, stars, crescents, and oblongs that used to enliven their lawns for a short time, at any rate, every autumn. As a result of this reaction, there are now an immense number of large, dull lawns, which as a rule slope slightly away from the house, and often to the south. They are wet in rain, and dry and brown in hot weather. They have their weekly shave with the mowing-machine, and lie baking in the sunshine. The poor plants, which would flower and do well in the open, are planted at the edges of the shrubberies, where – in a light soil, at any rate – they are robbed and starved into ugliness and failure by their stronger neighbours.

There are several ways of breaking up lawns. One is by turning the lawns into grass paths, along which the machine runs easily, and making all the rest into open, informally shaped beds. These can be planted in every kind of way – in bold masses of one thing alone, or at most in mixtures of two, such as Roses and Violas; Azaleas and Lilies; Carnations and more Violas, or mossy Saxifrages; Campanulas in succession, tall and low-growing; a bold group of Bamboos and *Bocconia cordata*; or simply with a selection of a few low-growing shrubs; and so on *ad infinitum*. Another way, and one that finds small favour with gardeners, and with considerable reason, because of the trouble of turning the mowing-machine round the plants, is to break up the lawn with sunshine-loving specimen plants – Mulberries, Savins, Sumachs, clumps of creeping Ayrshire Roses and Honeysuckles, poles covered with claret-coloured Vines, Clematis, &c. Yet another way is to have a double pergola running all round the lawn in a square, or only down both sides, with a grass path, broad and stately, underneath the pergola. This can be made of stone or brick, oak-trees or fir-poles; or, if wanted very light, of Japanese large Bamboos – to be got now in London, I believe. These Bamboos look best if two, three, or five are blocked together unequally, with different-sized openings in between, and used as supports for fruit-trees and flowering shrubs of all kinds. As these plants grow, bamboos and wires have to be put across the top to support the creepers. In the middle is a large square of grass; the openings are left turfed, but where the supports are put into the ground a narrow bed must be made for the plants. This enables them to be manured, chalked, watered, and generally cared for. I now come to what is, in my idea, by far the most enchanting plan for breaking up a lawn, which is to sink a small Dutch garden in the middle of it. The size of the Dutch garden must, of course, be in proportion to that of the lawn. If the proportion cannot be kept, it would be better to leave it alone. It should have a red-brick wall all round it, and be oblong or square, as suits the situation. The entrances to it are by brick steps, one in the middle of each of the four sides. The height of the wall is about three feet from the ground on the outside, and five feet on the inside. Along these walls, on the inside, are rather wide beds, bordered by paths made of rows of large, square red tiles, laid flat and not quite joining, so that tiny alpines and mosses may grow in between them at their own sweet will. If preferred, this narrow path can be made of bricks or broken paving-stones. The object of this path, besides the convenience of standing dry to pick the flowers or weed the beds, is that the front of the bed can be planted in groups, not in rows, with all sorts of low-growing things: –

Alyssums, Aubrietias, Forget-me-nots, Pinks of all kinds, Saxi-frages, and mosses. On the side shaded by the wall and facing north small ferns, Campanulas, and shade-loving plants are the only ones that will do well. Primroses, Auriculas, and the spring-flowering bulbs and Irises do best on the side facing east; and the summer and autumn plants like to face west and north, as they weary of the hot sun all the summer through. All the year round this little garden can be kept a pleasure and a joy by a little management, and by planting and replanting from the greenhouse, the seed-beds, or the reserve garden. The wall looks best if entirely planted with Tea-roses. As they grow, they send up long waving branches, which beautifully break the hard line of the wall. The middle of the walled garden is grass, and the mowing-machine can never cut or injure the plants, feather forward as they will on to the tiled path between the beds and the grass. In the centre there can be a sundial on a square base; or, if you have water laid on, a small square or oblong cement tank let into the ground, quite level with the grass, as a fountain and to be handy for watering. All day long the water in the tank is warmed by the sunshine. This kind of fountain is an enormous improvement, I think, to small suburban gardens, and it is prettier oblong than square . . .

To go back to the Dutch garden. I think at the corners of, or on each side of, the entrances there may be pots with plants in them, or balls of stone, or anything else in character with the rest of the stone or brick work, which should be formal and slightly constrained in design, as I consider all brickwork in a garden close to a house ought to be. If planted as I described, no two such gardens would ever be the least alike; no law could bind them, and no wind destroy them.

Mrs C. W. Earle, 1887

At Dumbarton Oaks

On either side of the door leading to the flower room and the Green Garden, a squatty plant is needed, such as a really dwarf Box, or *Taxus baccata repandens*. These are better in scale than plants which grow four or five feet high. Only an inconspicuous pair of markers is needed for this door, as it should be minimised in comparison with the south entrance door of the house and the south door of the orangery. Almost the whole south front of the orangery is covered with a groundwork of English Ivy (*Hedera Helix*) on which is applied a thinly trained *Akebia quinata*; but the main feature in spring is a beautiful *Wisteria*, which should be so trained that it carries its flowers high in the air as a floral entablature to the building over the tops of the windows. A flower border with Box edging was formerly planted on the south side of this building, but this was discontinued, partly in order to reduce costs of upkeep but also because the building itself is so low that any foundation planting tends to reduce still further its charming scale and lines.

Beatrix Farrand, 1941

I have come to see quite plainly, through several years of lost time, that balanced planting throughout is the only planting for a garden that has any design worthy of the name.

Mrs Francis King, 1915

A designer's response

I love all the things most gardeners abhor! – moss in lawns, lichen on trees, more greenery than 'colour' (always said as though green isn't a colour!), bare branches in winter, more foliage than flowers, root-ridden ground (wherein one never attempts to dig) with a natural covering of leaves, of grass or some amenable low-growing plant. I like the whole thing to be as wild as possible, to have to fight your way through in some places. I shall always like that architect who loved trees so much that he said he liked to have to fight his way to the front door! I like sheets and sheets of self-sown forget-me-nots, and anything else that will self-sow itself and look so beautiful. I like a mossy boulder more than I like a 'splash of colour'. I like soft grey-green leaves, and blue, mauve, white and pale yellow flowers and only the tiniest spot of red – looking exquisite as only red can against grey-brown bark and dusky blue flowers. I like white flowers, both in day-time and at night, in the house and in the garden. I like quite a lot of plants for their foliage alone (not 'VARIEGATEDS', just plain plants that are supposed to flower) and never care if they don't flower. I like quite large trees in quite small gardens sometimes. I like odd-shaped trees, and find the 'perfect specimen' rather dull. If there are two or three trunks coming up from the base so much the better. I like to throw myself into an inviting chair in the green shade of a large tree with my books on a low table beside me, but you might prefer to dig and to plant. I like to do that too . . . sometimes.

Edna Walling, 1948

PLANTSWOMEN

THIS IS where green fingers come in. I have met people who, through indifference or make-up, are by nature lethal to all forms of plant life. In spite of this, considerate planting and transplanting can be learnt and fingers and thumb trained to be more understanding.

Xenia Field, 1965

Ground-cover

Among other things there are two things I fuss about in the garden. I don't like weeds and I don't like to see great expanses of bare earth. I never see a weed without wanting to get rid of it then and there – and there is usually something else I am supposed to be doing then and there. And as for bare earth, well it has the same effect on me. I feel I must always be harassing it, to get rid of the weeds and to prevent the surface becoming dry and caked. In spite of all the nice things I give it, my clay soil always manages to come up on top, and I spend my life trying to cover it up and in the covering-up process conserve the moisture.

Another reason why I use a lot of ground-cover plants is to make a good background for my flowers. I like to grow interesting and colourful plants, but I don't want mine to be a garden of specimens but a cohesive design that is pleasant even when the major attractions are not in flower. I have seen too many gardens in which some things are very beautiful and the rest neglected in a bare or untidy way.

My idea of a good ground-cover plant is one that has good foliage all the year round, doesn't take too much nourishment from the soil, and is easy to control. Of necessity it must have a slightly invasive disposition, but should restrict its wanderings to the surface of the soil and not go burrowing feet down. I don't think it is necessary to be too superior about covering your ground, and sometimes the most ordinary plants are the most effective. I have seen the ordinary wild woodruff looking lovely in the shady part of a cultivated garden. It gets bigger and more luxuriant in cultivation. I have a lot of the cultivated woodruff, *Phuopsis stylosa*, which has small tufts of pink flowers at the end of every long trail. It does not insist on sun or shade, and covers a lot of ground. I like the way it goes on blooming from early summer until October and November, and the light green of its feathery foliage is a pleasant foil for many plants. London Pride (*Saxifraga umbrosa*) is another good commoner, and will do just as well in poor soils.

When I first started gardening I used the ordinary bugle in my flower-beds. It did the job very well, but had no idea when to stop. I have never met such an exuberant plant; it over-bugled everything, and I still find it trying to get another foothold in beds where I once grew it and from which it was banished – officially – many years ago. I still use it on banks and in odd corners, because I know no better foliage, so bright and shining and bursting with good health, and the sturdy spikes of blue are exceedingly pleasant. It always looks at home and when I find it trespassing it goes to my heart to have to fork it out, and I am always glad when I can find a good home for the poor, unsuspecting creature. I have a form with white flowers, but it is not very robust and I am having a hard time to get it to increase like its buxom sister.

There are refined forms of bugle which can be relied on not to overplay their hand. *Ajuga pyramidalis* (syn. *genivensis*) is a delightful plant, with slightly hairy and burnished leaves, and neat spikes of the most intense blue. Unlike the other bugles, it increases in itself instead of flinging out skinny arms far and wide, each finished with a tuft of a plant and ready to pin itself down in any available spot. The variegated bugle does this, but it is much less robust than the ordinary form and does its encroaching in rather a cringing, meek way. Red-leaved bugle (*Ajuga reptans rubra*) is a wonderful carpeter for silver plants. It will grow so thick that no weed could possibly find a space in which to grow. The three-toned variegated bugle always reminds me of a tortoiseshell cat. Its correct name is *Ajuga reptans multicolorus*, and that is what it is, with a metallic sheen to its bronze background. It makes a good background to either gold or silver plants, and associates well with plants with glaucous foliage.

I have one gardening rule – when in doubt plant *Geranium*

endressii. I have never known such an accommodating plant. It never seems out of place. Put it among the aristocrats and it is as dignified as they are, let it romp in a cottage garden and it becomes a simple maid in a print dress. There are flowers all through the summer, and they don't disagree with anyone. It creeps a little and so makes a fine ground-cover plant, but it doesn't prance over everybody like the bugle. I like the places in which it seeds itself, holes in the paving or crevices in a wall. It seems to know the bare patches that I want to cover with kindly vegetation. I am quite happy with the ordinary form, but the concensus of opinion is in favour of the improved Wargrave variety, with flowers a little warmer pink. Then there is *G. endressii* A. T. Johnson, with silver-pink flowers on fifteen-inch stems. It is pretty in a border, but is more tufted than my common plant and not so useful for ground-cover.

The prunellas make a nice thick carpet of dark green. The flower spikes are not very tall and they are usually about the same height so that in early summer we change from a green carpet to a rose or blue one. The pale blue 'Loveliness' is well named and has flower-spikes a little taller than the pink and red. The rich purple *P. grandiflora* is taller still. I have only one complaint against the prunellas and that is the way they scatter their young. I wouldn't mind so much if I knew to which family I should return the little dears, but there is no way of telling until they flower, except with *P. webbiana*, which has jagged leaves instead of the smooth ones of the rest of the family. Prunellas do well in shade as well as sun, but they need a thorough grooming after flowering and look unsightly until the untidy flower-heads are cut off and we get back to our green carpet.

Another family closely allied to the prunellas used to be called betonica, and now the awkward people who change names have decreed that it must in future be stachys. The only member of the green-leaved family that I use for ground-cover is the violet *S. grandiflora*. It has handsome hairy foliage and flower-spikes about nine inches high. The pink form I find less robust, with slender flowers and slender leaves, and the white version is even more restrained; in fact, I have no luck at all with her, whatever I do she remains a mean, wizened little thing with no appetite for life. The silver-leaved *Stachys lanata* is one of my favourite plants. It is a wonderful carpeter, and looks particularly well associated with bronze foliage such as *Lobelia cardinalis* and purple rhus. When used as a carpet I usually cut off the tall flower spikes but I give them their head when I grow it in paving or in a wall. It is quite effective under bush roses.

And this leads me to another branch of the labiataes – the lamiums. Yes, dead nettles can be quite decorative if used in the right way. The most plebeian, of course, is *Lamium maculatum*, which I find rather a trial as it seeds itself everywhere and is another of those complacent intruders I find it difficult to expel because it is really an attractive plant, whether we have just the striped grey-green leaves or when covered with orchid-pink flowers. I know one garden where it is used most effectively to cover bare earth under a hedge, and I know of nothing better for banks and stone work. I don't admit it to the more select domain of my terraced garden, but I would welcome the lovely pink form and the white. There is an interesting golden version of *L. maculatum*, which I would use all over the place if I had enough of it. I was given a small piece years ago; it did well for me and everyone wanted a bit. I used to meet it in the gardens of friends of friends, so it was distributed very widely. But I very nearly lost my own plant because of the depredations, and spent several anxious months nursing back to health the fragment I had left myself. I have discovered that it roots very easily in a cold frame in pure sand, and when good roots have formed it seems happiest in damp, heavy clay. I used to try peat to pep it up, but it didn't do the trick. One day I hope to have enough to make that glinting sheet of gold I'd like to see running up between some of my more sombre plants or for a gold and silver border, which is one of the things I hope to have one day. There is a larger, coarser lamium, *L. ovata*, which is useful when something bold in the way of ground-cover is wanted. In April it gets quite gay with cherry-red flowers.

One of the best ground-cover plants I know for a shady situation is *L. galeobdolon luteum variegatum*; in other words, a variegated dead nettle with yellow flowers. But that doesn't really describe this most attractive plant. The leaves are large and are mostly shining silver against a grey background, and the flowers are deep primrose. But it isn't a plant for a small part of a neat little bed. It likes to hurl itself down a shady bank, pegging itself down as it goes. I was so pleased with the first scrap I acquired that I gave it a place of honour at the top of the peat garden, but it didn't stay there long. Very soon it had covered one end of the garden, and was walking across the bottom of the ditch to get busy on the other side. Most of it had to be removed, and now it glints under silver birch trees. I often see unsightly shady spots in gardens, and think how nice they'd look if clothed with this symphony in green and silver. Used on a hillside, it would almost give the impression of a waterfall.

We grow *Aster yunnanensis* Napsbury for the lovely mauve and orange daisies in the summer, but it also makes a good thick carpet, and by the time autumn comes the ranks will be closed and there will be a close planting of shining leaves.

Symphytum grandiflorum is pleasantest in the spring when the cream, apricot-tinged flowers hang above large hairy leaves. There isn't much competition when it is in flower, and I can get quite a thrill seeing it thrusting through the railings of a forgotten garden or blooming away madly in a quiet corner of my own. I forget then that it grows coarse and dull in the summer, and I usually plant it in those places which become a tropical jungle in high summer, and so I don't see much of it after its glory is over.

Periwinkles lost their Victorian popularity early this century, perhaps because they were tangled up in our minds with 'rockeries', and grottoes and other Victorian horrors. Now they have come into their own again with a vengeance, not so much in flower-beds, where they'd be rather too busy, but to cover the ground among shrubs. Large nurseries who design labour-saving gardens of shrubs and trees use vincas by the thousand.

I have always had a few periwinkles in the garden and would hate to be without them. The large blue flowers of *V. major* have an innocence and purity hard to find in any flower. It put itself in the wall that shields me from the road and I am delighted to have it there, but I do curse it somewhat when it pops out of the wall for richer living in the border, although its wide-eyed flowers in winter soften me. In the right place it is an invaluable ground-coverer; there is nothing better for thickening up the bottom of a mangy hedge or providing a welcome green flurry at the bottom of a wall. I have seen it curbed to a narrow band at the edge of a path, and holding up a bank with loops and trails of shining green. The variegated form is nearly as lusty and often more effective. There is one form called *elegantissima* which looks as if white paint had been brushed on dark green and I don't wonder the flower arrangers use the long trails, each with its lovely floral ending, in winter bowls. The other, *V. major reticulata*, is variegated with gold.

The upright *V. difformis* is also in the large-leaved section, and has pale, pale flowers in winter. I have been told that it is not always hardy in cold parts of the country, but it grows happily in Somerset.

V. difformis is smaller in leaf than *V. major* and a little larger than *V. minor*, with curious shaped, rather spidery flowers in lavender blue.

The biggest group of periwinkles are the small-leaved ones, *Vinca minor*. Records show that there have been at least fifteen different forms, but, alas, I don't know if they all exist today. Has anyone the double form of *V. minor alba*, or *V. minor roseoplena*, a double red, or *V. minor cuprea*, which is a single in reddish-copper? I know two different white ones, the ordinary *V. minor alba* and Mr Bowles's variety, with different-shaped flowers, and two single blues, the ordinary one and the more intense La Graveana. There is a pink, a burgundy-coloured, and one that goes as *V. minor rubra plena*, which has a few extra petals but is not really double. *V. m. caeruleoplena*, sometimes called Celestial is really double, with flowers like little blue roses. The ordinary variegated form has silver markings and blue flowers, *alba variegata* has gold markings and white flowers; there is a blue-flowered form with gold variegations, and a gold-leaved vinca which can have white or lavender flowers.

I use violets to cover ground in shady places, and can also recommend alpine strawberries as carpeters of the most determined calibre.

Margery Fish, 1958

How I loathe being ill! How I fight it, rebel against it, garden up to the very last moment and get up tottering to go out and replant the Violet bed.

Mrs Leslie Williams, 1901

The south wind that came over the bed of violets, – the touching remark of Ophelia, who coloured all nature with the hues of her own sad thoughts, 'I would give you violets, but they withered all when my father died': these and many another sweet poetic passage, serve to show how men in all ages have prized our spring flower. Which of us could spare the violet from the memories of early life? And how many of us are even now reminded by its passing scent of scenes which may never be revisited, but whose verdure and sunshine and song make a picture on which the eye of the mind can linger as long as life itself shall last.

Anne Pratt, 1889

White Hellebore

By July, this Hellebore is in its strongest vigour. During that month the operation of lifting the clumps – only two or three at a time – is commenced, these clumps being at once wheeled to a cool shed.

In breaking up the plants in the ordinary way, the principal point is, to avoid as much as possible the loss of leaves; then cut off as much of the thick root-stock as can with safety be spared, leaving the true roots attached to the neck of the plant intact, and at once re-plant the divided clumps in their permanent quarters, watering carefully, and, if necessary, shading with a branch until evening, the object being to prevent flagging, to keep up the appearance of the bed or border during the summer, when this Hellebore is valuable for its foliage alone, and to ensure the flowering of the clumps. The growing plants safe, we commence cutting up the root-stocks . . .

Sitting down with a sharp thin strong blade, I cut up the root-stock into pieces from one to two inches in length, according to the appearance of the buds, or swellings; some of these may be 'blind', so close attention must be paid to the work, and at times you will have to sacrifice an 'eye' (so to speak), in making two plants of a piece of root, or, what is wiser for the amateur, be satisfied with one plant and keep all the eyes. But there is a dangerous fascination in seeing how many safe cuts you can make in a lump of root, and one turns it round and round before deciding on the best angle to take to make most, and lose least. In these doubtful cases, however, I now resist the temptation, and leave the piece whole, being sure that a finer plant will thus be all the more quickly secured.

I am particular in planting each day's roots that have been cut up the same day, leaving nothing for the morrow, and I therefore only lift what can safely be disposed of that day. Plenty of sand is needed in the shallow bed of light soil, and a gentle watering with a fine-rosed pot when the lines are filled up and the bed full, completes the business.

Frances Hope, 1881

Primroses

Some three years ago, when 'Wilson' blue Primroses were very precious, I bought three plants from an advertiser in some non-gardening paper. The first season one did not bloom; the others turned out to be – one a dark rich beautiful blue, the other an exquisite light blue between sky, porcelain and Cambridge. There were no seeds ripe this first year; the next summer I saved and sowed two pods, one from the pale blue and the other from the hitherto unbloomed plant, which was a dark blue. The resulting dozen plants are now in full swing in the Oblong, but, alas! there is not one sweet light blue among them. Eight are reds, one is a pretty shade of blue-lilac, not showy, one a darker shade of the same, one a nice purple, and one a washy lilac-purple . . . Some bought seed of the blue variety, sown later, has produced plants whose blooms are all very rich and deep self colours, violets, reds, and purples, with good yellow eyes, and grand in size, but up to the present not one real blue. I want a whole bed of those China blues!

Mrs Leslie Williams, 1901

The secret of getting bloom from lilies-of-the-valley in their first season is to plant the roots vertically, not spread out flat on the ground, and never disturb your bed again. Should the plants become poor after some years, take a sharp spade in November and cut square sods out here and there through the bed (you can either give these away or start a new colony for yourself); then fill up the holes with a very rich compost of loam, manure and leaf mould and tread this in firmly.

Lady Seton, 1927

Planting in dry shade

Today I put in some work in my dark and difficult corner. At the back of the flower-bed the rather splendid *Mahonia japonica* and the small-leaved bamboo, *Sinarundinaria nitida*, form a wall of shade and of course the earth underneath is very dry. In the late spring a spreading clump of *Polygonatum* (Solomon's seal), and *Smilacina racemosa* are beautiful, but as they die down the gap is depressing, and the Solomon's seal becomes a martyr to nasty grey sawfly caterpillars, which wreak unsightly havoc on the leaves. Recent browsing through books and some investigation at the Royal Horticultural Society shows produced some plants that may tolerate this situation.

I planted the common woodrush *Luzula sylvatica* 'Marginata' which the nurserywoman who sold it to me promised was absolutely foolproof for dry shade. I have seen luzulas in woodlands in Gloucestershire, certainly in shade though not apparently particularly dry. Laurels will usually survive difficult aspects, and if the *Aucuba*, variety 'Sparkler', does well its bright variegation should dispel some of the gloom.

The spotted-leaved *Brunnera macrophylla* flourishes under shrubs and *Symphytum* 'Goldsmith' (comfrey) has a well-variegated leaf in green and pale gold, so by using these variegations this dark patch may come to life. These and the fern for dry places, plus a few rooted pieces of the good-tempered spurge *Euphorbia robbiae*, have all been comfortably planted in well-dug soil enriched with leaf mould and some crumbled horse manure, followed by a liberal watering, and although all these plants should flourish in dry conditions they will appreciate regular watering in their first summer to give them a good start in life.

Sheila Jackson, 1994

The watering of a garden requires nearly as much judgment as the seasoning of a soup. Keep the soil well stirred and loose on the surface, going through the garden, where possible, with a rake; and if there is no room for a rake, stir gently with a trowel every five days or once a week. In this way moisture will be retained in the soil, since the loose earth acts as a mulch.

When watering, be generous. Soak the plants to the roots; wet all the earth around them, and do it late in the afternoon, when the sun is low. How often have I been obliged to chide the men for watering too early in the afternoon, and not doing it thoroughly, for, upon stirring the ground, I would find that the water had penetrated but a couple of inches. During long periods of dry weather, the garden, without water, will simply wither and burn.

Mrs Helena Rutherfurd Ely, 1903

Peonies

Long ago I learned that really to see peonies they should be so grown that one could sit near or actually beside them. So I sit now on this twenty-eighth day of June, the fragrance of countless mock-orange blossoms filling every air that blows and the most glorious flowers that we have for our gardens, bar none, close at hand on their respective plants.

Jubilee is before me in full sun, its milk-white feathers of petals moving in the breeze, its beautiful pale-lemon-coloured central cup very distinct in the bright light. Midsummer Night's Dream is beside my straw chair (all these peonies are set in round holes in grass) and I can lift one of its luscious heavy heads and see its creamy centre flaked with carmine and admire its guard-petals of pale lilac and the general look of its handsome flower. At a little distance is Reine Hortense, with its warm pink hue in the young flower and its fine tuft of white petaloids or true carpels. In the near distance stand two plants whose flowers glow like rubies: Felix Crousse, not new but so fine, and Ville de Nancy, beautiful in form as in colour, the clearest, most vivid of carmines.

Mrs Francis King, 1927

The Genus Rosa

Rosa Eglanteria

This species is the only British wild Rose which has always been permitted to rank as a garden plant; its compact habit and delicious fragrance have from very early days assured it a welcome place in English gardens. It is a vigorous and hardy Rose, and there are some well-known instances of its remarkable longevity. Some of them, of course, must be taken with reservation, but even so there is ample proof that the Sweet Briar under favourable conditions will live to a very considerable age. A large bush growing in a Touraine garden was cut down some sixty years since and upon the rings being counted they were found to number something like a hundred and twenty; the plant had shown no signs whatever of deterioration, and the thick gnarled stems were perfectly sound. In the garden of an old castle in Saxony there was a bush growing in a shady moist corner and reaching the height of some twenty feet, and it was still well furnished with leaves and blossomed and bore fruit in profusion. This plant was locally believed to have been growing there when Charlemagne's third son Louis was crowned Emperor of the West at Aix-la-Chapelle in A.D. 814!

Woods found that Sweet Briar fruit tasted mealy and insipid, whereas the fruit of its near relative *Rosa micrantha* Smith is slightly acid and pleasant to the taste. Although the fragrance from the Eglantine is so exquisite either after a shower of rain or when the leaves are touched, the water distilled from them yields a perfume far from agreeable unless mixed with some other ingredient.

Scotch Rose

These little Roses are so charming that they can never entirely disappear from our gardens. Flowering from three weeks to a month earlier than the generality of other Roses, they continue in bloom for a considerable time, and in autumn their bronze foliage and plentiful hips are an additional charm. The fruit apparently ripens but slowly, and is therefore not attacked by birds until towards the end of winter. Their compact habit and wealth of blossom makes them very beautiful objects for the rock garden. Care should, however, be taken not to plant them where their suckers are likely to interfere with the rarer plants. These Scotch Roses are seen to best advantage when growing on grass where they may increase unrestrained year after year, without requiring the least attention, except that the old wood should be cut out from time to time.

Stanwell Perpetual

This beautiful Rose has been for more than a century one of the greatest charms of our English gardens. In all ways it is good, in colour, fragrance, and habit. Never capricious, it will grow and thrive year after year, producing its beautiful flowers in profusion, shedding its delicious fragrance all around, and continuing in flower long after the other Scotch Roses are over. It flourishes even in poor soil, requires no attention, and will produce flowers even in the shade, although it undoubtedly prefers a sunny, open situation and so placed will attain to extreme old age and still preserve all its charms.

Ellen Willmott, 1910

Ispahan

A paragon amongst Damask Roses is Ispahan, Rose d'Isfahan or Pompom des Princes – a rose that grows wild on the hills of Persia and is particularly beautiful between Shiraz and the old caravan trading centre of Ispahan. Friends who have lived in that country tell us of the glories of this and other pink Damask Roses, and of the wild pink Persian lilac – which blooms at the same time as the roses – as they cascade over the hillsides. Residents of Shiraz grow the rose Ispahan in their quiet walled gardens, where ample water is led in to irrigate the trees and plants and also to create a cool and restful atmosphere in that hot dry land . . .

Our tremendous plant of Ispahan is growing in a pink border along one side of a sunken garden. When this Damask Rose is in full bloom, literally thousands of perfect flowers weigh down the long arching branches until the bush looks like a fountain or shower of several shades of pink. The buds, which come in sprays, are really exquisite, as they open to show a deeper tone in the centre – the many-petalled flowers being a soft, uniform pink when fully out. On a grassy terrace above this Damask Rose is a narrow border alongside the house in which are planted pink fuchsias, and roses; one rose, the lovely Tausendschön, reaches to the eaves of the house before weeping down in a pink cascade above the Persian Damask.

. . . Ispahan is a riot of bloom for over two months. It gives us endless pleasure and very little work; all we do is cut back the wood that has bloomed as soon as the first sign of fresh growth appears. The strong new shoots, covered with wonderfully healthy foliage, then develop rapidly and soon attain a height of over eight feet. These branches ripen well during the late summer and autumn; and are then in readiness to carry next season's heavy load of flower. Some of the longest branches can be shortened a little in the winter; and, if a number of stems are hooked over with strong wires, far more bloom will be produced.

Nancy Steen, 1966

Flowers that smell of other things

In some roses the foliage is aromatic. After rain or in muggy weather, particularly, *Rosa rubiginosa*, the sweet brier, gives off its stewed-apple fragrance; while *Rosa primula* is called the incense rose on account of the aroma of its leaves, not its dainty yellow flowers . . .

Many pinks and carnations smell like cloves – and indeed are commonly called clove pinks or clove carnations. The smell of cloves is present also in *Hesperis matronalis*, sweet rocket, and in other Cruciferae such as *Erysimum capitatum*, a rather tender wall-flower. Things get more complex when one reads that *Viburnum carlesii* smells like carnations; to me, it is more like a daphne. There is a close, but not perhaps exact, similarity between the scent of lily-of-the-valley and that of the flowers of *Mahonia japonica*, or of *Skimmia japonica* 'Rubella' and 'Fragrans'. It is hardly surprising to find that *Primula florindae* smells like cowslips, for it is closely related; but one expects less the cowslip perfume of *Corylopsis* species, or of *Clematis rehderiana*. The fragrance of *Clematis flammula* has been likened both to meadowsweet and to hawthorn, but to me it has nothing of the unpleasantly fishy smell of hawthorn flowers at close quarters . . .

The flowers of gorse smell of coconut, and of *Spartium junceum* like almonds. The powerful, far-carrying fragrance of *Viburnum* × *bodnantense* has a large almond content too. To all these foody smells, one could add the very characteristic perfume of the fallen leaves of *Cercidiphyllum japonicum*. It had never occurred to me that these smelled of anything other than hot toffee; the aroma is strong, and carries a fair distance on the air, so that one can confidently state at the right season that there is a cercidiphyllum about even if it cannot be seen . . . One writer took issue with my hot toffee, saying that on the contrary cercidiphyllum leaves smell of straw-berry jam. Well, if jam it must be, then it is definitely burnt jam. For the burnt toffee smell that you can have from *Leycesteria formosa*, you need to extract and crush the ripe black fruits; not a hint of fragrance is carried on the air.

Everyone expects conifers to give off a resinous smell, and *Hebe cupressoides* looks, until it flowers, so like a dwarf, glaucous-blue conifer that its unmistakable smell of pencil cedar is no surprise: until, that is, you realise that it is no conifer at all. Next time you sharpen a pencil, sniff the shavings, then rush out and rub a strand of *Hebe cupressoides* between your fingers to catch the likeness.

The hebe, with its rounded outline, assorts well with silvery foliage as of the pungent santolinas (which smell like nothing except themselves) and some of the needle-leaved helichrysums, in dry and sunny borders. Most of these smell of curry – that is, of the kind of inexpensive, general-purpose curry powder that would be recognised by no Asian but which is commonly used to make kitchen curry in Britain.

Most people dislike the smell of *Fritillaria imperialis* bulbs, which is usually described as foxy. This curious odour, which to me has strong overtones of garlic, is much the same as that possessed by *Phuopsis stylosa*, which looks like an unassuming pink woodruff. To anyone who shares my fondness for garlic (especially sliced thinly and eaten raw on rye bread with unsalted butter), this is not a wholly unpleasant smell. Less agreeable is the pigsty smell of *Escallonia viscosa* and *E. illinita*, which at a distance is reduced to an aroma not too far removed from the hot, peppery smell of phloxes, but close to is altogether too animal for comfort.

On the other hand the tackroom smell of aromatic rhododendrons such as *R. oreotrephes*, and most especially *R. glaucophyllum*, is unpleasant only to those whose childhood did not include shaggy ponies, neatsfoot oil and saddlesoap. The fronds of *Acacia pravissima*, when dried, smell very like the warm breath of horses.

Jane Taylor, 1989

Auratum Lilies

The auratum lilies planted last November are coming forward finely. They were grouped mainly in the bulb beds below the study windows, where they came the earliest in bloom. But for an experiment I scattered a couple of dozen bulbs at random, through the beds of the long walk, and the effect of the great golden-banded, ruby-spotted flowers is magical, giving depth of focus to the maze of phlox, as well as the thrill of oriental suggestion that the lily and iris tribes always bring with them. In an old-fashioned garden such as mine, this result must be by suggestion only; for if it is allowed to dominate, it becomes incongruous, and would wholly denationalise the garden.

Barbara Campbell, 1911

Border Phlox

There is no flower in the garden more beautiful, more easily cultivated, or giving so much bloom as the Phlox. I could certainly never have a garden without it. In mine there must be a couple of thousand. I have a great mass, of probably two hundred herbaceous Phloxes, growing together in one corner of my garden, the very tall varieties over four feet high. About the fifteenth of July, every year, this corner is a superb sight. Most of these plants are over fifteen years old. They have been kept fine by heaviest top-dressing every year, and by lifting all the plants every three years and digging in quantities of manure, and also by separating each plant into three, by cutting the roots with a spade, or pulling apart with the fingers.

The newer varieties of Phlox come in the most beautiful colours, – dark crimson, fiery scarlet, many shades of pink, pink striped with white, and pink with a white eye; all shades of lilac, lilac with white and purple, the beautiful pure white, and the white with the scarlet eye. Of all the varieties, my favourites are the snowy white, and the salmon-pink with the dark red eye. Buy fifty large field-grown plants; at the end of three years separate them, and you have a hundred and fifty. They present a picture of progression much surer than the tale of the eggs that were to do so much.

Many of the individual blossoms of my Phloxes are larger than a fifty-cent piece; a number of them larger by measurement than a silver dollar, and the heads also are very large. Always erect, neat and smiling, never needing to be staked (such a task in a large garden), when once grown they must always be dear to a gardener's heart. By breaking off the heads of Phlox immediately after bloom-

ing, a second crop of flowers will appear in about three weeks. The
heads will not be so large as the first, but they will amply repay
the slight trouble.

Every owner of a garden has certain favourites; it really cannot
be helped, although the knowledge that it is so makes it seem
almost as unfair as for a mother to have a favourite child.

Mrs Helen Rutherfurd Ely, 1903

Hydrangeas

Experiments in the production of blue flowers were reported in
the Horticultural Society's *Transactions* in 1818. Phillips tells a
touching story of a magnificent blue-flowered specimen that grew
in a cottage-garden on a 'dreary common' in Hampshire, at a time
when hydrangeas of any sort were rare: the owner, although
extremely poor, refused an offer of ten guineas for it, because it
had been 'reared by a child whom she had lost', but was eventually
persuaded to part with a few cuttings – all of which produced pink
flowers when transferred to a new environment. By 1875 it had
been discovered that watering with alum or mixing iron filings
with the soil would turn the flowers blue, but 'the natural delicate
rosy hue is preferable', says Burbidge primly, 'and we do not
recommend trickery in window-gardening'. It is now known that
hydrangeas will turn blue on an acid soil if 'free' aluminium is also
available and many recipes are given in horticultural works for
producing the desired result; but different kinds vary widely in
their capacity to change colour, according to the part played by the
wild species in their constitution. The white-flowered *H. japonica*
will not turn blue in any circumstances, whereas *H. acuminata*
blues readily; so pale shades bearing a high proportion of *japonica*
blood do not change colour so easily as darker ones.

Shirley Hibberd praised the hydrangea as a pet, because it
responds so willingly to any treatment that its owner may think fit
to give it; but Loudon drily remarks that it is 'particularly suitable
for persons who have little else to do than attend to their garden,
or greenhouse', as it requires so much watering. A large specimen

in warm weather will consume ten or twelve gallons of fluid daily. The name *Hydrangea*, though it means a water-vessel, has nothing to do with this excessive thirstiness; it was given to the first (American) species to be discovered, on account of its cup-shaped seed-vessels. The middle syllable, we are told, should be pronounced 'ran' not 'rain'; so Loudon's mnemonic 'head-ranger' leads us astray. In the language of flowers the Hortensia signifies a boaster, because the flowers are not succeeded by fruit, but are like fraudulent company-promotors offering shares in non-existent gold-mines.

Alice M. Coats, 1963

I know no summer-flowering shrub so beautiful as the *Hydrangea paniculata grandiflora*. I have tried over and over again to grow it, but it does badly and then dies. It is not the soil only, for I once saw a magnificent specimen growing under a wall at Ascot, where the soil is the same as ours. I suppose it never has had quite a good enough place. It should be cut back hard every spring, and, when growing freely, wants much watering; I am told that constant applications of soot-water does it good. I daresay I shall succeed in time.

Mrs C. W. Earle, 1897

'Giant Decorative Dahlia'

It is easy enough to love flowers but these
had never appealed to me before, so
out of proportion above my garden's
other coloured heads and steady stems.

This spring though, in warm soil, I set
an unnamed tuber, offered cheap and,
when August came and still no sign,
assumed that slugs had eaten it.

                 Suddenly it showed,
began to grow, became a small tree.
It was a race between the dingy bud
and the elements. It has beaten
the frost, rears now three feet above
the muddled autumn bed, barbaric petals
pink quilled with tangerine, turning
its great innocent face towards me
triumphantly through the damp afternoon.

I could not deny it love if I tried.

Molly Holden, 1968

... the Dahlia's first duty in life is to flaunt and to swagger and to
carry gorgeous blooms well above its leaves, and on no account
to hang its head.

Gertrude Jekyll, 1899

Dahlia and Fuchsia

The Dahlia, a native of Mexico, was first introduced in 1789 from
Spain by Lady Bute, but was lost and re-introduced in 1804 by Lady
Holland, and twenty years later the craze for these flowers reached

its height. The Fuchsia appeared in this country within the first five-and-twenty years of this century, although named by Plumier after Fuchs about a hundred years earlier. The story is told of how Lee saw a Fuchsia plant in a window of a small house in Wapping. He was so struck with the flower that he went in and asked the old woman to whom it belonged whether she would sell it to him. She, however, at first refused to part with it, as it had been sent to her by her husband who was a sailor, but was persuaded to let him have it when he offered her eight guineas and promised to give her two of the first plants he reared. He succeeded in getting some three hundred cuttings to strike, and presented the old woman with her share, while the rest, with their graceful hanging flowers, astonished the visitors to his Nursery, and brought him in a profit of about £300.

Alicia Amherst, 1895

Canna and Cosmos in India

Fashions in flowers are almost as evanescent as fashions in millinery. It is not long since canna was the rage; every garden I know was full of it, and people who had never gardened before became pronounced bores on the subject of canna, which appeals to the beginner as being a nice easy plant to grow. You planted it in any corner of your garden, the newer the soil the better, and no sooner had you planted it than – hey presto! it flowered gorgeously, sending up a quantity of suckers for the furtherance of its species. In fact, canna seemed almost too good to be true.

It was barely a year before a doubt crept in. The canna groups had a way of getting untidy, and the *mali* forgot to cut down the stems that had flowered. In time it dawned on us that canna was a greedy and ungrateful creature, an insatiable feeder, a thirsty drinker. It speedily exhausted the soil about it, and clamoured for more. We discovered that canna loved change, and must be transplanted every three months or so, and gradually we fell out of love with it. It was still gorgeous, but so easily propagated that every garden blazed with it; we wearied of its magnificence. And so canna fell into its proper place. It serves to fill a space, and it flowers often when there is little else in the garden, but it is in no sense to be relied on, and it is deceptive in that it requires more care than it professes to.

Cosmos is now the fashion, and its starlike blossoms are dainty and easy to arrange.

Kathleen Murray, 1913

August

If, in the early days of my gardening life, I had been asked to name a flower for each month of the year I would probably have replied something like this. January – snowdrops, February – crocuses, March – hellebores, April – daffodils, May – tulips, June – roses, July – lilies, August – dust, dead grass and black spot! Certainly I would have been appalled to be asked to enthuse about the garden in what is possibly the most disheartening month of the year. Or rather it can be, and used to be in my case.

Living as I do in the driest part of East Anglia, we are always concerned with drought. Desiccating winds following pathetically mean showers of rain, left-overs of downpours before the rain clouds reach us – are very much the pattern of our growing season. Even in wet summers our rainfall is still only average, between 1½ and 2 inches a month. In this part of the country, the garden in August is often a sad sight, the grass burnt brown, early plants finished and cut down, leaving perhaps weary looking stands of mildewed phlox and michaelmas daisies. If you do plenty of bedding out followed by copious watering the picture can be brighter, but I prefer more permanent planting.

I am very fortunate that my garden at Elmstead Market, near Colchester, is situated in a shallow hollow between two farms. Because there is a wide range of soil conditions we have been able to make several different types of planting. We began about twenty years ago, bulldozing away the bramble tangles, tall bracken and nettle beds, and found we had everything, including dry hungry gravel, moist black silt, and sticky wet clay in the hollow where there ran a spring-fed ditch. Over the years the ditch has been dammed and transformed into five large pools, set in sloping green grass, reflecting the bog-loving plants that we have grouped around them.

However, three quarters of my land is very dry, free-draining gravel, and it was the need to find something which would furnish this difficult situation for most of the year that started my great interest in leaves. Once you stop waiting for plants to produce flowers to hide their leaves – and begin to find how many exciting shades of colour, not to mention variety of forms and textures there are to be found in leaves – you find yourself designing with foliage, and the flowers follow incidentally.

I am now often quite relieved with the coming of August for the confusion of flowering plants to ebb away, and the new fresh patterns of leaves to take over. Walking along one of my dry sunny borders at this time of year, I enjoy stands of tall feathery bronze fennel above silver mounds of santolina, with Miss Willmott's ghost, *Eryngium giganteum*, seeded among them. Perhaps the loveliest of the sea hollies, she opens green, but slowly turns to a silver milky-blue. There are many eryngiums, some very spiny and prickly, others with soft and exquisite lace-like ruffs surrounding their central cones. Their deep indigo blue colouring, silvered veining and metallic texture look well with velvety carpets of *Stachys olympica*, or lambs' ears, as we called it as children.

All the artemisias, and there are so many, improve as the summer passes. Silky, feathery, almost white foliage glows in the dusk of late summer evenings, and, together with the cistus bushes, thymes and santolinas, fills the air with warm southern scents. Among them little lizards rustle over the dry soil, seed pods of euphorbias explode and pop, bees hum busily in the calamint bushes. I thought my first plant of *Calamintha nepetoides* was a dull little thing, but as summer fades into autumn these little plants produce more and more clouds of tiny pale blue flowers until they are a charming sight, crowded and humming with honey bees. They look well in the herb border surrounded with golden or variegated thymes, and the matt-leaved sages. The golden sage, *Salvia officinalis* 'Icterina', is a lovely foliage plant with soft gold and green variegated leaves, brightest in late summer. I have never seen it flower. The purple-leafed sage has just finished flowering, spasmodically, and will continue to produce its velvety purple leaves, some splashed with pink or cream.

Looking across the Dry Garden at this time of year, with its background of grey and silver plants, the dominant flower colour seems to be yellow. Outstanding is the Mount Etna broom, *Genista aetnensis*, not nearly so commonly planted as Laburnum, I wonder why not. Just now it is a fountain, fifteen feet high and across, dripping with millions of tiny yellow pea flowers, while the sweet spicy scent drifts over the garden. At ground level, yellow is repeated with *Coreopsis verticillata*, and lovely sharp, almost luminous yellow in the daisy *Anthemis tinctoria* 'Wargrave'. Shrubby potentillas are there in creamy white, primrose yellow, soft tans and apricot. Cool contrast is provided for these warm colours with shades of blue and purple. Tumbling over a raised bed sheltered under a west wall is *Convolvulus mauritanicus*, a very superior bindweed which never becomes a nuisance; it is massed with shallow fluted saucers in a lovely rich blue. This warm raised bed is a novelty for me, providing in flat Essex somewhere for tumbling plants to trail and where tiny treasures can be placed at a level where it is easy to see and care for them. Two plants, not in the least tiny, are demanding attention against this wall just now. *Crepis incana* is covered with hundreds of rose-pink dandelion flowers on thin branched stems, about nine inches high; it is a delight. Further along *Penstemon isophyllus* has shot up tall elegant stems hung with vivid scarlet and pink tubular flowers.

For the large border the double and semi-double forms of Shasta daisy, *Chrysanthemum maximum*, will go on producing new flowers for weeks to come. And so too will the *Acanthus mollis*, already holding stately stems above its mounds of handsome shining leaves. They have such strong moulded flowers of a curious dull maroon, with a clean white frilly petticoat held out seductively to encourage some insect to enter and fertilise the large cherry-like seed pod that will eventually be formed.

More white flowers will be added with the summer hyacinths – *Galtonia candicans*. They seem such luscious plants to be flowering in August. Their well-fed bulbs send up tall strong stems heavy with drooping white bells. Much nearer the ground are the soft grey mounds of *Anaphalis triplinervis* which will be massed with bunches of small white papery everlasting daisies. I hang these upside down and when they are quite dry I fill a large bowl with them to bring summer into the house in winter.

Round the corner of the house below the west wall, and on

slightly better soil is a surprising riot of rich growth. The purple leafed vine is mixed up with trails of *Eccremocarpus scaber* whose burnt-orange flowers are intertwined with the soft scarlet of the Cape figwort, *Phygelius capensis. Clematis tangutica* adds to the tangle, smothered with tiny lemon flowers, while bold contrast is made with the great white crumpled petals of *Romneya coulteri*, the Californian tree poppy. Looking from the house across this jungly border I have enjoyed a tall bush mallow, *Lavatera olbia* 'Rosea', massed with large rosy-mauve silken flowers – it should be a feature for several weeks to come.

If we leave the Dry Garden and go down a shallow flight of steps we shall come on to the cool grass of the lower garden and arrive by the ponds. Here is a different world. The impact of lush green growth around is almost overpowering. Huge upturned parasols of *Gunnera*, each leaf more than four feet across, intricately puckered and crinkled to form a frilled and fluted edge, are lifted above our heads on great thick stems covered with green prickles. Protected between these barriers stand the curious flower spikes or fruiting bodies. About two feet high, they consist of close-packed fleshy fingers or cones, covered with small green dots which ripen to become small orange seeds. Extraordinary that such a vast plant produces such ridiculously small seeds.

More dramatic foliage is provided by the great phormiums, or New Zealand flax, which can be plain, purple, or variegated, while a towering grass, *Miscanthus sacchariflorus*, is ten feet tall, its drooping strap-shaped leaves catching the light like a waterfall. For the really large water garden there is *Petasites japonicus*, the gigantic Butter-bur, which I have planted to cover the banks of the neighbouring farm reservoir at the end of my garden. This plant makes thick underground stems (disastrous in a small garden) fine for stabilising sloping sides which could be washed down by winter rain. The enormous round leaves make overlapping mounds which smother the toughest weeds. In spring the bare clay bank will be dotted with its curiously attractive flowers, demure posies of white heliotrope-like clusters surrounded by a ruff of primrose-coloured bracts.

Adding lightness to these architectural giants are such plants as Mr Bowles's golden sedge (a form of *Carex stricta*) – a lovely grass-like plant, like a bright golden sunburst overhanging the water's edge, and repeated across the pool by a dainty shrub which has golden leaves all the growing season. It used to be called *Spiraea opulifolia*, but now it is *Physocarpus opulifolius* 'Luteus'.

Too many flowers out at the same time can spoil the atmosphere of tranquillity by the waterside, but somehow there is a spaced effect, of colour coming and going, among the rich foliage. Most of the candelabra primulas and water iris are over now, but *Primula florindae*, the mealy Himalayan giant cowslip, is reflected in the dark water, with yellow musk nearby, and not far away the yellow is repeated in the tall *Thalictrum flavum* which holds fluffy masses of tiny yellowish-green flowers high above wax-blue leaves.

Astilbes are good in August, and especially I love the small ones like Sprite, which has finely cut bronze green foliage and wide airy sprays of shell pink flowers. More pink is provided by several meadow sweets. *Filipendula rubra* 'Venusta' runs about in the Bog Garden sending up six-foot stems topped with swirls of tiny pink flowers – like sticks of candy floss.

There is a race of moisture-loving daisies among which I find myself still confused. *Ligularia*, *Inula* and *Buphthalmum* – they are all handsome looking creatures, flowering and leafing well into late summer provided they are in good soil which does not dry out. I have at least three that are similar, yet not the same. One makes enormous basal leaves, dock shaped, which send up six-feet stems carrying wide heads of large yellow daisies whose petals are cut to narrow ribbons. Nearby, with similar foliage is a smaller version with orange-peel shredded petals, with a large central disc that goes brown with age. Finally by the waterside is silhouetted yet another, with impressive foliage and towering stem, up to eight feet high, narrowly set with green knobby buds which open out into a spire of smallish yellow daisies, and eventually make a gigantic seedhead – useful for decorating a large room.

Tapering spires are needed I think among rounded clumps like day lilies, or scented border phlox, both flowering now. Two I like specially. The first is *Lysimachia ephemerum*; it is, surprisingly perhaps, related to the modest little Creeping Jenny. However, this plant makes clumps of four-foot stems elegantly set with blue-grey leaves and topped with neat spires of small white flowers. *Veronica virginica* 'Alba', faintly washed with lilac, creates a similar effect – the flowers set more closely on narrower spires.

Both in my ponds, and in cool borders, in well-prepared sites, I grow several forms of *Zantedeschia*, which we know better as arum lily. Although they grow wild in South Africa, they can be grown here with some protection in winter. In natural ponds they are protected from frost when established in the deep mud floor, while in a border a thick covering of straw or bracken keeps them safe. The form known as 'Crowborough' is now at its best on the edge of one of my shrubberies. Few flowers have such purity of line, each single 'petal' rolled and spiralled like an old-fashioned sweet-bag. Beside it towers the green-flowered form, known as 'Green Goddess'. Standing tall as I am are enormous fluted funnels whose wide green tips disappear into ivory throats. The great leaves form a feature in themselves – indeed you have to look twice to spot the flowers among them.

Beth Chatto, 1980

Knowing how to grow things is important if you want to make a garden, but not as important as people make out; it's knowing where to put them that matters.

Mary Keen, 1987

No year passes that one does not observe some charming combination of plants that one had not intentionally put together. Even though I am always trying to think of some such happy mixtures, others come of themselves. This year the best of these chances was a group of pale sulphur Hollyhock seen against Yews that were garlanded with *Clematis Flammula*; tender yellow and yellow-white and deepest green; upright spire of Hollyhock, cloud-like mass of Clematis, low-toned sombre ground of solemn Yew . . .

One of the happiest mixtures of plants it has ever been my good fortune to hit on is that of St. Bruno's Lily and London Pride . . .

Gertrude Jekyll, 1900

The Crossing House garden

When we moved to the Crossing House, Shepreth in March 1959 my first impression was of a wilderness. Closer investigation revealed a small triangular flat plot of which the two longest sides were bounded by a busy country road and by the King's Cross to Cambridge railway line on which my husband was level crossing keeper. Four outhouses were in an advanced state of decay. A sleeper pigsty sagged under the weight of a venerable ivy. None of the four rickety, peeling fences matched. There were paths of rotten sunken sleepers leading nowhere in particular. Waist high nettles hid the rusted remains of the wire netting hen run, but at least indicated fertile soil. The seven fruit trees were so badly diseased as to be a menace. Two elderly rose bushes and a tangled forsythia were hardly worth saving. First efforts at digging produced a rich crop of tin trunks, meat paste jars and corroding batteries.

With a backdrop of telegraph poles and ugly railway clutter, we felt it essential to draw the eye into the garden. What we aimed at was masses of colour, but first we had to think what we could do to disguise the surroundings. Round the outside of the site we planted fast growing shrubs and trees for shelter. A single, large low shed was built from the best of the salvaged sleepers providing a south wall for the protection of *Chimonanthus praecox* 'Grandiflorus' and *Clematis* 'Barbara Dibley' as well as a home for our collection of horseshoes. We disguised a telegraph pole and its wires with honeysuckle, rambler roses, clematis and wisteria . . .

Shortage of funds drove us to learn to raise seeds and cuttings ourselves. With three small home-made frames and beginner's luck we soon filled the wide open spaces with the old-fashioned plants which were our first loves: single hollyhocks, tall purple Canterbury bells, common foxgloves, laced pinks and forget-me-nots. There were the giant oenothera and verbascum to tower over delphiniums and a small purple viola to decorate every empty space for three quarters of the year. We also discovered the value of annuals especially larkspur and eschscholzia to cover the dying leaves of spring bulbs. Trial and error have left us with fifty or more self-perpetuating annuals and biennials, while solidity was added by small shrubs, rosemary and lavender and hebe grown from cuttings given by our friends.

Something, however, was still missing. It was all too flat and featureless. I peered out of bedroom windows for hours trying to see what was lacking. Our garden is often viewed from above by passengers on trains and the upper decks of buses, a fact easily overlooked by us during planning. Raised beds of alpines, that was the answer. Fired with enthusiasm I persuaded my long-suffering husband to build five wooden beds in rapid succession and a crisis occurred when we ran short of turf to lay between drainage and compost. We successfully improvised with old railway uniform overcoats and the final result fully justified his strenuous efforts.

Now we had homes for a whole new range of plants. Blue and white *Gentiana dahurica* seedlings promptly put down such roots that we have never succeeded in thinning them out. *G. verna* and a packet of lewisia seed took care of one small bed, which replaced the prostrate conifers we had used to disguise ugly metal drain tops. An extra peaty bed was intended for special primroses, but the hose-in-hose and Jack-in-the-green varieties grew so strongly that they were soon moved into the open ground, leaving room for such treasures as December flowering *Galanthus caucasicus hiemale*, the black leaved *Ophiopogon nigrescens* and *Sanguinaria canadensis* 'Flore Pleno'.

Saxifrages abound, 'Marie Louise' regularly being the first to flower in company with the crimson winter cyclamen, of which we have many types, mostly grown from our own seed. *Cytisus* × *kewensis* dominates a sunny bed, spilling over the side in a primrose waterfall with *Hacquetia epipactis* nestling in its shade. Bulbs pop up everywhere between the alpines. *Crocus boryi* increases very slowly. *Tulipa saxatilis* sometimes rewards us with a solitary flower but *T. sprengeri* can be relied upon to produce a blaze of scarlet every May. In summer miniature roses and crimson-magenta semi-procumbent *Caladrinia umbellata* carry on the show.

Despite our obsession with colour we make room for quieter treasures such as ferns, *Origanum rotundifolium*, or *Saxifraga squarrosa*, which after six years was a hummock barely half an inch across and in constant danger of being smothered by a neighbouring *Phlox douglasii*. And in winter too we have many green hellebores as well as the showier types. All except *H. odorus* do well, as might be expected when *H. viridis* grows wild a few fields away. *Viburnum* × *bodnantense* and *V. farreri* 'Candidissimum' never fail to make a show in the short days. *Iris histrioides major* increases well, particularly in a shady spot so ill drained that the soil turns green with moss. *Abeliophyllum distichum* sulked for years against a west wall, but soon settled down to flowering every February when moved into the open. *Ceanothus dentatus* planted in its place shot up the wall with great enthusiasm.

A present of a load of Westmorland limestone led to the making of a rock bed. Cash being particularly short at the time, we were forced to skimp on sand and peat, the result being too thin a layer of heavy compost barely covering the rubble foundations. However, this turned out to be a blessing in disguise once we had accepted its limitations. *Oenothera missouriensis* covers the crown and blooms as nowhere else in the garden. Creeping phloxes are reduced to manageable proportions. *Lonicera implexa* makes a neat miniature bush with red and cream flowers followed by scarlet berries. *Saxifraga* × 'Jenkinsae' clings bravely to a rocky face, as does *Sempervivum* 'Mrs Guiseppi'. The mat-forming *Potentilla eriocarpa*, with grey leaves and yellow flowers seeds freely in the granite chippings which cover the rock bed, raised beds and paths, giving a neat all over effect.

Then my grandfather died and we inherited his African grey parrot Polly Flinders. Her raucous screeching drove us to dip into our savings and buy a greenhouse where she could live. We chose a six-sided cedar wood model which blended into the background as if it had grown there. A year later we bought another to house the damp-hating alpines and hundreds of show auriculas I had raised from seed. So now we were able to overwinter *Chrysanthemum frutescens*, pineapple scented sage and a huge plant of *Senecio petasites* as well as raise quantities of bedding annuals to push into every gap. French and African marigolds give a tremendous display for space occupied; zinnia 'Chippendale Daisy' never seems to fade before the first frost; aster 'Pepite' will make the most of the smallest crack; a ruby chard adds a wonderful patch of crimson.

The kitchen-copper sunk by the back path made a home for the heavily scented *Aponogeton distachys* and whetted our appetites for more water. A cement pond was made by the concave curve of the lawn. Mistakenly we set it a fraction lower than the garden behind, hoping for a natural effect. It looked fine, but came the rain and a steady trickle of earth washed down into the water. The goldfish were ploughing their way through a murky soup until I filched some of the less essential rocks from the rock bed to form a low barricade. The gaps between were plugged with stones and planted with sempervivums.

We have always been short of space and have cultivated every inch but even so we found we had not room for both flowers and vegetables. We made our vegetable plot along 150 yards of the up railway track. Clearing the foot deep layer of ballast stones, the brambles and the hawthorn bushes kept us busy for years. We also used a strip on the far side of the track from our main garden for the strong growing plants which we could not find room for nearer the house. Here the soil is poor and thick with ballast stones but it proves a home for crambe, globe artichokes, kniphofia and orange alstroemeria. Shrub roses now spread unhindered. A gigantic heap of ash from the crossing hut fire nearly defeated me until I tried flag iris. An almost soil-less patch of stones has been covered by *Mentha rotundifolia*, a large white mossy saxifrage and muscari.

We have also cultivated the narrow strip between our fence and the tarmac path along the road side. The warm pink, shrubby *Aethionema grandiflorum* covers an ugly stopcock at the foot of *Clerodendrum trichotomum*, the shrub with improbable turquoise berries and deep red calyces which delights our flower arranging friends. The soil is 'sun baked' and thick with shrub roots but our planting provides a colourful welcome to visitors.

Throughout the garden dryness is our main problem. Small sedums and *Cyclamen hederifolium* clothe most of the bad spots. One arid patch between rambler rose 'Excelsa' and a vigorous honeysuckle was tamed with bluebells planted under *Vinca minor* 'Variegata' with a bedding of love-lies-bleeding as soon as the bluebells faded.

Two long narrow boxes fixed to the front fence also need careful planting because of the danger of the soil drying out. *Saponaria ocymoides* is reduced to a neat mat. Silver thyme remains tight and shapely. *Leucanthemum hosmariense*, the large white daisy with feathery silver foliage, flowers well into the winter and phlox 'Chattahoochee' is seen at its best at almost eye level.

Climbers take up little space. Forty or more clematis have been slow to establish in the dry soil under the shrubs. *Jasminum nudiflorum* has been allotted walls by the front and back doors and is now being trained across an arch over a stepping-stone path. Between these stepping-stones we grow double-flowered chamomile, *Mentha requienii* and various thymes which give off their scents when crushed by passing feet. These are only some of the perfumed plants we grow. Round the seat are dwarf catmint, bergamot and rose 'Little White Pet', while Cretan dittany grows by the front door.

More recently arthritis has led us to look for ways to making the garden easier to maintain. Regretfully we have had to abandon the vegetable plot and are drastically reducing the number of plants which need staking and constant division. Michaelmas daisies are being replaced with Japanese anemones and as our stock increases, with *Colchicum* and *Cyclamen hederifolium* . . .

Over the years the number of visitors has grown steadily, people returning with their gardening friends, and the exchange of plants has greatly accelerated. So many people were peering over the fence in curiosity that we were emboldened to hang a notice by the front gate 'Plant lovers are welcome to walk round this garden'. Since then a steady stream has taken up the invitation. The paths have had to be widened slightly to accommodate visitors encumbered with prams, tots on tricycles and the occasional invalid chair. Extra path raking is a small price to pay for so many new friends.

Margaret Fuller, 1980

All this planting, which I admit I can't resist – especially when I see ravishing things in other people's gardens which we haven't got and I long to have – has led to furious arguments. I firmly believe that more planting, particularly in corners, steep banks and awkward places which are difficult to keep, saves work. My husband is just as convinced it makes work. I say weeding needn't be done every week – mowing and tractoring does. So he is always cutting down on my planting and I am always trying to reduce his mowing. As a result of these disagreements and of always being greeted by, 'Good God – not more plants', each time I returned home with some exciting shopping or even gifts from friends, I finally resorted to hiding everything under rugs or plastic bags or locking them in the boot of the car and only getting them out late at night, hoping they wouldn't be noticed until they were safely tucked into their new home.

Joan Payne, 1987

The thing most worth doing

It is not possible to use to any good effect all the plants that are to be had. In my own case I should wish to grow many more than just those I have, but if I do not find a place where my critical garden conscience approves of having any one plant I would rather be without it. It is better to me to deny myself the pleasure of having it, than to endure the mild sense of guilt of having placed it where it neither does itself justice nor accords with its neighbours, and where it reproaches me every time I pass it.

I feel sure that it is in a great measure just because this is so little understood, that gardens are so often unsatisfactory and uninteresting. If owners could see, each in their own garden, what is the thing most worth doing, and take some pains to work out that one idea or group of ideas, gardens would not be so generally dull and commonplace.

Often in choosing plants and shrubs people begin the wrong way. They know certain things they would like to have and they look through catalogues and order these, and others that they think, from the description, they would also like, and then plant them without any previous consideration of how or why.

Often when I have had to do with other people's gardens they have said: 'I have bought a quantity of shrubs and plants; show me where to place them'; to which I can only answer: 'That is not the way in which I can help you; show me your spaces and I will tell you what plants to get for them.'

Gertrude Jekyll, 1900

COLOURISTS

PLAYING WITH colour and form in the garden is the nearest that most of us will ever get to painting.

Mary Keen, 1991

An artist's border

The planting of the border is designed to show a distinct scheme of colour-arrangement. At the two ends there is a groundwork of grey and glaucous foliage – Stachys, Santolina, *Cineraria maritima*, Sea Kale and Lyme Grass, with darker foliage, also of grey quality, of Yucca, *Clematis recta* and Rue. With this, at the near or western end, there are flowers of pure blue, grey-blue, white, palest yellow and palest pink; each colour partly in distinct masses and partly inter-grouped. The colouring then passes through stronger yellows to orange and red. By the time the middle space of the border is reached the colour is strong and gorgeous, but, as it is in good harmonies, it is never garish. Then the colour-strength recedes in an inverse sequence through orange and deep yellow to pale yellow, white and palest pink, with the blue-grey foliage. But at this, the eastern end, instead of the pure blues we have purples and lilacs.

Looked at from a little way forward, for a wide space of grass allows this point of view, the whole border can be seen as one picture, the cool colouring at the ends enhancing the brilliant warmth of the middle. Then, passing along the wide path next to the border the value of the colour-arrangement is still more strongly felt. Each portion now becomes a picture in itself, and every one is of such a colouring that it best prepares the eye, in accordance with natural law, for what is to follow. Standing for a few moments before the endmost region of grey and blue, and saturating the eye to its utmost capacity with these colours, it passes with extraordinary avidity to the succeeding yellows. These intermingle in a pleasant harmony with the reds and scarlets, blood-reds and clarets, and then lead again to yellows. Now the eye has again become saturated, this time with the rich colouring, and has therefore, by the law of complementary colour, acquired a strong appetite for the greys and purples. These therefore assume an appearance of brilliancy that they would not have had without the preparation provided by their recently received complementary colour.

Even when a flower border is devoted to a special season, as mine is given to the time from mid-July to October, it cannot be kept fully furnished without resorting to various contrivances. One of these is the planting of certain things that will follow in season of bloom and that can be trained to take each other's places. Thus, each plant of *Gypsophila paniculata* when full grown covers a space a good four feet wide. On each side of it, within reasonable distance of the root, I plant Oriental Poppies. These make their leaf and flower growth in early summer when the Gypsophila is still in a young state. The Poppies will have died down by the time the Gypsophila is full grown and has covered them. After this has bloomed the seed-pods turn brown, and though a little of this colouring is not harmful in the autumn border, yet it is not wanted in such large patches. We therefore grow at its foot, or within easy reach, some of the trailing Nasturtiums and lead them up so that they cover the greater part of the brown seed-spray.

Delphiniums, which are indispensable for July, leave bare stems with quickly yellowing leafage when the flowers are over. We plant behind them the white Everlasting Pea, and again behind that Clematis Jackmanni. When the Delphiniums are over, the rapidly forming seed-pods are removed, the stems are cut down to just the right height, and the white Peas are trained over them. When the Peas go out of bloom in the middle of August, the Clematis is brought over. It takes some years for these two plants to become established; in the case of those I am describing the Pea has been four or five years planted and the Clematis seven. They cannot be hurried, indeed in my garden it is difficult to get the Clematis to grow at all. But good gardening means patience and dogged determination. There must be many failures and losses, but by always pushing on there will also be the reward of success. Those who do not know are apt to think that hardy flower gardening of the best kind is easy. It is not easy at all. It has taken me half a lifetime merely to find out what is best worth doing, and a good slice out of another half to puzzle out the ways of doing it.

In addition to these three plants that I grow over one another I am now adding a fourth – the September-blooming *Clematis Flammula*. It must not be supposed that they are just lumped one over another so that the under ones have their leafy growths smothered. They are always being watched, and, bit by bit, the earlier growths are removed as soon as their respective plants are better without them.

Then there is the way of pulling down tall plants whose natural growth is upright. At the back of the yellow part of the border are some plants of a form of *Helianthus orgyalis*, trained down . . . But other plants can be treated in the same way; the tall Rudbeckia Golden Glow, and Dahlias and Michaelmas Daisies. The tall Snap-dragons can also be pulled down and made to cover a surprising space of bare ground with flowering side-shoots.

As it is still impossible to prevent the occurrence of a blank here and there, or as the scene, viewed as a picture, may want some special accentuation or colouring, there is the way of keeping a reserve of plants in pots and dropping them in where they may be wanted. The thing that matters is that, in its season, the border shall be kept full and beautiful; by what means does not matter in the least . . .

An important matter is that of staking and supporting. The rule, as I venture to lay it down, is that sticks and stakes must never show. They must be so arranged that they give the needful support, while allowing the plant its natural freedom; but they must remain invisible. The only time when they are tolerated is for the week or two when they have been put in for Dahlias, when the plants have not yet grown up to cover them . . .

Now is the time to begin to use our reserve of plants in pots. Of these the most useful are the Hydrangeas. They are dropped into any vacant spaces, more or less in groups, in the two ends of the border where there is grey foliage, their pale pink colouring agreeing with these places. Their own leafage is a rather bright green, but we get them so well bloomed that but few leaves are seen, and we arrange as cleverly as we can that the rest shall be more or less hidden by the surrounding bluish foliage. I stand a few paces off, directing the formation of the groups; considering their shape in relation to the border as a whole. I say to the gardener that I want a Hydrangea in such a place; and tell him to find the nearest place where it can be dropped in. Sometimes this dropping in, for the pots have to be partly sunk, comes in the way of some established plant. If it is a deep-rooted perennial that takes three or four years to come to its strength, like an Eryngium or a Dictamnus, of course I avoid encroaching on its root-room. But if it is anything that blooms the season after it is planted, and of which I have plenty in reserve, such as an Anthemis, a Trades-cantia, or a Helenium, I sacrifice a portion of the plant-group, knowing that it can easily be replaced. But then by August many of the plants have spread widely above and there is space below. *Lilium longiflorum* in pots is used in the same way, and for the most part in this blue end of the border, though there are also some at the further, purple end, and just a flash of their white beauty in the middle region of strong reds.

In order to use both blue and purple in the flower border, this cool, western, grey-foliaged end has the blues, and the further, eastern end the purples. For although I like to use colour as a general rule in harmonies rather than contrasts, I have a dislike to bringing together blues and purples. At this end, therefore, there are flowers of pure blue – Delphinium, Anchusa, Salvia, Blue Cape Daisy and Lobelia, and it is only when the main mass of blue, of Delphiniums and Anchusas, is over that even the presence of the pale grey-blue of *Campanula lactiflora* could be tolerated. Near the front is another pale grey-blue, that of *Clematis davidiana*, just showing a few blooms, but not yet fully out.

Gertrude Jekyll, 1911

Mauve and blue

Immediately round the house, or climbing on the house, I have mixed up wild and cultivated flowers and can indulge in various weaknesses – some passing manias, others more durable – like my present fancy for mauve and blue flowers blooming together in close proximity: purple crocus and scillas, bluebells and aubrieta, or candytuft and flax, or chionodoxa and dame's-violet. The latter is a great favourite with the orange tip butterfly – only the male has orange tips to its wings, the female is white – both as a nectar source and food for its caterpillars.

Miriam Rothschild, 1983

Good-taste gardener

At Hadspen House I was a 'good-taste gardener', planning plant associations based on leaf colour, texture and form, with seasonal flowers just as a bonus. As I started to read Gertrude Jekyll, and through her began to study the theories of the French Impressionists, I began to see the infinite possibilities of weaving colour pictures with plants. The more I learnt about colour behaviour, the more I wished to practise and experiment with harmonies and contrasts, using the 'hottest' colours as well as the pale pastel tints, not only in pleasing compositions, but also to manipulate perspective and to evoke definite moods.

Penelope Hobhouse, 1985

The spectrum

Victorian colourists, whose legacy persists in gardens today, liked to use complementary colours for strong contrasts. This means that you use each primary colour with a secondary made of the other two primaries: yellow with purple (blue and red), red with green (blue and yellow) and blue with orange (yellow and red). For me these intense contrasts are too strong for everyday life and too dominant in borders where other colours are included. With the exception of blue and orange, where the cold-warm contrast is so beautifully balanced that it is exciting, I dislike combinations of complementary colours under temperate skies. But this is a personal veto: others may and do enjoy complementaries together. And I wonder whether the word complementary has gone some way towards prejudicing our taste, because it sounds like compli*mentary*, suggesting flattery? What complementary means as a colour description is that colours that are opposite one another on the spectrum will annihilate each other when mixed together. This technical point may not appear relevant to garden planners, but the fact that a mixture of the pigments of these colours produces black could explain my lack of enthusiasm for groups of complementaries. An impression of black in the garden is not what most of us want to see.

Mary Keen, 1991

True colours

I am always surprised at the vague, not to say reckless, fashion in which garden folk set to work to describe the colours of flowers, and at the way in which quite wrong colours are attributed to them. It is done in perfect good faith, and without the least consciousness of describing wrongly. In many cases it appears to be because the names of certain substances have been used conventionally or poetically to convey the idea of certain colours. And some of these errors are so old that they have acquired a kind of respectability, and are in a way accepted without challenge. When they are used about familiar flowers it does not occur to one to detect them, because one knows the flower and its true colour; but when the same old error is used in the description of a new flower, it is distinctly misleading. For instance, when we hear of golden buttercups, we know that it means bright-yellow buttercups; but in the case of a new flower, or one not generally known, surely it is better and more accurate to say bright yellow at once. Nothing is more frequent in plant catalogues than 'bright golden yellow', when bright yellow is meant. Gold is not bright yellow . . .

The same irrelevance of comparison seems to run through all the colours. Flowers of a full, bright-blue colour are often described as of a 'brilliant amethystine blue'. Why amethystine? The amethyst, as we generally see it, is a stone of a washy purple colour, and though there are amethysts of a fine purple, they are not so often seen as the paler ones, and I have never seen one even faintly approaching a really blue colour. What, therefore, is the sense of likening a flower, such as a Delphinium, which is really of a splendid pure-blue colour, to the duller and totally different colour of a third-rate gem?

Another example of the same slip-slop is the term flame coloured, and it is often preceded by the word gorgeous. This contradictory mixture of terms is generally used to mean bright scarlet. When I look at a flame, whether of fire or candle, I see that the colour is a rather pale yellow, with a reddish tinge about its upper forks, and side wings often of a bluish white – no scarlet anywhere. The nearest approach to red is in the coals, not in the flame. In the case of the candle, the point of the wick is faintly red when compared with the flame, but about the flame there is no red whatever. A distant bonfire looks red at night, but I take it that the apparent redness is from seeing the flames through damp atmosphere, just as the harvest-moon looks red when it rises . . .

Crimson is a word to beware of; it covers such a wide extent of ground, and is used so carelessly in plant-catalogues, that one cannot know whether it stands for a rich blood colour or for a malignant magenta. For the latter class of colour the term amaranth, so generally used in French plant-lists, is extremely useful, both as a definition and a warning. Salmon is an excellent colour-word, copper is also useful, the two covering a limited range of beautiful colouring of the utmost value. Blood-red is also accurately descriptive. Terra-cotta is useful but indefinite, as it may mean anything between brick-red and buff. Red-lead, if it would be accepted as a colour-word, would be useful, denoting the shades of colour between the strongest orange and the palest scarlet, frequent in the lightest of the Oriental Poppies. Amber is a misleading word, for who is to know when it means the transparent amber, whose colour approaches that of resin, or the pale, almost opaque, dull-yellow kind. And what is meant by coral-red? It is the red of the old-fashioned dull-scarlet coral, or of the pink kind more recently in favour.

The terms bronze and smoke may well be used in their place, as in describing or attempting to describe the wonderful colouring of such flowers as Spanish Iris, and the varieties of Iris of the *squalens* section. But often in describing a flower a reference to texture much helps and strengthens the colour-word. I have often described the modest little *Iris tuberosa* as a flower made of green satin and black velvet. The green portion is only slightly green, but is entirely green satin, and the black of the velvet is barely black, but is quite black-velvet-like. The texture of the flower of *Ornithogalum nutans* is silver satin, neither very silvery nor very satin-like, and yet so nearly suggesting the texture of both that the words may well be used in speaking of it. Indeed, texture plays so important a part in the appearance of colour-surface, that one can hardly think of colour without also thinking of texture. A piece of black satin and a piece of black velvet may be woven of the same batch of material, but when the satin is finished and the velvet cut, the appearance is often so dissimilar that they may look quite different in colour. A working painter is never happy if you give him an oil-colour pattern to match in distemper; he must have it of the same texture, or he will not undertake to get it like.

What a wonderful range of colouring there is in black alone to a trained colour-eye! There is the dull brown-black of soot, and the velvety brown-black of the bean-flower's blotch; to my own eye, I have never found anything so entirely black in a natural product as the patch on the lower petals of *Iris iberica*. Is it not Ruskin who says of Velasquez, that there is more colour in his black than in many another painter's whole palette? The blotch of the bean-flower appears black at first, till you look at it close in the sunlight, and then you see its rich velvety texture, so nearly like some of the brown-velvet markings on butterflies' wings. And the same kind of rich colour and texture occurs again on some of the tough flat half-round funguses, marked with shaded rings, that grow out of old posts, and that I always enjoy as lessons of lovely colour-harmony of grey and brown and black . . .

Snow-white is very vague. There is nearly always so much blue about the colour of snow, from its crystalline surface and partial transparency, and the texture is so unlike that of any kind of flower, that the comparison is scarcely permissible. I take it that the use of 'snow-white' is, like that of 'golden-yellow', more symbolical than descriptive, meaning any white that gives an impression of purity. Nearly all white flowers are yellowish-white, and the comparatively few that are bluish-white, such, for example, as *Omphalodes linifolia*, are of a texture so different from snow that one cannot compare them at all. I should say that most white flowers are near the colour of chalk; for although the word chalky-white has been used in rather a contemptuous way, the colour is really a very beautiful warm white, but by no means an intense white. The flower that always looks to me the whitest is that of *Iberis sempervirens*. The white is dead and hard, like a piece of glazed stoneware, quite without play or variation and hence uninteresting.

Gertrude Jekyll, 1899

Malignant magenta

It has been the custom of late to sneer at crimson in the garden, especially if its vivid colour gets a dash of purple and becomes what Miss Jekyll calls 'malignant magenta'. It is really more vulgar than malignant, and has come to be in textile products a stamp and symbol of vulgarity, through the forceful brilliancy of our modern aniline dyes. But this purple crimson, this amarant, this magenta, especially in the lighter shades, is a favorite colour in nature. The garden is never weary of wearing it. See how it stands out in mid-summer! It is rank in Ragged Robin, tall Phlox, and Petunias; you find it in the bed of Drummond Phlox, among the Zinnias; the Portulacas, Balsams, and China Asters prolong it. Earlier in the summer the Rhododendrons fill the garden with colour that on some of the bushes is termed sultana and crimson, but it is in fact plain magenta. One of the good points of the Peony is that you never saw a magenta one.

This colour shows that time as well as place affects our colour notions, for magenta is believed to be the honoured royal purple of the ancients. Fifty years ago no one complained of magenta. It was deemed a cheerful colour, and was set out boldly and complacently by the side of pink or scarlet, or wall-flower colours. Now I dislike it so that really the printed word, seen often as I glance back through this page, makes the black and white look cheap. If I could turn all magenta flowers pink or purple, I should never think further about garden harmony, all other colours would adjust themselves.

Mrs Alice Morse Earle, 1901

'I love ...'

I love the English country scene
But sometimes think there's too much Hooker's green,
Especially in August, when the flowers that might have lent a
Lightness, don't; being gamboge or magenta.

Stevie Smith, 1975

Non-U

Nature's favourite colour is a washed-out magenta ... the preferred colour of the unsophisticated is firehouse red, the winner among tulips, zinnias, dahlias, salvia, impatiens, begonias, etc., by a wide margin. Orange and yellow come next, then pink, with blue and white, both comparatively rare in nature, last on the list – a spectrum that runs from hot to cold.

It follows that blue and white are the choices of the discriminating, and your real garden snob will go so far as to cast whole gardens in one or the other. White has perhaps the higher status. White flowers have always had an aura of luxury and expense, partly because so many of them are imported from warmer climates and must be grown under glass. In the eighteenth century, which put a much higher value on scent than we do, the fact that they were also heavily perfumed made white flowers such as the gardenia and the tuberose favourites with collectors. But white is also a distinctively modern colour, or un-colour, because of its cool neutrality. It will even take the curse off otherwise unacceptable objects, including flowers. Syrie Maugham's all-white rooms, famous in the 1920s and 1930s were full of rococco pieces pickled and rubbed with white paint, a form of vandalism that imparted instant chic. White gardens came into fashion during the same period and for some of the same reasons. Though flowers were still massively grown in borders, doubts arose as to whether they were really in good taste. To have them all white met the objection, and still does. Even a white gladiolus may get by – just – while one in any other colour is beyond the pale.

The blues are a little different – not chic exactly, though Edith Wharton's all-blue garden at her Pavillion Colombe outside Paris was the ultimate in elegance. But they also have overtones of class distinction, and this may be as good a place as any to admit that there is such a thing in gardening. When, for example, I say that gladiolas are beyond the pale, I am not making a strictly aesthetic judgment. What I crassly mean is that they are non-U, that objectionable if handy phrase coined *not* by Nancy Mitford but by a rather pompous professor who mined her books for upper-class speech patterns and later expanded the definition to include other things such as clothes and food – but not flowers, an odd omission in garden-loving England, where they bear the marks of caste just as fatally as 'notepaper' and 'putting the milk in first'. So do they here, though no class-conscious English person would admit it, everything 'transatlantic' being non-U by definition. Never mind. We, too, have U and non-U gardens, with the same taboos: gladiolas, scarlet salvia, wax begonias, red-hot pokers, orange marigolds, and many more it would be tedious to enumerate are all non-U, too obviously, perhaps, to merit mention.

Eleanor Perényi, 1981

Scarlet may be used

Personally I am delighted that the more vibrant hues are again to light our gardens – red, scarlet, orange, purple. I have had a bit of border at the back of my garden this summer that has given me much pleasure. It is primarily a red and white border but there are here and there a bit of pale pink, a little cool blue and some light yellow to take the edge – or the curse, if you like – off the brilliance. It began in May with the Tulips, Halley (Chinese red) and Colonel Cuney, a warmer hue, and several creamy and lemon-coloured sorts, and progressed to masses of Sweet William Scarlet Beauty, a superb colour, white Peonies, a pink Peony or two, pinky-scarlet *Lychnis Arkwrighti*, tall white and pale yellow *Aquilegia chrysantha* and a yellow Potentilla whose name I do not know. Now as I write it is bright with red and white Hollyhocks, dark red and salmon-coloured Zinnias, Snapdragons, Dimorphotheca, and so on, the whole very gay and refreshing to look upon.

I do not personally care for grey foliage used as a foil for red and scarlet flowers. There is something hard and sharp, metallic in the association that offends my eye, while white, cream and pale lemon used in the same connection seem always fresh, gay and stimulating. Blood red is more difficult to adjust in the garden scheme than is scarlet. A little spectrum red goes a long way, while scarlet may be used with fair freedom. The latter is happy in association with orange, apricot, gold, cream and white, as well as with all the cool lavenders and blue purples. Red on the other hand likes the complement of maroon, some crimsons, pure purple, and may be used with white and cream.

Louise Beebe Wilder, 1924

Green is a colour too

My fellow-gardener at the dinner table was dismissive . . . 'Oh, I dislike any colour in gardens: I never have it in mine.' Obviously he meant *flower* colour, perhaps the bright confusion of a traditional herbaceous border, or even the gaudy mixture of annuals in a public park. I imagined his garden (he was a Frenchman) full of low-toned greens, textured foliage in clipped hedges or topiary, elegant limes and chestnuts reflected in still water: no place for intrusive or vivid eye-catching flowers.

I should have answered that *green* is a colour. That I had spent months observing the multiplicity of shades and tones in 'plain' green foliage, and searching for ways to describe the subtleties of what I saw: even the simplest specimen tree shading a green lawn conveys a constantly changing pattern of colour as the light alters from minute to minute, and as the seasons modulate the tones of the leaves.

Of course, it did not occur to the Frenchman that I might be concerned with these fine distinctions of green. Perhaps he thought I was writing for that other gardening school, for our modest neighbour who says, 'Please don't come and see my garden now, there's no colour in it.'

Penelope Hobhouse, 1985

Elizabeth's German garden

It is to-day a garden of wallflowers, and I think I have every colour and sort in cultivation. The borders under the south windows of the house, so empty and melancholy this time last year, are crammed with them, and are finished off in front by a broad strip from end to end of yellow and white pansies. The tea rose beds round the sun-dial facing these borders are sheets of white, and golden, and purple, and wine-red pansies, with the dainty red shoots of the tea roses presiding delicately in their midst. The verandah steps leading down into this pansy paradise have boxes of white, and pink, and yellow tulips all the way up on each side, and on the lawn, behind the roses, are two big beds of every coloured tulip rising above a carpet of forget-me-nots. How very much more charming different-coloured tulips are together than tulips in one colour by itself! Last year, on the recommendation of sundry writers about gardens, I tried beds of scarlet tulips and forget-me-nots. They were pretty enough; but I wish those writers could see my beds of mixed tulips. I never saw anything so sweetly, delicately gay. The only ones I exclude are the rose-coloured ones; but scarlet, gold, delicate pink, and white are all there, and the effect is infinitely enchanting. The forget-me-nots grow taller as the tulips go off, and will presently tenderly engulf them altogether, and so hide the shame of their decay in their kindly little arms.

Elizabeth von Arnim, 1899

Where the sunset strikes

One of the nicest things about gardening is the sudden surprise we may get when something that we arranged years ago comes into its own and is at last doing what we had intended it to do. We must admit that dusk is probably the kindest hour, lengthening the shadows, intensifying the colours, and obliterating the weeds, but nevertheless, I was not disappointed in the glare of the following morning by the great golden group I had observed in the after glow of a lingering sunset.

It was a group composed of ordinary, easy things, and it was simply their collusion in flowering all together at the same time that made them so effective. In the foreground was a rounded shrub of cinquefoil, *Potentilla fruticosa*, with silvery leaves spattered by lemon-yellow flowers. Behind this arose the taller, flat-headed yellow yarrow, *Achillea eupatorium*, and then behind that the feathery meadow-rue, *Thalictrum glaucum*, a fluffy, saffron version of the brush we used to push up lamp-glasses before we had electric light. A few pale evening primroses had poked their untidy way upwards through a huge bush of the truly aureate St John's Wort,

Hypericum patulum forrestii, already massing the varnished buttercup of its half-crown-sized flower, and many buds coming on in promise. All this was good enough, but towering above the lot came the dripping glory of a great Mount Etna broom, *Genista œtnensis*, 10 ft high, an arrested fountain of molten gold.

Now all these are easy-going plants, within the scope of every purse and experience or lack of experience, and if anybody had the space requisite to repeat this grouping in some lost corner where the sunset strikes, I think he would be pleased. Since one is never satisfied, however, I started making mental notes for improvement. The Hidcote variety of the St John's Wort, for instance, is a finer thing than the type introduced by Forrest from China. Why hadn't I planted the Hidcote hypericum in the first instance? One should always plant the best, but one is ignorant to start with, and it takes years of floundering before one learns. And why had I not sent up some rockets of the giant mullein, *Verbascum olympicum*, to match the suspended fireworks of the Mount Etna broom? Why, indeed? I hope next year to repair my half-misspent time, but meanwhile my golden group gives me more pleasure than all the nuggets in the cellars of the Bank of England.

V. Sackville-West, 1958

'Rose of Sharon' (St John's Wort)

The flat and golden pentagonal bud
opens one June morning, mathematically –
five strap-shaped petals, a great handful
of trembling stamens that astonish one.
Yet nothing really exotic. It will only last
three days at most, at best. On the first day
the golden stamens have ox-blood-red heads,
on the second brown. By the third day,
the blossom is twisting, the cupola-shaped fruit begins
to form, the stamens are not in such accord.
Brown stains the petals too.

Dead-head immediately.
Dozens will follow hard upon its heels.
No nourishment – sun, damp soil, long days –
is wasted. This flower has haunted me since
I was twelve.

They must be tough flowers,
I suppose; they will take over any patch
of poorish soil left vacant. The leaves
are tough too, a shiny evergreen.

It is the heart though, the heart of golden stamens,
the sweet shared shuddering of all,
that draws me in. These are not tough.
Certainly they re-form with grace
after the blundering entry of some clumsy bumble bee,
but one thing finishes them immediately, even
on the day of their birth. Rain is their downfall.
Because they are so delicate rain clots them
bends them, ruins their sisterhood;
not the strongest sunlight brings them up again
into that first astonishing golden genesis.

Another of the 'things that come not back'.

Molly Holden, 1975

The blues

I must declare an interest. Whatever the reasons (and I don't think anyone knows or has studied why people respond to colours as they do – snobbery aside, there are unplumbed depths in the psyche that affect whole nations: why do the liberty-loving choose blue and white for their flags, while those who opt for tyrants invariably prefer red and black?) I love blue more than any other colour. I am inordinately attracted to any blue substance: to minerals like turquoise and lapis lazuli, to sapphires and aquamarines; to cobalt skies and blue-black seas; Moslem tiles – and to a blue flower whether or not it has any other merit.

Take anchusa, the Italian bugloss, a hairy perennial that looks like an outsize borage (which it is) and does little credit to the well-groomed border. But an anchusa in bloom is like a Christmas tree with lights so intensely azure they shine out clear across a garden, and I always keep at least one. I harbour the royal blue perennial cornflowers (*Centaurea montana*) for the same reason and in spite of their floppy, undistinguished foliage; and over some opposition (my mother can't abide their prickly, bristly appearance), the steel-blue globe thistle (*Echinops*), whose unopened buds are little balls covered with spikes, miniatures of those weapons one sees in the medieval armory. I doubt if I would care for the veronicas, which are somewhat nondescript and require to be massed to make an effect, if they didn't come in a variety of stained-glass window blues (the pinks and whites leave me cold); and I wouldn't tolerate the invasive, floppy *Tradescantia virginiana* (spiderwort) if it weren't for the cultivar Blue Stone. (Save the tradescantias for rough spots where you want a little colour – they don't belong in a border.)

All the above have the advantage of being tough as well as blue. They are perennials you can plant and more or less forget. What they lack is the elegance that doesn't necessarily go with hardiness. For that combination among the blues I look first to the campanulas, especially *C. persicifolia*, the peach-leaved bellflower that will produce flush after flush of enchanting bloom on the wiry stems if you have the patience to go out every morning and remove the faded flowers. These campanulas need only to have their basal rosettes divided every so often to last practically forever, and they are my favourites, though fancier, doubled varieties exist. (*C. glomerata*, dark purple, is one, and to my mind the flowers are too heavy for the stalks.) The same plant in little is *C. carpatica*, and I like it too. Both are to be had in white as well.

Platycodons (blue, white, and a dim pink) are next. Closed, they are lanterns, and they open into stars. Platycodons, too, will be with you forever if you remember where they are and don't wield a careless trowel in early spring. They vanish over winter and don't emerge until mid-May, camouflaged as baby asparagus, and if these easily overlooked shoots are damaged they are done for. Otherwise, they come up in the same place year after year, don't encroach on their neighbours, must not be divided. (Many gardeners get the idea that all perennials should be split up after a few years, often with fatal results. If the clump doesn't increase in size, leave it alone. I lost the best flaxes I ever had, and the only ones to last longer than two years, because some demon whispered that the time had come to separate them; and since that day I have learned to look twice at the structure and growth habits of plants before I start moving them around. In general, those that want dividing will have already started the process for themselves, forming obviously distinct off-sets. Those that don't do this, or go to ground leaving no trace, should be left to their own devices – unless, of course, they are bulbs or rhizomes, like iris, which must always be divided.)

Other blue perennials, as handsome as they are durable, that shouldn't be tampered with once established, are the monkshoods and *Baptisia australis*, the false indigo. Monkshoods (*Aconitum*) are tall, elegant plants with glossy, deeply incised foliage and helmeted flowers. Most bloom in the fall, like shade and have a slightly sinister air, perhaps because one knows they are poisonous. 'Very danger-ous if eaten or if their juices get into scratches,' one authority advises. To my knowledge, neither animal nor child has ever nibbled on my thirty-five-year-old clumps and my hands, perpetually scratched like those of most gardeners, have survived unscathed the staking, tying, cutting down of the stalks. But it is a thing to know, and I pass it on. The baptisia poses no such problem. It can be a great big perennial, the size of a small shrub, and it is covered with pea-like flowers that are the true indigo blue. (Though called false, the baptisia must be related to the true indigo, which it resembles, because the stems will, I read, produce a weak blue dye.) These and one or two other standbys – Virginia bluebells, the powder-blue *Phlox divaricata*, both semi-wildings; Stokes's asters, fringed like sea-anemones – complete the list of blue perennials in residence here. Now for the trouble-makers, those I can't grow for the life of me.

The giant delphiniums come first. I don't mean the garland lark-spurs (Belladonna and Bellamosum, light and dark blue respectively, are the classics), nor the Chinese species, nor Connecticut Yankee, developed by the photographer Edward Steichen. All these are of moderate height with loosely organised flowers like big larkspurs, very pretty and easy to grow – if I couldn't succeed with a flower called Connecticut Yankee, I really would die of shame – and given my contempt for the grosser hybrids, they should do me nicely. Alas, where delphiniums are concerned, good taste flies out the window. I want the biggest and showiest, those rulers of the race whose densely packed spires can reach to six feet, the glory of the English herbaceous border. I can do without the pinks and purples. The myriad blues are what I want, all the sapphires and azures of a Chartres window, and an occasional white.

It is hopeless. Delphiniums like a cool damp climate, neither too hot nor too cold, and a sweet soil, what the English call a chalk garden. (Does anyone remember the play of that name and the entrance of Gladys Cooper in a floppy hat, limp dress, garden basket of the type called a Sussex trug over her arm – or have I invented the trug? – deathlessly beautiful at age seventy? Eighty? When I think of delphiniums, that apparition comes back to me.) I supply the lime they need, surround their tender shoots with ashes to keep off slugs, water them tenderly. I tie the stalks individually to slim bamboo poles. The commoner types respond handsomely, but not the giants. They bloom once and never again. I tell myself the climate is at fault, and to an extent that is true. The giant delphiniums thrive along the Maine coast and in the Pacific north-west, home of the Pacific hybrids that even the English now carry in their catalogues, for they are the world's best. Here, better gardeners than I am treat them as biennials and start them early under glass.

I can't do that and excused myself accordingly – until a few years ago when I pulled up to a derelict gas pump on a nearby back road, magnetised by the sight of five-foot delphiniums (and columbines nearly as large) growing in a grassy little pasture that showed no sign of having been cultivated. Queried, the rustic who ran the pump allowed that he raised them both from seed he got from an English firm called Thompson & Morgan. Had I heard of it? I had. At that time it had no American outlet, and I was rather smug about having got hold of a catalogue. Their delphinium seed (Blackmore & Langdon hybrids, the equivalent of our Pacific giants) hadn't done badly either. It was and is the most viable I have tried and once produced a respectable stand that lasted all of three years, a record, but nothing like these beauties in bloom among the weeds. How *he* had got hold of a catalogue was impossible to ask without implying an insulting incredulity. All I could do was humbly ask to buy a few plants, which naturally died on me, and to speculate that the real right way to cultivate giant delphiniums is to scatter the seed in an unploughed field.

Then there is the dustily blue *Catananche caerulea*: Cupid's dart, a daisy with a purple splotch and petals trimmed with pinking shears. Catananches aren't much to look at individually. They should be grown in large clumps drifting through a border, as I first saw them in an Oxford college garden – a garden that also had two white peacocks trailing their fans across a faultless lawn. The lawn and the peacocks are beyond me to imitate. The catananches ought not to be. They aren't rare plants, yet I can't grow them in sufficient quantity to make those blue clouds, or make them last. They tolerate the seed bed; they won't endure transplanting to the perennial beds, and that is that.

Still, they can't be classified as total disasters. I reserve that category for, first, *Meconopsis betonicifolia*, the fabled Himalayan poppy, the colour of a summer sky, with golden anthers – and my abominable snowman. It grows in England but I have never seen it – not the tiniest shoot having come up from repeated sowings. (Nurseries don't carry it: poppies of this type are notoriously difficult to transplant.) I would give anything for a glimpse of it, even in somebody else's garden. The fact that nobody I know or have heard of grows it ought to console me. *Wyman* says this poppy 'always makes a great impression on American tourists visiting England, for it is practically unknown in the US', and I would bet that it is practically unknown in the Himalayas, too, these days, given the record of third-world countries in stripping their forests and wilderness lands, a record considerably worse than our own. What I can't understand is why, if it is practically unknown in the US, the seeds are sold by a number of companies. Somebody, somewhere, is cultivating this elusive blue papaver. It is clear I never will.

Another total failure is the gentians. One thinks of these as wild flowers, but some are in cultivation and can be found at nurseries, and since the wild gentians are all on the endangered-species list, growing them in the garden may be the only way to preserve them. I can't do it. There was a moment when I had four little *G. septemfidae* in the seed bed, a whole year old. These aren't the most exciting of the gentians, not to be compared with the exquisite fringed gentian (*G. crinita*) that is now almost extinct. But I am not fussy and was looking forward to transplanting my little specimens to a spot under the apple tree. Some unknown force put an end to that hope, and I didn't see them again.

Meanwhile I have embarked on yet another, probably doomed project. It is now my ambition to grow agapanthus, the so-called lily-of-the-nile, not a lily and with no connection to the Nile. (It comes from South Africa.) The flowers are blue or white, and it used to be considered a pot plant only, the tubers to be stored indoors over winter. Now, however, a hardy strain has been developed (*A. òrientalis*) which we are promised will grow outdoors, with some protection, where temperatures don't fall below zero. Absent for some years from Wayside's catalogue, these were offered again in 1980 and I ordered the blue, which now sit in the perennial bed. They didn't bloom the first summer and don't have the air of looking forward to their winter season. Neither do I. Something tells me they won't make it. In that case I will try something else. There is no shortage of frustrating blue perennials. I might have another go at the maddening little shrub called caryopteris, a kind of spirea that bursts into a cobalt-blue bloom at summer's end, a time when other blue flowers are absent or hard to come by. *C. × clandonensis*, Heavenly Blue, is the variety to order, and reorder. Three have been given homes here and quickly made their exit to a better world. According to *Wyman*, in a curiously worded sentence, caryopteris 'may be killed back by severe winters and, if not, a severe pruning in early spring will usually force it to produce better flowers'. Which seems to mean that being killed back is good for them. Mine haven't taken this view, and as for pruning them, they haven't given me the opportunity. Once killed back, they have chosen to leave it at that.

Eleanor Perényi, 1981

One-colour gardens

It is extremely interesting to work out gardens in which some special colouring predominates, and to those who, by natural endowment or careful eye-cultivation, possess or have acquired what artists understand by an eye for colour, it opens out a whole new range of garden delights.

Arrangements of this kind are sometimes attempted, for occasionally I hear of a garden for blue plants, or a white garden, but I think such ideas are but rarely worked out with the best aims. I have in mind a whole series of gardens of restricted colouring, though I have not, alas, either room or means enough to work them out for myself, and have to be satisfied with an all-too-short length of double border for a grey scheme. But, besides my small grey garden I badly want others, and especially a gold garden, a blue garden, and a green garden; though the number of these desires might easily be multiplied.

It is a curious thing that people will sometimes spoil some garden project for the sake of a word. For instance, a blue garden, for beauty's sake, may be hungering for a group of white Lilies, or for something of palest lemon-yellow, but it is not allowed to have it because it is called the blue garden, and there must be no flowers in it but blue flowers. I can see no sense in this; it seems to me like fetters foolishly self-imposed. Surely the business of the blue garden is to be beautiful as well as to be blue.

Gertrude Jekyll, 1911

Silver leaves among the green

Ever since Miss Sackville-West opened her garden at Sissinghurst there have been many attempts at copying the white border and some gardeners seem to have the idea that silver foliage plants have to be segregated and planted in a special bed. This seems a pity as far as the shrubby types are concerned for most retain their foliage throughout the year, and with a little pruning at the right time can be persuaded to hide the gaps left when other plants such as delphiniums have had their day. Furthermore grey is the perfect contrast for any colour, and it is surprising how much impact a few flowers will make when seen against a backcloth of silver.

Clever positioning of these shrubs can, in fact, be the making of small gardens, enabling their owners to grow a few herbaceous plants and yet keep their borders well furnished and tidy throughout most of the year.

To do this well entails careful pruning. The aim should be to have the shrubs well covered with fresh young growth in June ready to spread across and hide the gaps left when early flowering herbaceous plants have had to be cut back. Later in the year one has to plan for winter cover of mature growths.

It is unwise to start pruning too early in the year. For one thing immature shoots are prone to frost damage, and for another if one prunes too early the plants will have passed their zenith and have started to flower just when one wants them to be at their best. The end of April and early May is about the right time and most types can be cut back ruthlessly, though the very slow growers such as *Convolvulus cneorum* and *Senecio compactus* only need tidying up.

The appearance of flowering growth can be a nuisance; very few silver shrubs have attractive flowers, and much of this growth comes up from the base and forces the plant out of shape. In the case of the santolinas and senecios it is as well to cut these shoots away as soon as possible, but in any case if the shrubs are wanted for winter effect the flowers must not be allowed to set seed.

Even trimming out this flowering growth will encourage the appearance of some shoots, but in order to achieve a good winter effect the shrubs may need to be shortened back in the first fortnight in August. This leaves just enough time for the young breaks to harden sufficiently to withstand frost.

Mrs Desmond Underwood, 1975

Ghost gardens

In America 'ghost gardens' are rather the fashion. Here everything is dim and subdued. Under cool, creeper-clad pergolas or shady trees are arranged such misty effects as can be got by the use of large masses of *Gypsophila paniculata*, the great silver thistle, tall grey mulleins, and of the broad-growing silver salvia or sage as a flat carpet from which rise fragile white campanulas, white moondaises, or white lilies of Bermuda. Near a grey stone seat may be found a large clump of white datura, with heavily scented trumpet flowers; or, if no frost-proof shed can be found to store the datura, then a group of white *Nicotiana sylvestris* or *Nicotiana affinis*, which comes up year after year. Then there are white foxgloves, with white jasmine as a background, on some old wall or pillar; and *Clematis Flammula* (or, earlier in the season, *montana*) wreaths itself in and out of bay or box, and even tall junipers standing like sentinels do not escape, but are caught in its embrace. A small marble basin with water-lilies growing in it is sunk in the cool green turf, the water reflecting the early moonbeams; for no one walks in the ghost garden except at evening.

Lady Alice M. Martineau, 1924

The manor of Sutton Courtenay

Some gardens, like some people, have a charm potent to enslave and yet as intangible as dew or vapour. The gardens of the manor of Sutton Courtenay have this shining quality. Maybe the lack of grandeur, though not of formality, pleases, and the absence of any bedding out, through distaste and economy combined, produces a sense of flourishing ease and naturalness which is their most lovable feature. There is an air of spontaneity in the planting, as if the flowers and trees had chosen their own positions and, like the house, been overlooked by the rushing tide of men. This is what you have missed and what, unconsciously, you have been seeking all your life . . .

These gardens seem always to be in bloom. Even the lean winter days have their button-hole in the starry, lemon jasmine, the mysterious pale flowers of *Chimonanthus fragrans*, and the frail candles of the various crocus species. If there is the slightest interval between hailstorm and snowstorm, the bare ground is immediately powdered with a hundred thousand aconites, their golden blobs frilled elegantly in the newest green, while cyclamen unwind from winter sleep and the pale hellebores raise freckled faces to the new year. But as the earth warms to the sun and the wrinkled trees entertain the nightingale and black-cap, and doors are open till midnight, the tide of colour and scent rises till the whole garden blooms like one enormous nosegay. It is impossible to come

indoors, for magic is abroad, and who would want to shut themselves up when the 'High Pomps of Midsummer' are here and will
too soon be passing? In a garden where labour is scarce and the soil
beneficent, all manner of tiny seedlings get overlooked till, lo and
behold! a handsome clump has established itself in the most unlikely
position, claiming squatters' rights and in nine cases out of ten
succeeding in establishing its claim. The Long Garden . . . set with
high black yews and punctuated with heavy green humps of box,
contains many such vagrant but successful colonies cunningly
inserted among bold groups of ordinary herbaceous plants. Lupins,
anchusas, mulleins, all the easy English flowers raise their tinted
spires in spring and summer, and treading on their heels come
mallows, thalictrums, hollyhocks, the tall bushy campanulas and
the tropical rods of the magnificent eremuri. All these look comfortable and healthy growing in big informal drifts. One group
follows another in rapid succession, so that there is never an inch
of bare earth to be seen, and they require no attention beyond
their annual weeding and staking. Though the whole effect is that
of thoughtless abundance, there is an underlying colour scheme
most carefully considered. For the rich blues, deep purples and
various pinks and lemons are kept away from the hot scarlets of
the sizzling great poppies, the burning alstroemeria and all the
metallic golds of the rudbeckias and sunflowers. With these flaming
fellows are planted the cool silver grasses, the fascinating bloodless
candelabra of *Salvia turkestanica* (one of the most persistent and
welcome of squatters) and the grey fish-bone thistle, with its frosted
prickly wings. Old box hedges, 2 ft high and as much across,
surround this radiant parterre and in their clipped decorum
produce the perfect finish to the jungle they encircle. There is a
running accompaniment of lilies and crown imperials just inside
these box hedges, and who shall say which season is the loveliest:
spring, with the ardent 5 ft high amber Turk's-caps, their downcast
eyes filled with tears, their gold or tawny reversed bells crowned
with a valiant tuft of leaves; or summer, with the pure stainless
Madonnas, their long, waxy buds pointing this way and that, their
alabaster chalices drenching the air with honey-sweetness in which
lie embalmed precious memories of Venice and Perugia. Indeed,
there is more than a memory of Italy in my garden.

. . . An old wall covered with choice shrubs divides this herbaceous garden from the one next door, called the Persian Garden.

On it magnolias offer us their cream kid goblets in August, while in July enormous mauve ostrowskias shoot up like Jack-in-the-bean-stalks, holding their fragile fluted faces high above our heads. Akebia, with its early crop of raspberry-coloured trefoils; piptanthus, the robust Nepalese laburnum; *Abutilon vitifolium*, with felted stems and clusters of white or heliotrope blossoms; the fascinating *Fendlaria rupicola*, with its argosy of milky buttercups; various ceanothus in continuous clouds of powder blue, many of them laced with deeper purple clematis; and feijoa, that shy-flowering member of the myrtle family, all occupy permanent seats here. There is also an overgrown thicket of *Choisya ternata*, 12 ft long and very aromatic, a gaunt and ancient gum cystus with dark sticky leaves, and one lolloping bush of *Phlomis fruticosa* whose woolly white foliage and gaudy golden cockades have broken all bounds and lie heaped on the path below . . .

An old ironwork gate, almost hidden under a splendid tangle of pomegranate, leads into the Persian Garden, where beds of roses pour out their attar unstintingly and are hemmed with spicy early pinks and backed by a tall screen of Penzance and sweetbrier mixed. Sweet-smelling hedges are a great feature of this garden, and in the twilight of a hot summer's day the perfume from each one is distinct and intoxicating. At one end, against the wall of the house, is a brickfloored enclosure . . . furnished with great fat tree peonies, a tall, glossy, vanilla-flavoured Azara, two Hoherias and a grand bush of *Calycanthus floridus* with its rufous rosettes of clove. Here is a favourite seat, for the wall behind is papered in that flimsy adorable rose, Fortune's Yellow, called after the lucky Mr Fortune who espied it flowering in some secret Chinese valley. Round the enclosure runs perhaps the prettiest hedge of all, made of the old-fashioned *Rosa Damascena*, York and Lancaster. It is about 4 ft high and flowers so profusely that for six weeks there is hardly any foliage to be seen. The colour and diversity of the petals, now all crimson, now all white, now carefully striped, and now deli-cately feathered as if with a fine brush, the eager buds of close bright rose held well aloft as if waiting to be picked, and carrying their particular scent with them into the house, places this hedge high in the love of the inhabitants. When this supply is finished the next hedge begins, a tall screen, 10 ft high, of honeysuckle, *Lonicera Etrusca* . . . from which it is a delight to gather the crisp nankeen-tinted sprays, which are just the right size for vases, and no amount of cutting for the house or for friends disturbs its bloomy surface. The old grey stone wall is hung in spring with huge sponges of aubrietias in full tone of purple, lilac and puce, straggling, dazzling golden wallflowers and neat tuffets of ham-pink arabis. As they die down our old accommodating friend, the valerian, in shades of crimson, pink and white, springs to life, so that the whole length of the wall flushes into a rosy cloud, tremulous in beauty, but so stout in intention that it only melts away in late autumn . . . The contrast of the severe grey stone and the frolicking valerian is a perpetual delight. A conspicuous example of this perfect mating is to be seen on the twin *tapis verts* which lie in the middle of the Long Garden, where the old lichen-stained vases in the centre are entirely surrounded by the crimson plumes of the self-sown valerian . . . Wherever the flowers themselves have planned the garden I gracefully retire, for they are the guiding intelligences and strike where we fumble.

Norah Lindsay, 1931

COUNTRYWOMEN

On a summer afternoon

THE PRIDE of my heart and the delight of my eyes is my garden. Our house, which is in dimensions very much like a bird-cage, and might, with almost equal convenience, be laid on a shelf, or hung up in a tree, would be utterly unbearable in warm weather, were it not that we have a retreat out of doors, – and a very pleasant retreat it is. To make my readers comprehend it, I must describe our whole territories.

Fancy a small plot of ground, with a pretty low irregular cottage at one end; a large granary, divided from the dwelling by a little court running along one side; and a long thatched shed, open towards the garden, and supported by wooden pillars, on the other. The bottom is bounded, half by an old wall, and half by an old paling, over which we see a pretty distance of woody hills. The house, granary, wall, and paling, are covered with vines, cherry-trees, roses, honeysuckles, and jessamines, with great clusters of tall hollyhocks running up between them; a large elder overhanging the little gate, and a magnificent bay-tree, such a tree as shall scarcely be matched in these parts, breaking with its beautiful conical form the horizontal lines of the buildings. This is my garden; and the long pillared shed, the sort of rustic arcade, which runs along one side, parted from the flower-beds by a row of rich geraniums, is our out-of-door drawing-room.

I know nothing so pleasant as to sit there on a summer afternoon, with the western sun flickering through the great elder-tree, and lighting up our gay parterres, where flowers and flowering shrubs are set as thick as grass in a field, a wilderness of blossom, interwoven, intertwined, wreathy, garlandy, profuse beyond all profusion, where we may guess that there is such a thing as mould, but never see it. I know nothing so pleasant as to sit in the shade of that dark bower, with the eye resting on that bright piece of colour, lighted so gloriously by the evening sun, now catching a glimpse of the little birds as they fly rapidly in and out of their nests – for there are always two or three birds-nests in the thick tapestry of cherry-trees, honeysuckles, and China-roses, which covers our walls – now tracing the gay gambols of the common butterflies as they sport around the dahlias; now watching that rarer moth, which the country people, fertile in pretty names, call the bee-bird; that bird-like insect, which flutters in the hottest days over the sweetest flowers, inserting its long proboscis into the small tube of the jessamine, and hovering over the scarlet blossoms of the geranium, whose bright colour seems reflected on its own feathery breast: that insect which seems so thoroughly a creature of the air, never at rest; always, even when feeding, self-poised, and self-supported, and whose wings, in their ceaseless motion, have a sound so deep, so full, so lulling, so musical. Nothing so pleasant as to sit amid that mixture of the flower and the leaf, watching the bee-bird! Nothing so pretty to look at as my garden! It is quite a picture; only unluckily it resembles a picture in more qualities than one, – it is fit for nothing but to look at. One might as well think of walking in a bit of framed canvass. There are walks to be sure – tiny paths of smooth gravel, by courtesy called such – but they are so overhung by roses and lilies, and such gay encroachers – so over-run by convolvulus, and heart's-ease, and mignonette, and other sweet stragglers, that, except to edge through them occasionally, for the purposes of planting, or weeding, or watering, there might as well be no paths at all. Nobody thinks of walking in my garden. Even May glides along with a delicate and trackless step, like a swan through the water; and we, its two-footed denizens, are fain to treat it as if it were really a saloon, and go out for a walk towards sun-set, just as if we had not been sitting in the open air all day.

Mary Russell Mitford, 1832

A garden journal

1943 March – The most perfect of days – warm as midsummer – mown grass, birds and my large garden hat. Everything soaked in sunshine that burns ... Continuation of Midsummer Madness! *Clematis armandii* Apple Blossom is exquisite delicate blush pink – but the one on the pillar by steps to Open Air Theatre is not too happy ... We badly need some more magnolias standing out in the grass against dark backgrounds – not enough blossom to be seen ... *Stellatas* are wrongly placed – should be against yews or something very dark.

July – The real excitement of the past week has been the opening of *Magnolia grandiflora* on the study corner and by the morning room. Jerry brought one branch actually into his study. What a flower – what utter purity, and never have I seen such smooth texture and such rhythmic curves of the petals, and added to the visual beauty – such an unearthly scent – the essence of lemon. How noble this flower is.

September – A lovely planting day. Calthorpe and I put in crocus under three old pines in Courtyard ... Then we planted three groups of *Colchicum* above grassy bank of rock garden ... We also put in four sets of cyclamen in rock garden ... Then two dozen mixed *Erythronium* ... This p.m. we planted two hundred bluebells.

... Planted out forty-eight white foxgloves, twenty-four Lutz hybrids in Wilderness. Took up all violets in Dell – forked in peat and replanted them, adding twelve Princess of Wales. Moved *Daphne mezereum* to new place among hellebores.

Dorothy Elmhirst, 1968

First sighting of 'Daffodils'

We first rested in the large Boat-house, then under a furze bush opposite Mr. Clarkson's. Saw the plough going in the field. The wind seized our breath. The Lake was rough. There was a Boat by itself floating in the middle of the Bay below Water Millock. We rested again in the Water Millock Lane. The hawthorns are black and green, the birches here and there greenish, but there is yet more of purple to be seen on the twigs. We got over into a field to avoid some cows – people working. A few primroses by the roadside – woodsorrel flower, the anemone, scentless violets, strawberries, and that starry, yellow flower which Mrs. C. calls pile wort. When we were in the woods beyond Gowbarrow park we saw a few daffodils close to the water-side. We fancied that the lake had floated the seeds ashore, and that the little colony had so sprung up. But as we went along there were more and yet more; and at last, under the boughs of the trees, we saw that there was a long belt of them along the shore, about the breadth of a country turn-pike road. I never saw daffodils so beautiful. They grew among the mossy stones about and about them; some rested their heads upon these stones, as on a pillow, for weariness; and the rest tossed and reeled and danced, and seemed as if they verily laughed with the wind, that blew upon them over the lake; they looked so gay, ever glancing, ever changing. This wind blew directly over the lake to them. There was here and there a little knot, and a few stragglers a few yards higher up; but they were so few as not to disturb the simplicity, unity, and life of that one busy highway.

Dorothy Wordsworth, 1802

Pond life

There is a dip in the rye-fields about half a mile from my garden gate, a little round hollow like a dimple, with water and reeds at the bottom, and a few water-loving trees and bushes on the shelving ground around. Here I have been nearly every morning lately, for it suits the mood I am in, and I like the narrow footpath to it through the rye, and I like its solitary dampness in a place where everything is parched, and when I am lying on the grass and look down I can see the reeds glistening greenly in the water, and when I look up I can see the rye-fringe brushing the sky. All sorts of beasts come and stare at me, and larks sing above me, and creeping things crawl over me, and stir in the long grass beside me; and here I bring my book, and read and dream away the profitable morning hours, to the accompaniment of the amorous croakings of innumerable frogs.

Thoreau has been my companion for some days past, it having struck me as more appropriate to bring him out to a pond than to read him, as was hitherto my habit, on Sunday mornings in the garden. He is a person who loves the open air, and will refuse to give you much pleasure if you try to read him amid the pomp and circumstance of upholstery; but out in the sun, and especially by this pond, he is delightful, and we spend the happiest hours together, he making statements, and I either agreeing heartily, or just laughing and reserving my opinion till I shall have more ripely considered the thing.

Elizabeth von Arnim, 1899

Flowers in the field

After the cowslips, come the bird's-foot trefoil – a liberal layer of scrambled eggs rather than eggs-and-bacon – and the faint memory of pale spring grass disappears in a sea of bright green. Buttercups follow and suddenly the quaking-grass is nine inches tall and the oxeye daisies are in full flower. It is the variety of plants in the hay which is so attractive. I have gradually accumulated a hundred species in mine, by the simple method of collecting seed (in a paper bag) along road verges and from a nearby derelict airfield, then wire-raking a patch of the 'field' and scattering, more or less at random, the contents of the bag in the small raked patches. This is usually effective with all the clovers and vetches, and with lady's bedstraw and knapweeds. Field scabious is more capricious and after several failures I sowed these in rows in the garden and transplanted them into the field as seedlings. I did the same with harebells and ragged-robin. Of plants which I collected in this fashion I think the most attractive nectar flowers to hayfield butter-flies and moths – of which the common blue is my favourite – have proved to be (1) common ragwort (which, on the Ministry of Agriculture's prohibited list, came in by itself), (2) field scabious, (3) knapweeds, (4) red clovers, (5) bird's-foot trefoil (Lepidoptera are said to take the nectar without effecting pollination), (6) campions, (7) ragged-robin, (8) yarrow, (9) thistles, (10) selfheal and bugle (the upper lip of these labiates is missing, which makes them good butterfly flowers), (11) hawkbits and cat's-ears, and (12) wild thyme (these get easily swamped by the grass). But I have seen the small white feeding in a leisurely fashion on harebells when the flowers were in a suitable position. I introduced the black-and-red burnet and cinnabar moths to this site, and both flourish. They prefer field scabious, vetches, clovers and knapweeds – if they are in bloom early enough – and ragworts.

Miriam Rothschild, 1983

Beekeepers

Dear Mother,

Well, this is the last letter I will be writing before you come! ... I have been working so hard physically out in the garden that I am inarticulate and ready for bed by evening, hence my long silences. I don't know when I've been so happy or felt so well. These last few days I have been weeding our strawberry patch and setting the runners, just as I did on Lookout Farm, and at night I shut my eyes and see the beautiful little plants with the starry flowers and beginning berries. I love this outdoor work and feel I am really getting in condition . . .

Today, guess what, we became *beekeepers*! We went to the local meeting last week (attended by the rector, the midwife, and assorted beekeeping people from neighbouring villages) to watch a Mr Pollard make three hives out of one (by transferring his queen cells) under the supervision of the official Government bee-man. We all wore masks and it was thrilling. It is expensive to start beekeeping (over $50 outlay), but Mr Pollard let us have an old hive for nothing, which we painted white and green, and today he brought over the swarm of docile Italian hybrid bees we ordered and installed them. We placed the hive in a sheltered out-of-the-way spot in the orchard – the bees were furious from being in a box. Ted had only put a handkerchief over his head where the hat should go in the bee-mask, and the bees crawled into his hair, and he flew off with half-a-dozen stings. I didn't get stung at all, and when I went back to the hive later, I was delighted to see bees entering with pollen sacs full and leaving with them empty – at least I *think* that's what they were doing. I feel very ignorant, but shall try to read up and learn all I can. If we're lucky, we'll have our own honey, too!

Sylvia Plath, 1962

Leafcutter Bees

Perhaps the wrens were having a go at some kind of
   abstract beauty.
Anyhow they built a nest they didn't use in the thick
   yew-tree.
And a few days afterwards when someone gave it a poke
With a concerted high-pitched buzz the dim thing spoke.
Little gold bees like quarter-scale bumbles
Tumbled out of it in response to the fumbles.
'Oh the little darlings' some female utters,

'Leave them alone, they're only leaf-cutters,
They won't harm your potherbs or your posies,
Only cut round holes in the leaves of the roses.'
Huh! They by-passed the roses as if they'd been nettles.
They wrapped up their eggs in geranium petals.
They took a dead set at a thing that really matters,
They cut the flame geraniums into shreds and tatters.
We knew where they lived. We could have gone at night
And done them all in and served them all right.
But we could not penalise them for their childish folly,
Any more than little girls who want to dress their dolly,
Who take their little scissors and with uncertain
Snips cut a great piece from your red silk curtain.

Ruth Pitter, 1966

Mowing the orchard

The moment for mowing has come. We go into the shed and look at our scythe. From the fields around comes the drone of the reaper, sending us almost to sleep with the bee-like hum, now nearer, now further, of its graduated waves of sound. Even the voice of the mower as he calls to his horses has a humming quality. So deeply are we under the spell of this drone that we have hardly the energy to think of our own mowing. The scythe seems heavy as we lift it from its hooks on the shed wall. If that soothing hum would only stop, we could brace ourselves to start. We linger and pause, and look about us, eager for any excuse to delay work. Perhaps the daffodil leaves are not as dead as we had imagined last evening in the half light? But when we go to the orchard to look, we see that there is no excuse for us, they lie crinkled and brown among the roots of the grasses.

The grasses undulate in the breeze, with the motion of a slight swell at sea. As we walk round the orchard, now facing, now backing the sun, they change colour; they are pale silver fawn with the sun full on them, and darker and redder against the sun's light. And as the men and women in a vast crowd have their unremarked, individual beauty and character, moulded each in his own fashion, differing each from the other in shape and colouring, so are the grasses in the orchard composed of multitudinous varying forms, some frail and fine, some erect and sturdy, each with its own pattern of life. I look closer. Where the rapid glance perceives a mere shimmering stretch of fawn, I now see the cock's foot grass, with violet-tinted flecks of pollen still sticking to its rough spikes; rye grass and vernal grass are light against brown plantain; the flowered green timothy grass towers smooth and erect, austere of form among the shaking, quivering totter grasses. Shorter, in this vast crowd, clump the 'backbone' grasses, familiar to us from our childhood's game of 'Tinker, Tailor'. Pale meadow soft grass and meadow poa add to the waving buff, a background to some still blossoming pink vetch. Aristocrat amidst this multitude stands the lovely yellow melilot, like a beauty in the market place. Burnt spire tells of seeding dock that we have overlooked in our weedings. Bladder of white campion looks strangely smooth against fringed grasses. At the far end of the grassland grows a white clot of moon-daisies. We did not dig the orchard land when we made our garden, merely cultivating the ground that surrounded each fruit-tree; so to-day it blossoms with stray lucerne and white clover, heritage from the days when it was pasture.

Beneath these towering, tapering grasses, in the thick tangle of undergrowth, creep little yellow hop trefoil, and scarlet pimpernel. The gilt downy seeds of the goat's beard lie low in the grass, seeking the earth. Below this carpet of flowering weeds are the dark homes of insects. Moss covers the nest of the wild bee, which hums in the short stemmed clover. Butterflies are a brown and blue mist among the grasses. Ripened vetch pods burst in the heat with sudden crackles.

Clare Leighton, 1935

Cuckoo in the nest

There are many reasons not to plant × *Cupresso-cyparis leylandii*, the Leyland cypress. It is characterless. It is depressing. It is like a cuckoo in the nest. It almost always outgrows its home, engaging its keepers in an exhausting battle with shears, loppers and saw to keep its greedy branches from taking all light and space to itself. Few trees look as uncomfortable in our landscape as the Leyland cypress. There are just two places where I have seen it looking at home: in a cemetery and screening an electricity sub-station.

Leylands do not change with the seasons. They have no blossom and no fruit to speak of. There is neither shape nor shine to the leaf, and no architecture about the things at all.

What they *can* do is grow, sometimes up to 2 ft/60 cm a year. If you are fighting to establish some privacy in a pocket handkerchief of a plot surrounded by nosy neighbours, this may seem a great advantage. And so it is, for the first three years or so. After that, it is a curse. For each extra couple of feet that the thing reaches into the sky, there is a corresponding shadow on the ground. It does not take long before the whole handkerchief may be cast in gloom, confined in a suffocating, dark green prison.

There is a small brick cottage that I used to pass every week on my way to town. It sat in the middle of a small field hedged round with the usual country mixture of blackthorn, field maple, hazel and ash. After almost a hundred years of unpretentious life as a farm worker's cottage, it was sold for improvement.

Plastic windows replaced the wooden casements and the Welsh slate roof made way for Marley tiles of an uncompromising colour, but it was the day the bulldozers moved in to grub out the old hedge that I felt like throwing myself in the juggernauts' path.

None of my business, I know. An Englishman's home is his castle. But why murder a perfectly good hedge at great expense to plant instead hideous lines of Leyland cypress that look as at home in the country as heifers in Piccadilly? 'Die, you beasts, die,' I used to mutter vindictively as I drove past each week. They have not, but the cottage has not sold. Perhaps there is a moral in this tale after all.

Hoping that I may be witnessing the beginning of a reaction

against the dreaded conifer, I hurried along to the local garden centre to check out sales figures for Leyland cypress. 'Definitely our best line,' said the foreman, depressingly. 'People like it because it is a good, fast grower.' Why should fast growth automatically be an advantage, I wonder? Instant gardening is no more satisfying to the soul than thirty-second snatches of Mozart, condensed novels or fast food.

Anna Pavord, 1992

Rain after drought

The whole garden is singing this hymn of praise and thankfulness. It is the middle of June; no rain had fallen for nearly a month, and our dry soil had become a hot dust above, a hard cake below. A burning wind from the east that had prevailed for some time, had brought quantities of noisome blight, and had left all vegetation, already parched with drought, a helpless prey to the devouring pest. Bushes of garden Roses had their buds swarming with green-fly, and all green things, their leaves first coated and their pores clogged with viscous stickiness, and then covered with adhering wind-blown dust, were in a pitiable state of dirt and suffocation. But last evening there was a gathering of grey cloud, and this ground of grey was traversed by those fast-travelling wisps of fleecy blackness that are the surest promise of near rain the sky can show. By bed-time rain was falling steadily, and in the night it came down on the roof in a small thunder of steady downpour. It was pleasant to wake from time to time and hear the welcome sound, and to know that the clogged leaves were being washed clean, and that their pores were once more drawing in the breath of life, and that the thirsty roots were drinking their fill. And now, in the morning, how good it is to see the brilliant light of the blessed summer day, always brightest just after rain, and to see how every tree and plant is full of new life and abounding gladness; and to feel one's own thankfulness of heart, and that it is good to live, and all the more good to live in a garden.

Gertrude Jekyll, 1900

'News from Stump Cross'

Rain. More rain. Waterbutts full for the first time in a year. A soft grey mist hanging in the hedgerows. The snowdrops did their best in dry, warm ground, and quickly went their way. Now the scillas and the narcissi and the wood anemones are keeping their jubilee, their petals sleeked by the damp air, glowing against the new green that is rushing up over the land. Under the beech trees a clump of sweet violets has appeared; by the pond in the wood is another. A dome of frog spawn nudges the surface of the water and the white marsh marigold is in flower. Up on the chalk hill Farmer Hamilton's beet is beginning to show.

The grass grows like mad, and the geese graze like mad upon it, for the time of their brood is almost at hand. They are already so plump that the folds of fat beneath their bellies drag up on the new grass, leaving trails like the slime of a giant snail . . . We have a thousand or so rabbits and about the same number of rats on my three acres because there is nowhere else for them to go. The population that should be spread over the 100-acre field lives with me because I neither plough nor poison my ground with fungicides, herbicides, insecticides and fertilisers. Because of the environmental stress none of the critters who lives under my hedgerows and my poultry houses is quite sane or quite well. The rabbit population is full of myxomatosis. Because none of the predators will take a sick rabbit, the myxy ones are compelled to live out a normal life-span, and to reproduce. When the ferreters come these days they get no hassle from me. Strange to relate they get no hassle from the anti-blood sports people either. Funny that, when you think about it. Foxes live by hunting and could expect to die the same way, but rabbits? What harm did rabbits ever do?

Well, I'll tell you. Rabbits are bloody bastards. Absolute bloody bastards. They don't kill other animals. They kill plants. Foxes, unlike dogs and mink, kill for food for themselves and their young. Rabbits don't kill trees for food. I don't know why they kill trees. They will do just enough damage to a young tree to ensure that it dies, and then they will move on to the next one. They will nose their way through spiral guards and gnaw out a neat half-inch strip all the way round the tree; that's all it takes to kill even a mighty tree. They will climb on each other's shoulders to attack the tree above the guard — I reckon, because otherwise I don't know how the hell they do it. Build a cage for a young tree and they will burrow under it. If they can't get at any other part of the tree, they will dig under it and eat the roots. They will kill larch, oak, sycamore, hornbeam, whitebeam, beech, birch, horsechestnut, willow, alder, poplar, aspen, apple, medlar, cherry, maple, cedar, cypress, hazel, pine, spruce, juniper, whitethorn, blackthorn, but not brambles or bracken or elder. I have just planted twenty planes and they have yet to kill one, but they will. I have planted more than seven hundred trees since I have lived in this house and they have destroyed four hundred of them, some when they were already twenty centimetres in girth. They have eaten whole yews and lived to tell the tale. They even managed to strip a monkey puzzle of its scales.

I do not protest when rabbits eat bulbs or gnaw their way into the cage to eat my salad. But I cannot bear it when for the sake of slightly different taste, some sort of oral novelty, they kill one of my trees. Do something for our struggling tree population. Kill a rabbit today.

Germaine Greer, 1992

You must not, any of you, be surprised if you have moments in your gardening life of such profound depression and disappointment that you will almost wish you had been content to leave everything alone and have no garden at all

Mrs C. W. Earle, 1897

Rabbits

Rabbits are an intolerable nuisance in a flower garden, and in some country places they abound most destructively. A light wire fence about two feet high, closely lattice-worked, or a net of the same height, carried round the garden, is a sure defence from these marauders. But where these conveniences are unattainable, there are other modes which answer the purpose, but they require a little trouble and patience.

It is the well-known nature of Rabbits and Hares to dislike climbing or entangling their feet; and very simple inventions deter them from attempting to gnaw the roots and hearts of flowers. They will not walk upon straw or ashes strewed thickly round any plant: they equally dislike a fence of sticks placed round a plot, with bits of white paper or card fastened to each stick; or a string carried round the sticks a foot or two high. If they cannot creep under a slight fence, they never attempt to leap over it. If a stick is run into the ground close to a plant, and other sticks are slanted from the ground towards that centre, the plant will remain untouched, be the frost of ever so long duration.

Louisa Johnson, 1843

The 'Fantaisie'

The garden's story. It is only eleven years old, though the place itself is an old place – an old place without a history, for scarce a record remains of it anywhere that we have ever found . . . The borders are filled with the dearest old-fashioned plants; the main entrance is removed to the north side; the stable-yard is removed also, and instead thereof are turf and straight walks, and a sun dial, and a parterr for bedding-out things – the sole plot allowed here for Scarlet Pelargoniums and the like. In this parterre occurs the only foliage plant we tolerate – a deep crimson velvet-leaved Coleus. The centre bed is a raised square of yellow Stonecrop, and little white Harebells; with an old stone pedestal, found in a stonemason's yard, bearing a leaden inscription – 'to Deborah' – surmounted by a ball, on which the white pigeons picturesquely perch. There are green walks between Yew hedges and flower borders, Beech hedges, and a long green tunnel – the *allée verte* – so named in remembrance of a bower-walk in an old family place, no longer in existence. There are nooks and corners, and a grand, well-shaded tennis lawn, and crown of all, there is the 'Fantaisie'! This is a tiny plantation in the field, – I mean the Park, – date 1874, connected with the garden by a turf walk, with a breadth of flowers and young evergreen trees intermixed, on either hand. Here all my most favourite flowers grow in wild profusion. The turf walk is lost, after a break of Golden Yew, in a little wood – a few paces round – just large enough for the birds to build in, and with room for half-a-dozen wild Hyacinths and a dozen Primroses under the trees; with moss, Wood Sorrel, and white and puce coloured Periwinkles, and many a wild thing, meant to encourage the delusion of a savage wild! I am afraid I never can be quite serious about a garden; I always am inclined to find delight in fancies, and reminiscences of a child's garden, and the desire to get everything into it if I could. This 'Fantaisie' was a dream of delight during the past summer – from April, when a nightingale possessed in song the half-hidden entrance under low embowering Elm branches and Syringa – through all the fairy days and months, up to quite lately. Yes, even last week, it was fragrant with Mignonette and Ragged Jack (I mean that Alpine Pink *Dianthus Plumarius*), gay with yellow Zinnias and blue Salvia in rich luxuriance, with a host of smaller, less showy things – with bunches of crimson Roses, and pink La France, blooming out from a perfect mist of white and pinkish Japan Anemones, white Sweet Peas, and a few broad Sunflowers towering at the back – their great stems coruscating all over with stars of gold; and here and there clusters of purple Clematis, leaning sadly down from a faggot of brown leaves and dead, wiry stalks, – or turning from their weak embrace of some red-brown Cryptomeria elegans. Even last week the borders throughout the garden looked filled and cheerful – brilliant with scarlet Lobelia and tall deep red Phloxes, and bushes of blue-leaved starry Marguerites, and the three varieties of Japan Anemone, with strange orange Tigridias and auratum Lilies and Ladies' Pincushion (*Scabious*, the 'Saudades' of the Portuguese language of Flowers), and every kind of late as well as summer Roses, the evening Primrose (Œnothera) making sunshine in each shady spot, with here and there the burning flame of a Tritoma; though these last have not done well this autumn.

Out near the carriage drive are Golden Rod and crimsoned patches of Azalea, and a second blow of late and self-sown Himalayan (so called) Poppies. In one narrow bit of south border one finds that pretty blue daisy (Kaulfussia Amelloides) – such an odd, pretty little thing. I remember a bed of it in the garden of my childhood, and I possess a portrait of it, done for me by my mother; and then, never met with it again till a year or two ago, when unexpectedly it looked up at me, somewhere in a remote country churchyard. I am afraid our present stock comes from that very plant. Until now, the long border of many-coloured Verbenas was still rather gay, and the three east gables of the house were all aflame with Virginian Creeper. But two days of rain spoilt us entirely. The variegated Maple slipped its white garment all at once in the night, causing a melancholy gap. In the kitchen garden a bright red Rose or two remains, but along the east border the half-blown buds are rotted away. In the centre of one drenched pink bloom I saw a poor drone, drowned as he sat idly there. Small black-headed titmice are jerking about among the tallest Rose trees, insect hunting; and still tinier wrens flit here and there bent on the same quest. Great spotted missel thrushes are now haunting the pillar Yews, beginning to taste the luscious banquet just ready for them. While thus perched amongst the sweet scarlet Yew berries and dark foliage, the thrushes always bring to one's mind a design in old tapestry.

And this reminds me of the good and abundant fruit-feast we have ourselves enjoyed this season. Strawberries and Raspberries were not much, but such Gooseberries, Apricots, and Nectarines! Peaches, plenty enough, but no flavour. Figs, enough to satisfy even *our* greediness, – though we have but one tree, on a west wall. Pears, especially Louise Bonne, first-rate and plenty. Apples, a small crop, but sufficient. Wood Strawberries have been ripening under the windows till within the last few days: I planted them there for the sake of the delicious smell of the leaves when decaying – a smell said to be perceptible only to the happy few. Nuts (Filberts and Kentish Cobs) were plentiful, but we were only allowed a very few dishes of them. A large number of nuthatches settled in the garden as soon as the nuts were ripe; they nipped them off, and, carrying them to the old Acacia tree, which stands conveniently near, stuck them in the rough bark and cracked them at their ease (or rather punched holes in them). The Acacia's trunk at one time quite bristled over with the empty nutshells, while the husks lay at the roots. The fun of watching these busy thieves at work more than made up for the loss of nuts. We had a great abundance of large green and yellow wall Plums, also a fair quantity of purple. Of sweet Cherries, unless gathered rather unripe, my dear blackbirds and starlings never leave us many. But there were a good lot of Morellos; they don't care a bit for them. Whilst on the subject of fruit, let me say that never a shot is fired in the garden, unless to destroy weazels. Our 'garden's sacred round' is free to every bird that flies – the delight of seeing them, and of hearing their music, compensates to the full any ravages they may indulge in. Thanks to netting without stint, and our Gardener's incomparable patience and longsuffering, I enjoy the garden and my birds in peace; and if they ever do any harm, we never know it; fruit and green Peas never fail us! . . . Here is a sunny morning; and the cows are whisking their tails under the Elms, as if it were July. But indeed the last lingering trace of summer has vanished: the garden is in ruins, and already the redbreast is singing songs of triumph.

E. V. Boyle, 1889

TOWNSWOMEN

I WOULD put the drawbacks in town gardening in the following order: – First, WALLS; second, AIR; third, CATS; fourth, SOIL . . . Cats can almost break a gardener's heart.

Lady Seton, 1927

A dilemma

As I reside in town, and am known among my friends as a lover of the country, it has often happened that one or other of them would bring me consolation in the shape of a Myrtle, a Geranium, an Hydrangea, or a Rose-tree, &c. Liking plants, and loving my friends, I have earnestly desired to preserve these kind gifts; but, utterly ignorant of their wants and habits, I have seen my plants die one after the other, rather from attention ill-directed than from the want of it. I have many times seen others in the same situation as myself, and found it a common thing, upon the arrival of a new plant, to hear its owner say, 'Now, I should like to know how I am to treat this? Should it stand within doors, or without? should it have much water, or little? should it stand in the sun, or in the shade?' . . .

Although it is true that near London plants in general will not thrive so well as in a purer air, and that people in the country have usually some portion of ground to make a garden of, yet such persons as are condemned to a town life will do well to obtain whatever substitute for a garden may be in their power; for there is confessedly no greater folly than that of refusing all pleasure, because we cannot have all we desire.

Elizabeth Kent, 1831

What kind of garden?

The elements that must be fitted into the space at your disposal will depend on how you are going to use the garden; there might be a sitting-out place, provision for children's play, flower beds or vegetable patch, plus a small working area for compost and a tool shed – an essential in all but the smallest gardens – and arrangements for dustbins and other household needs. Some of these will be competing for the sunniest spot or that nearest the house, so it is important to decide which has first claim. Access in all weathers must be provided: a path to the working area, for example, or to dustbins outside the back gate. These are the factors that control where the paved areas are to be, and how large.

The overall character of a town garden is determined by two basic design principles: it is either an extension of the rooms of the house . . . or an illusion of country come to town . . . Many gardens contain elements of both, but to be successful, one kind of design should dominate. Personal inclination – the pull towards formality or romanticism – will be the deciding factor, modified by the requirements of daily use.

One striking difference between the two types of garden is the way the boundaries are handled. Where the garden is treated as an outdoor room, these are clearly seen and the shape of the enclosure is important, though this should not mean that the whole garden can be taken in at a glance. The floor pattern is also prominent. And since this type of design is based on geometry, one way of arriving at an overall sense of harmony is to relate the measurements of all spaces and structures to the dimensions of whatever paving slab has been chosen. This is similar to the Japanese *tatami* system, where the standard size of the small mats covering the floor of a house is the basis of the proportions of all the other elements of the structure . . . Pursued to an extreme, the results can be boring; fortunately, every garden has irregularities that cause slight variations which, with the help of the planting, prevent monotony.

The success of the country-style garden depends almost entirely on concealing the boundaries and using loose, informal planting, rather than screens or hedges, to create separate compartments within the garden. This is not, however, a natural garden, but one where nature is under strict control ('organised woodland' is one owner's description of her north London garden). To be effective, the vegetation should be on a fairly bold scale, but a constant watch is necessary to prevent the garden from turning into an impenetrable jungle – concealed order as opposed to the more obvious order of the outdoor room.

Whether you settle for romanticism or geometry, or a combination of both, one further general point should be borne in mind. This is the question of scale: the furnishings of the garden – trees, shrubs, sculpture, etc. – should not dwarf the house or garden, nor should they be so small as to look insignificant.

Susan Jellicoe, 1977

In the heart of the city

I realise now that the purpose of gardening in London – and presumably in any city – is to be able to do as I've been doing this afternoon: to sit in the sun in a deckchair recovering from 'flu, conscious of the quietness all around because my neighbours are at work; to give the birds, used to skylarking all day on the edges of flower pots and playing hopscotch on paving-stones, the fright of their lives as I emerge into the garden at lunch-time; and to be able to climb my own silver birch, survey the surrounding gardens, each a walled yard 14 ft × 23 ft (4.2 × 7 m) or thereabouts, and decide (as I suspect all the garden pests for miles around have long since decided) that mine is nicer than anyone else's within range. Trains from one of central London's main rail termini trundle past on the other side of the very high wall at the foot of the garden, but apart from that it can be astonishingly quiet here in this green oasis. So I want to tell people who may be hovering on the brink of buying a terrace house with a back garden, however small, something about what can be done on a modest scale; and, perhaps more important, on a trial-and-error basis. Too many people, I think, are put off by the idea that beautiful town gardens are expensive luxuries; but this only need happen if basic structural work is needed, if costly herbaceous and bedding plants must be purchased afresh each year, or if you fall for gimmickry.

In the ten years since I came here, the tiny space has evolved into the nearest thing to a cottage garden imaginable in the centre of a city . . . Pots and tubs jostle each other, their positions being changed as their occupants come into bloom, and the first impression given is always of the extent and variety of greenery – 'All that green!' – visitors exclaim, confronted with a sudden view through glass as they round the corner into the long sitting-room which faces west into the garden. This perhaps is the first rule of London gardening – to realise that, whatever can be achieved in the way of colour, the basis is greenery and it behoves the gardener to aim for as many contrasting shapes and shades, textures and growing habits as possible. There is another important variation too – between movement and stillness. *Hosta marginata alba*, for instance, strikingly contrasts with the restless birch above it.

The second rule is that, to avoid excessive expense and the impression that a hasty assembly job of pots and tubs has just been done, your garden must be a real working garden and not an exhibit. This means that you must arrange a small nursery area for letting bulbs die back, storing pots and so on, in the shade, and screened by tubs. You must learn to handle cuttings, and to grow plants from seed, and that can mean seed pods, sometimes unidentified, as well as packet seed.

Pruning and cutting back are important skills in a small garden, especially as you have to bear constantly in mind the need to allow for the enhanced effects on growth of sun and rain confined to a small area. Arising naturally from this is another precept – something you must brace yourself to do – which is to discard temperamental or downright unsatisfactory doers. It is easy, but fatal, to give a year's stay of execution to a plant which is healthy enough, producing luxuriant greenery even in the poorest soil, but which sturdily refuses to earn its keep by flowering. Two years to get into its stride, three perhaps to be generous, but after that . . . a present to friends is my solution to the problem.

Audrey le Lièvre, 1981

Seen from the train

In these days of motors, when we are quickly whirled through the approaches to London and other towns, we do not see as much of suburban gardens as when the train slowly slackens speed upon a high railway-embankment and we look down from it upon rows of small houses. The buildings may all be alike, but how varied in taste, order, arrangement is each plot of ground. Such a bird's-eye view somewhat recalls to mind the jumble of mixed garden designs seen at some of our big flower-shows at Chelsea or Holland House. Here each nurseryman naturally endeavours to outdo his neighbour in striking effects, and side by side we find dry wall gardens with natural-looking rock-plants in their chinks, whilst almost touching them is a stiff treillage garden of Le Nôtre's time. Excellent as are some few of these flower-show effects, we sometimes wonder if they are altogether healthy as regards building up good taste in garden craft. Those who have not made any real study of the progressive history of garden design, who have never been taught to think of the lie of the ground or 'suitable surroundings', are here led to choose a garden much as they would select a wedding present. They like it for itself and hope that it will look well in the new home. It is natural that those who invent pergolas, arbours, and garden temples should wish to show them to the public and thus quickly obtain orders; but to build up a garden in a night is no criterion of the true qualifications as a garden designer.

Viscountess Wolseley, 1919

Container gardening

Round every city corner lurks yet another window-box filled with cheerful scarlet pelargoniums, cascading lobelia and ample clumps of softly hued petunias. A glance upwards reveals plants perched on inhospitable balcony 'cliffs'. Full-sized trees grow in urns and superbly grown camellias flower in astonishingly small pots. Of course, there are also many sad, neglected conifers and bay trees standing glumly in tubs on pavements, but however unsuccessful the plantings, or unhealthy the inmates, containers make it possible for us to grow so much more in a small area.

I often use several plants in one container. A large *Salix caprea* sharing a nineteen-inch-diameter (48 cm) terracotta pot with a well-grown *Arbutus unedo*, is underplanted with ivy and a thick planting of annuals. The compost level is kept below the rim for easy watering, and the top few inches replaced with fresh compost every year. This seems to keep the permanent occupants happy and gives the summer bedding a good start.

Thomasina Tarling, 1988

Preparing the pots

It was necessary to go to the garden centre today to stock up with John Innes Compost No. 2 (a good grade of compost for most pots), some sharp sand, which is essential for potting, and a sack of grit – used for drainage at the bottom of pots and for spreading liberally around plants prone to slug damage. I also mix grit with John Innes to form a more open and free-draining compost and find that many plants flourish in it, as the soil in pots can become clogged and sticky.

Sheila Jackson, 1994

Infinite riches in a little room

The garden I describe is in London, in South Kensington. It is divided into two, by the house lying in between. Thus there are two plots, each about twenty-five by thirty-five feet. Working in the front means working in public. You get used to this, in fact like it on some occasions, such as when a passer-by once said to me: 'You've made a little Sissinghurst'.

I began by growing herbaceous plants and many bulbs followed by annuals, resulting in the inevitable winter gap. In my ignorance I thought this was town gardening. Admittedly there was what is often (critically) referred to as 'a good show' at the appropriate times of the year. This type of gardening entailed much work and expense, and somehow brought no fulfilment.

About six years ago I set out to create a garden with a basis of permanent plants, chosen chiefly for their foliage. It was Miss Jekyll who said 'People forget that green is a colour'. Add purple, silver, variegated and glaucous-leaved plants, and a garden is alive with contrasts. Miss Jekyll also remarked 'The size of a garden has very little to do with its merit. It is merely an accident relating to the circumstances of the owner.'

In the making of a town garden the first matter to consider is the quality of the soil . . . I had to renew most of mine, and as with many town houses, it had to come through the house, in my case (for my back garden) the sitting-room – an anxious procedure, though made less of a strain by the modern polythene sack.

The vital humus in the new soil will be used up in proportion to the intensity of cultivation. Therefore fresh humus must be constantly added to the soil . . .

My next consideration was the boundary fences . . . Not everyone seems to realise that flowering shrubs, *trained flat*, are excellent wall coverers, and in my opinion should be one of the main features of town gardening. By doing this you can effectively cover boundary divisions. Unnatural? Yes, but so are many aspects of gardening from topiary to lawns. Less flower? Yes, but you cannot have everything both ways, and you can grow different clematis between each shrub to flower through and above them, and these appreciate the root shade given by the shrubs. Half hardy and tender shrubs like to have their 'backs to the wall', and if you do not train them flat, there is no room for any other type of plant in front of them, at least not when your borders are only two and a half feet wide, as mine are.

The lace-cap *Hydrangea serrata* 'Grayswood' is a good one for this purpose; let it grow to the same height as your boundary fence, and spread to a width of eight feet or so. It flowers profusely, starting white and ending up four months later as a dark crimson.

Cytisus battandieri, from Morocco, has laburnum-like grey leaves with a unique silky sheen. This is essentially a foliage plant, and will grow to a tree of fifteen feet or so if you choose, and it stands cutting back. Its yellow flower smells of pineapple. I grow *Euphorbia wulfenii* tied back to a four-foot wall . . . ; it has blue-green leaves the year through, and its exciting lime-coloured flower bracts are out for four months (it also seeds itself). *Cotinus (Rhus) coggygria* 'Foliis Purpureis' gives you a dark contrast, but it is deciduous. *Hydrangea petiolaris* (really a natural climber) does well facing north and makes a good hat-stand for clematis, as does *Hydrangea villosa* in the same aspect . . . My plant of the latter is three years old, so has not yet been tested out in a hard winter. London is several degrees warmer than the surrounding counties, and surprising plants survive which might not in more open country. *Camellia japonica* is a superb shrub for a north aspect. *Chaenomeles* is an easy one to train flat. This shrub is still often referred to as Japonica, a word meaning 'of Japan', where so many good garden plants come from, but to refer to this particular genus as Japonica is frowned upon by the élite. *Garrya elliptica* likes to grow flat, the long pale green catkins of the male plant are enchanting. Always make room for the yellow winter jasmine; put it in the worst position in your garden and it will do, and flower for over two months. I make the large-leaved dead nettle (*Lamium galeobdolon variegatum*) grow up my three-foot street wall, and fall down the other side. This evergreen plant can be a curse or a blessing; it is definitely the latter when you learn to make it do what *you* want. It climbs, or covers, and will conceal any small eye-sore you wish to hide.

A good tip is to grow a hardy flowering shrub between two half-hardies. Laurustinus (*Viburnum tinus*) is a good plant for this purpose. Let its side-shoots grow over the tenderer plants and prune them in the spring. I use it as a protector for *Senecio leucostachys*, a bright silver plant which likes to climb. The dying summer foliage of clematis can often be drawn across half-hardies as some protection. In a hard winter you must augment these, of course, by branches of fir trees or broom, bracken or plastic secured to wire netting with sticks through the sides, leaving six inches free at the bottom to put firmly in the ground. You must resist putting on this winter protection too soon, and even more important do not take it away too early.

This so-called unnatural method of growing shrubs entails the right pruning at the right time of year, much tying back, *and* strong supports in front of the main stem . . .

Among the natural climbers that I grow is *Vitis coignetiae*, though again unnaturally treated, because as well as hard pruning in early winter, I stop the ends of the shoots at least three times in the growing season, and thus keep it to its allotted space, which is about twelve feet in breadth and eight feet high. Two branches are allowed to turn a corner on to a higher wall and meet the evergreen leathery-leaved *Clematis armandii* which covers the equivalent area. This clematis is usually more successful in coastal gardens, and the vine acts as an insurance against the clematis succumbing to a hard winter, as it would cover the latter's space the same year. I have about thirty other clematis which seem to thrive, due to a good mulch of manure in the spring and autumn, and a lot of watering in the summer. These vary from species and small-flowered hybrids, to the many large-flowered varieties and include one *C. montana* 'Tetrarose', also a non-clinging herbaceous type called *C. davidiana*; its flowers look and smell like a pale blue hyacinth. An unusual clematis is *C. durandii* which is semi-herbaceous and indigo-blue in colour. A red equivalent is 'Gravetye Beauty'. Clematis must have water to flower well, and to a lesser extent this applies to town borders generally, on account of their lack of depth. I have found it wiser not to have a nozzle on a hose as it is easy to use it with too much force.

One of the best small evergreen shrubs is *Viburnum davidii*; this needs no unnatural treatment, in fact you must have a male and female plant for the latter to produce its bunches of azure blue berries. Plant the pair about five feet apart, and they will meet in about three years. I keep a space pruned between them at their back, where I have established *Alstroemeria* Ligtu Hybrids, whose deep apricot flowers rise above these two-foot high viburnums, and are protected by the shrubs and show each other off to advantage. The best grey shrub is *Senecio laxifolius*, a perfect joy the whole year through; you can hardly have too much of it . . . Keep it bushy, by nipping out growing shoots constantly; you must learn to do this to many plants, particularly grey ones, also hebes. One hates doing it, but do it you must to make good shaped plants; if you don't they become leggy and straggly.

The choice of plants to grow between flat trained shrubs and edging plants, depends on what space you have. I would advise you to look for some of the many euphorbias and choose the ones of suitable height. They nearly all have sour-yellow flowers which look so lovely next to grey plants such as santolinas and artemisias. Hellebores do well in towns, my favourite is *corsicus* (now sometimes called *argutifolius*) as the pale apple-green flowers start to come out in December and last till April or May; the evergreen foliage is light grey-green, netted with dark veins and scolloped at the edges . . . It is a really perfect plant, and likes slight shade. Bearded irises are excellent, their sword-like leaves being of such architectural charm. Shape, size and texture of leaf in a foliage garden is as important to vary, as contrast in colour. Hebes, or shrubby veronicas, provide a wide range to choose from and are of infinite variety, originating from New Zealand. Have as many different ones as your space allows. These are medium-sized, evergreen shrubs with small leaves ranging from pale grey to bronze, often with white to lavender flowers, but some are tender. A useful small shrub, with purplish leaves is *Berberis thunbergii* 'Atropurpurea Nana'. *Daphne mezereum alba* flowers in November and smells delicious. A rather special plant is *Oenothera missouriensis* with pale yellow flowers and prostrate red stems. *Sedum* 'Autumn Joy' grows three feet high with me, and has bright red flowers from August to November which then turn a good brown for the rest of the winter. I fill up the odd space with annuals, in particular white and lime-green nicotiana. I also have a few herbaceous plants and several strong-smelling geraniums and herbs.

Rosa rubrifolia (a bush-rose), is essential in a foliage garden having such unusual coloured purple grey leaves. This is the only rose I grow and to many people a garden without roses can hardly be called a garden . . .

A successful planting in a south corner has been *Artemisia arborescens* now about eight feet tall (it may be cut in a hard winter) . . . and a dark-leaved *Ceanothus russellianus*, both growing up a wall. In front grows *Acanthus mollis*, flanked by two groups of regale lilies (followed by white Japanese anemones later), under-planted with glaucous blue rue (*Ruta graveolens*) 'Jackman's Blue'. For a north aspect a pleasing combination is a group of dark evergreen *Euphorbia robbiae* . . . about two feet tall, with rosette type of foliage; it is vigorous and invaluable for giving offsets to one's friends; behind this grows white astrantia that flowers for three months.

On either side are the greyish-blue-leaved *Hosta sieboldiana* (syn. *H. glauca*) and in front *Primula florindae* with primrose coloured flowers and *Saxifraga fortunei* 'Wada', the leaves of which are dark red underneath, sometimes colouring the surface, and its unusual white flowers have a long flowering period through September and October. Beside them grows *Arum italicum marmoratum pictum*, a plant which throws up its bright green marbled leaves in the winter and disappears in the summer. It is practical to mark its place.

The edges of small borders are important . . . Edging plants are legion – various evergreen campanulas, bergenias with their large leathery leaves colouring in the autumn. *Ajuga reptans purpurea* makes a dark patch, next to which I grow a blue-grey flow of *Hebe pageana*, a neat tailor-made plant as opposed to the more fluffy artemisias. Heucheras cover edges well and will spill over to any extent you want and flower for three months; there are many varieties of them. *Artemisia stelleriana*, and *A. schmidtii nana* are good bright silvers for this purpose. Helianthemums (rock roses) will provide colour in sunny aspects. It is not difficult to find edging plants to your taste, but try to achieve contrasts of silver- and dark-leaved plants, and the occasional one which sweeps onto the path and makes an uneven line . . . What is taste? No one seems able to define the word. In the choice of plants, each must have its special appeal to your own individuality, thus if you are not a schizophrenic, the chances are the plants you choose will merge into a balanced whole. The main theme of my garden is grey, and plants with green or white flowers are shown up by others with bronze foliage, obviously the smaller the garden, the greater must be the discipline of choice.

However small a garden, some attempt should be made to achieve different levels. Raising the borders, even by six inches, is a help. In my back garden I have raised a corner bed to eighteen inches high and grow tall plants in it to accentuate the height, shrubs such as *Choisya ternata*, *Cornus alba* 'Variegata Elegantissima' and a white buddleia. These are backed by clematis, which climb a wall made higher by squared wooden trellis. The sides of this bed are hidden by 'hangers down' such as *Iberis*, *Cytisus kewensis*, the dark-leaved *Vinca minor alba*, and the humble *Cerastium tomentosum* ('Snow-in-Summer'). Learn to keep it in the space you want and it makes a lovely patch of grey, hanging down beside a

dark-leaved plant; it will grow in any soil or position, the poorer
the better.

This garden is stone paved, and in the middle is a large raised
bed on two levels, paved with York stone, in which are fourteen
planting pockets of different sizes and shapes . . . The lower level is
fourteen inches high, and the higher part is twenty inches
and forms a bed of eighteen inches wide. Emphasis is given to the
difference in levels by tall shrubs in the high part, and flat plants in
the planting pockets of the 'table bed'. *Weigela florida* 'Foliis
Purpureis,' *Cotinus (Rhus) coggygria* 'Drinkstone', *Phormium tenax
purpureum* and *Senecio laxifolius* are the high plants in the bed. Among
the pocket plants are *Euphorbia myrsinites*, *Ajuga reptans purpurea*,
Helichrysum petiolatum (grown flat) and gazanias . . .

Town gardeners constantly have to be hiding or disguising something and I have disguised the manhole in the front by making it
into a sunk garden. It was at a slightly lower level anyway, so to
accentuate this I made a 'wall' round it, eight inches high and
six inches broad, and planted *Armeria maritima alba*, *Polygonum affine*
'Donald Lowndes', rock phlox and *Salix argentea repens* at a corner,
but the important plant here is *Cotoneaster dammeri* to cover the
actual manhole itself, its long branches being easily held up when
necessary. This sunk 'bed' serves as a sheltered standing ground
for rooted cuttings in pots; in severe weather I can cover the area
with panes of glass or plastic . . .

As well as different heights, you must try to have some 'hidden
aspects'. In my back garden the tall plants in the two-foot high part
of the middle bed succeed in hiding the border behind them . . .
In the front garden is a slightly raised square bed, covered over
with cement. I originally put tubs on this, and planted bulbs and
annuals in them. When I started on my permanent foliage garden,
I cut about six different sized holes in the cement, and everything
I planted in these spaces did remarkably well, and thus I discovered
the importance of a cool root run in the shallow beds of town
gardens. I now put bits of York stone round the roots of many
plants in the borders, and examine these regularly for slugs who
like to shelter beneath them.

Cecily Mure, 1968

Flower relationships, in the place of counting sheep, is an excellent exercise for anyone who happens to be suffering from a bout of sleeplessness. To conjure up a window-box of flowers immaculate in growth and bloom, in brilliant patterns, can be helpful in lulling one to sleep.

Xenia Field, 1965

In Paris

Two months ago my neighbour was jealous of my yellow laburnum and then of my wistaria, vigorous even in its youth, that throws from wall to lime-tree, from lime to the climbing roses, its snake-like shoots dripping with mauve clusters and heavy with perfume. But at the same time I cast an envious look at his double-flowering cherries; and, with July here, how to compete with his geraniums? At full noon their red velvet achieves an indescribable violet, mysteriously evoked by the vertical light . . . Patience! He'll see my purple sage in October and November, my neighbour will.

And, without having to wait, he can always catch sight of those ambitious crossed poles that I dignify with the title 'rose-pergola', the heavy clumps of roses, capsized like drunken heads. I have left for my other neighbour the shade flowers, the clematis as blue as it is violet, the lilies-of-the-valley, the begonias made blowzy by an hour's sunshine. An old garden nearby nurtures a giant mallow to which the rest of the plant kingdom has been sacrificed; ancient and untiring, it bears a dazzle of blossoms, pink when they open, mauve as they fade. A little farther away flames the red hawthorn, glory of the Breton spring, and a bushy vine, arranged like a mosaic on the façade of a small mansion, appeases with its vertical lawns the rustic taste of an inhabitant of Auteuil whose land has only the width and breadth of an orange-box. Friendly rivalry that summons old folk and well-conducted children to the threshold of these captive gardens, brandishing of rakes and hoes, clashing of curved beaks of secateurs, truck-garden odour of manure and mown grass, how much longer can you save Paris from the mournful cubism, the rectangular shadow of apartment blocks? Every month in the sixteenth *arrondissement* sees the felling of an avenue of limes, a thicket of spindle-trees, an old-fashioned arbour rounded to the measure of the crinoline.

On my outer boulevard, drowned in foliage, there has risen in six months a block of flats with the shape and self-importance of a glaring new tooth. A charming low dwelling, content for a hundred years to flourish in the middle of its garden like a sitting hen on its nest of straw, has now – flanked by seven new storeys – lost for ever its right to the sun, its scarab-coloured mornings, its fiery grave sunsets. It stays mute and frozen like an extinct planet, clad in its own mourning.

Colette, 1971

'The Trees are Down'

> – and he cried with a loud voice:
> Hurt not the earth, neither the sea, nor the trees –
>   (Revelation)

They are cutting down the great plane-trees at the end of the
    gardens.
    For days there has been the grate of the saw, the swish of
    the branches as they fall,
The crash of trunks, the rustle of trodden leaves,
With the 'Whoops' and the 'Whoas', the loud common talk,
    the loud common laughs of the men, above it all.

I remember one evening of a long past Spring
Tuning in at a gate, getting out of a cart, and finding a large
    dead rat in the mud of the drive.
I remember thinking: alive or dead, a rat was a god-forsaken
    thing,

But at least, in May, that even a rat should be alive.

The week's work here is as good as done. There is just one
  bough
    On the roped bole, in the fine grey rain,
        Green and high
        And lonely against the sky.
           (Down now!–)
        And but for that,
        If an old dead rat
Did once, for a moment, unmake the Spring, I might never
  have thought of him again.

It is not for a moment the Spring is unmade to-day;
These were great trees, it was in them from root to stem:
When the men with the 'Whoops' and the 'Whoas' have carted
  the whole of the whispering loveliness away
Half the Spring, for me, will have gone with them.

It is going now, and my heart has been struck with the hearts of
  the planes;
Half my life it has beat with these, in the sun, in the rains,
      In the March wind, the May breeze,
In the great gales that came over to them across the roofs from
  the great seas.
      There was only a quiet rain when they were dying;
      They must have heard the sparrows flying,
And the small creeping creatures in the earth where they were
  lying –
      But I, all day, I heard an angel crying:
        'Hurt not the trees.'

Charlotte Mew, 1929

A proud curtaining

Even the tiniest garden, a few rods, maybe, between the stares of buildings is ennobled by the planting of trees. Otherwise the walls lean in, and there is nothing to lift your garden above the level of the eye and hide the peering windows, the lavatory and the clothes line of the house next door.

Trees give a privacy, a proud curtaining, and the gardener who can complacently tend a treeless garden without a sense of nakedness, is less easily shamed than Adam and Eve. Better dub it allotment at once!

Muriel Stuart, 1936

Tower block

The idea of making a garden on the topmost twenty-third floor of a council tower block in east London might be compared with a brave but astonishingly foolhardy attempt to make a garden in the crow's nest of an old-fashioned sailing ship. After all the weather conditions are more or less the same. That is to say, impossible. Parching sunshine in summertime or teeming rain pouring remorselessly down into the tiny area, no protection from frost, ice or snow, and above all the winds, galeforce winds, at their worst measured *officially* at 100–120 mph raging and roaring within the tiny structure, tearing leaves and petals to shreds, loosening plants in their pots, and, unless everything is firmly battened down, sending them crashing from their positions. In winter these same winds hurl sheets of icy up-current rain over anything in their path, including me.

I doubt if any gardener endures such extremes of climate as I undertook to fight when I moved into my tiny top floor flat in 1971. But I wanted to realise a dream I had cherished for many years, a dream of a garden, and the top floor flat was the only one with a miniscule patio. So, it would be a garden some 230 feet up in the sky. I would encourage highrise and nature to combine.

My pocket handkerchief space is really very little larger than a balcony being about eight feet by ten feet (2.4 m × 3 m) and without any shelter from the elements. An L-shaped wall about six feet high (1.8 m) forms the south and west sides. The sitting-room wall and the bedroom wall complete the enclosure. The aspect is good, on the south-west corners, so in fine weather there is a great deal of sunshine lost only when the sun sinks below the level of the wall. This wall is not high enough to act as a barrier against the tremendous gusts of wind which can blow at such a height, reinforced and strengthened in their power because of up-currents produced by the design of tower blocks. On days when at ground level all is still at my height there is a breeze

I calculated that in winter, the very inefficiency of the building's design might be turned to my advantage to some small degree. With the heat loss through the single glazing of the large windows of the sitting-room combined with other factors I intended to create, a micro climate could be induced to keep the garden blooming and to cloak those plants nearest to these windows with a little sheltering warmth.

Between 1971 and 1974, the year when I was ready to make my garden, I spent a great deal of time thinking about it, working out solutions to the many problems anticipated, for instance how to use the minute space most effectively. After all, I intended to make a small scale country garden with trees, climbers, shrubs of all kinds, soft fruits, herbs, vegetables, perennial and annual flowers, flowers all the year round. Mine was to be a twelve-months garden. And of course there would have to be one or two garden features, a small statue or two to add an air of sylvan tranquillity to the scene.

New compost (John Innes) would be used, bought in large bags and lightened by the introduction of peat to produce the acidity preferred by so many plans and especially by those which were my favourites. There could be no heavy containers. Everything must be light enough for me to move if necessary. All of these, therefore, would be of plastic or polystyrene, but, so that they should not look garish I planned to 'paint them out'. Such weight as there was would be spread around the sides of the plot so that there would be no unacceptable strains on any part of the paving. The centre of the area would be kept clear and, on sunny days, suitably shaded from the fierce, concentrated heat.

A real garden must have climbing plants, but I had no anchorage on the inside of the wall. I decided to fix strong, six-foot bamboo canes (1.8 m) to the inner wall edge of the benching I would make. The tops of the canes and the plastic netting used to cover the inside wall were secured by threading strong garden cord around the canes through the netting and then attaching it to screws which anchor an aluminium strip already fitted along the top of the wall. This had to be very secure because once the plants were growing well the weight would increase dramatically, especially in wet weather.

In hot weather the containers would dry out very quickly and keeping everything healthily watered would be another problem as I would be out all day. By keeping most bases of containers in shade I could partly solve this.

I made many visits to gardens open to the public in London and nearby, looking for ideas I might adapt. Whenever I encountered experts I talked to them, telling them what I intended to do and asking for suggestions. I soon became used to the expressions which appeared on their faces or in their eyes, quickly and politely hidden, as I described the location, height and size of the garden-to-be and then sketched in what I thought I would grow in my small area, leaving the centre clear, of course! Undoubtedly most of them thought they were dealing with a vain eccentric who liked to talk about gardening, and seemed to know a bit about it, but who had no intention of doing anything so extraordinary as making a typical English country garden in the middle of London.

Even books on the small garden held little which was of use to me. Either I already knew the difficulties described, or plants and facilities were recommended that I had no space for. It seemed that no one had ever tried to make such a garden in such circumstances, or, if they had, they had failed.

I planned a three level garden, containers on the paving, narrower ones on benching to be made, the third tier comprising the climbers, perennial and annual. The benching would be strong but lightweight, around three sides of the patio and about ten to eleven inches deep (25 cm). For next to nothing I bought a gigantic packing case nine feet wide (2.7 m), which was dismantled for me. The best pieces were chosen and some were cut to the required size, the rest brought home to cut down to a 'tailor-made' fit. A broken U-shape left corners open for climbers to grow through while shading their roots. The benches were all about eighteen inches (45 cm) high, leaving space beneath for storage of large pots and extra boxes.

For quite a few years I had been collecting plastic containers from local waste grounds. Discarded narrower polystyrene troughs were also garnered. They varied in colour. Using paints, stainers and thinners left over from recent interior decorating I invented a new colour 'Paving Stone Grey', a 'nothing' shade matching almost exactly the terrace slabs. All benches and boxes were painted in this tone.

The benches were positioned. The boxes were 'holed' for drainage where required and set on blocks to lift them from the floor. The more fragile polystyrene troughs were confined to the benching. All were filled with a few inches of peat, then with a handful of charcoal, and then topped up with compost to within about an inch and a half of their edges.

I had carefully timed all this work to be ready to stock my garden with plants in spring 1974. Indulgent advisers, humouring me had said 'Stick to tough plants only'. So I bought everything *tough* and tender, starting with a clematis 'The President' in one corner and another 'Comtesse de Bouchaud' in the opposite corner. They would be encouraged to grow *sideways* towards each other. A third clematis, *montana rubens* in the middle corner was to grow out to meet them both, but it did well and had to be given away. 'The President' and the 'Comtesse' are still with me.

Small trees were added, shrubs, bedding plants of all kinds, seeds were sprinkled. That first year all was experiment and much continues to be experimental today. Early June was my main planting time. By early August the garden was beginning to 'take' and look good and by early September it was a riot of colour and a joy to come home to. Because space was so restricted a careful colour harmony had been worked out, omitting 'hot' shades of glaring yellow and orange, instead moving through white to cream, pinks of various intensities, violet, mauve, light and dark blues, light and dark reds.

Soft fruits were added, strawberries, raspberries, red currants, black currants. The raspberries, red currants and a *Symphoricarpus* romped away and they too have been handed on as have so many other plants since 1974.

Some forty to fifty plants flourished in that first year, including winter and early spring 1975 introductions. Until late autumn 1974 the tiny plot bloomed. The containers held a varying symphony of trailing lobelia, alyssum, carnation, pinks, verbena, geranium, nasturtium, salvia, stock, antirrhinum, heliotrope, pansy, fuchsia, wallflower, gypsophila, sweet pea, and many more. In that first season I kept to annual flowers for the most part. Scarlet runners and climbing sweet peas grown for speedy coverage of the trellis complementing the clematis.

A fairly mild autumn, regular deadheading, and the success of the microclimate which managed to combat the chill dawns and colder evenings kept the garden blossoming until, with much reluctance, in late October and early November I removed the last of the summer annuals to make room for bulbs and corms for early spring and early summer flowers, perennials which I have never disturbed, except inadvertently to add more and which delight me as they return each year, increasing but so circumspectly. Scilla, iris, narcissus, chionodoxa, snowdrops, tulips, hyacinth, crocus, grape hyacinth, creamy white daffodils and anemones all appear.

In such a small space and living over so many people, garden hygiene is of the greatest importance. Mine must be the cleanest garden in England. A regular routine of sweeping up all plant debris, of vacuum cleaning on dry days (much to the merriment of visitors, since I use my domestic cylinder vacuum cleaner, making sure meanwhile that no large leaves jam the hose), of weekly rinsing out with disinfectants, washing down all pots and containers and dousing the soil with a much used garden disinfectant known to many gardeners, the meticulous collecting of stray leaves and petals keeps my garden looking tidy and prevents the build up of any nuisance. Regular inspection of the undersides of leaves and flowers keeps in check any invasions of greenfly or any other ills and at the first sign of trouble I leap in to the rescue with a suitable remedy.

I can hardly believe it myself but I now have about a hundred different trees, shrubs, climbers, herbs, soft fruits, evergreens, roses, annuals and perennials making an appearance in my garden.

As the years have passed I have added perennial plants such as winter-berried shrubs, clerodendron, callicarpa, cotoneaster, pernettya and others. There is a red maple which flames into autumn richness. Winter jasmine, my only real concession to yellow, a colour which I must admit, does much to brighten grey days, is installed and has grown away against the north and east facing walls in the corner. A juniper, bought as a tiny plantlet and now some three to four feet tall (1.2 m) holds at its base winter erica. My bay tree flourishes. A slim beech grown originally as a bonsai specimen but freed from its bondage, is now six feet tall (1.8 m). Soon it too will have to go.

The little plot was devised to make a small but useful contribution to housekeeping quite apart from the fact that it is most pleasant to step out into the garden to pick my own fresh chives, mint, parsley (which grows for me in huge fluffy clouds of vivid green), basil, thyme, sage and other herbs. I also grow spring onions, beetroots, radishes, dwarf beans as well as runner beans and carrots. All these vegetables are grown among the flowers where their foliage adds another decorative note. I have no space for a separate vegetable garden and in any case close planting keeps weeds down, these arriving with bedding plants.

There are always perfumed flowers. In winter *Daphne odora* and *Sarcoccoca*. Later in the year, tobacco, carnation, pinks, petunia, sweet peas, lavender and a honeysuckle, as well as roses, which waft their fragrances into the sitting-room on a warm summer evening.

Many of my plants attracted fat, golden brown bees from a nearby apiary, very welcome if somewhat surprised visitors. My garden also attracted humming 'insects' of a much larger and more sophisticated kind. Amazed helicopter pilots spotted me as they made their river runs during the day. Amused I used to watch them as they hovered nearby, watching me as I gardened. They still keep an eye on me nowadays.

Hester Mallin, 1980

A barrel of water

Spare a thought, as you pace your herbaceous borders and stroll about the lawns, for those of us whose boundaries can be defined by the four legs of a deck-chair. See those half-dozen paving slabs in front of the potting shed? Imagine that were your entire acreage. How would you feel? Depressed? Ah – then you're not a city gardener.

We urban muckers and mulchers are strangers to despair. After all, there's nothing you've got in your rolling acres that we can't have in our backyards. It's just a matter of scale. Once, when idly flicking through a book on water gardens, I was struck by a picture of the cascade at Chatsworth, with water emerging from a temple and descending a stone staircase. 'The way water has been used successfully in other gardens can teach a good deal to those interested in incorporating a water feature – even on a more modest scale – in their own garden.' I poked my head out of the window and craned my neck to assess the possibilities. Well, it might be feasible to channel a stream from my roof onto next door's lean-to, then ricochet it off the shed through a length of guttering, but perhaps another type of feature would be more suitable.

A water-lily lake to enjoy 'reflections in the pool's surface of the sky' sounded nice, but would need to cover the whole of my garden plus the lady's across the back to get much of an effect. The shed would have to be hoisted up on stilts, oriental fashion, or sat on an artificial island.

I turned the page and there it was. Eureka ! A half barrel covered in lily pads and three pink, saucer-sized flowers, a clump of spiky reeds for dramatic interest and a hovering dragonfly to top it all off. There may not have been much sky reflected in the surface, but the dragonfly had room to admire itself.

Getting hold of a barrel was less of a problem than how to treat the inside. The library yielded a surfeit of theories. Paint it with rubberised paint. If it smells of beer (you started singing rugby songs if you bent over mine), either line it with polythene or let it stand outside for the winter. One source had the incendiary idea of lighting a small bonfire and upending the barrel over the top. Picturing a pile of ashes and an iron hoop, I lined mine with polythene.

Then the real fun began – what to plant. When you've scarcely room to plant anything, choosing is half the enjoyment. Walling myself in with the entire aquatic section from the library, I agonised. Just one tiny water-lily. Just one small iris. Was it possible to choose? Would it work? Needing a Spiritual Advisor to nurse me through the crisis, I phoned the information desk of the local garden centre. Succour was at hand. A warm, honeyed voice remarkably like that of Sir Roy Strong oozed down the receiver. Did the barrel sound an attractive feature, I asked?

'Oh, a most attractive feature,' he enthused. 'And, as you know, very popular in Edwardian times.'

Of course I knew – didn't everyone? But what variety of water-lily should I choose?

'I once saw an "Escarboucle" looking extremely happy in a barrel,' he confided.

An hour later I was at the information desk, pencil and paper at the ready. I recognised him at once, as he *looked* remarkably like Sir Roy, down to the moustache and glasses. We spent several hours, happy as two 'Escarboucles' in a barrel, agonising together. What did he think of a *Nymphaea pygmaea*?

'Well I've got a *pygmaea* in my shallow end and my dear, it simply flowers and flowers.'

He jotted down a few possibles and I headed for the comprehensive, if slimy, aquatic section. By peering into the gloomy tanks I could just make out some pots, sulking on the bottom, keeping their contents a secret. To read the labels I had to plunge a hand through the green scum and go in as far as my elbow, then haul them up. Hmm. 'Laydekeri Purpurata' – 'deep crimson with bright orange stamens'. Add green leaves and you've got a traffic light, perfect for the city. After all, at twelve pounds fifty I want everyone to notice my water-lily. Fling in some *Acorus calamus* 'Variegatus', *A. gramineus* and *Iris laevigata* for height, a selection of underwater oxygenators, a *Lobelia cardinalis* and a *Mimulus cardinalis* to disguise the edge of the polythene, and Bob's your uncle. Better throw in a pair of water hyacinths for the children to play battleships.

Laying all the library books on the square of cement I laughingly call 'the patio', I prepared to plant. First, fill the barrel with water. Then line each planting crate with hessian, slide the plant plus attendant gunge out of its pot and pack aquatic soil, i.e., mud, around it. Even the children were disgusted and only agreed to help sprinkle a layer of gravel on top. Book in hand, I set about planting the expensive water-lily. 'Disturb the lily as little as possible,' advised the experts. Very carefully I slid the plant out of its pot, to find a pile of mud and a bare rhizome at my feet. It only took an hour to get the crown sticking out at the correct angle.

Then I dropped several bricks into the barrel to balance the planting crates at their appropriate levels. Water surged over the edge into my shoes. I'd forgotten all about Archimedes. In went the crates. Result – swirling brown water, like a mud Jacuzzi.

A few days later a lot had happened. One oxygenator had reached the surface, the water hyacinths had doubled in size and grown roots the length and texture of Tennyson's beard, and the water had turned into a thick green soup. I fled to the books. 'Keep your nerve,' they said. My husband, sitting beside our attractive feature that evening with a bottle of Bulgarian, kept peering from its depths to the charming photograph that had started it all, and shaking his head.

I kept my nerve and a week or two later the pond became, quite suddenly, as clear as a glass of gin. The *Acorus calamus* was two feet tall and hurtling skywards, the *gramineus* filling out like a fan, and the lobelia stood a good eighteen inches. Only the mimulus looked unhappy. Another read of the label revealed I'd planted it two inches below the surface rather than two inches above. I hastily raised it on another brick while no one was looking, and started to swank about the garden . . .

The following summer the iris produced brilliant blue butterfly-like flowers and a bud appeared on the 'Laydekeri Purpurata'. It looked a bit pale for deep crimson. Gradually it opened – white, with a saffron middle. When almost closed that evening it looked like a boiled egg with the top cut off. Next day it turned pale pink. Next day it was dark pink – a perfect example of 'Laydekeri Lilacea'. When the third pink saucer opened beside a clump of spiky reeds and a dragonfly hovered above, it reminded me of something. I dashed down to the library and got out the same old water gardens book that had set it all going. There was the picture of the half barrel, looking distinctly inferior to my own.

It's all very well for me to boast about my triumph, but not every metropolitan gardener has room for a half barrel, nor even a bucket. Don't give up. Why – if I had no garden at all I would simply prune my vision and create (pedestrians below beware) a water feature on my window-sill. I'm sure Sir Roy could find me a water-lily which would be extremely happy in a teapot.

Jean Holden, 1992

VISITORS AND TRAVELLERS

ON FIRST going into a garden one knows by instinct, as a hound
scents the fox, if it is going to be interesting or not.

Mrs C. W. Earle, 1897

Conducted tours

When I take first-timers round the garden they fall into three
categories. There are those who go round chattering about something else completely, and pass each specially prepared view with
unseeing eyes, even walking over a brand new bridge without so
much as a 'My, oh my!' They are the ones who take gardens for
granted. That was me before I came to this. Next, there are the
recently converted enthusiasts, who never stop asking questions
and telling you about their own gardening problems – 'How
exactly do you grow begonias from seed?' and 'When are you
meant to prune ceanothus?' As I don't know the answers to
any of these questions, the journey round the garden becomes
fraught as opposed to serene. The last category are the old hands,
who walk round in virtual silence. When they pass an evidently
glorious display of tulips, they do not say, 'What wonderful tulips',
but 'What are you going to follow those tulips with?' Then, when
walking round the carefully contrived vegetable garden, they say,
'If you want to see a *really* beautiful vegetable garden, then you
ought to go and look at Rosemary Verey's.'

Candida Lycett Green, 1987

'All has been done wrong'

... when Mr Lock's or the Captain's gardeners favour our grounds with a visit, they commonly make known that all has been done wrong. Seeds are sowing in some parts when plants ought to be reaping, and plants are running to seed while they are thought not yet at maturity. Our garden, therefore, is not yet quite the most profitable thing in the world ...

Fanny Burney, 1794

Not a place to be happy in

I have been much afflicted again lately by visitors – not stray callers to be got rid of after a due administration of tea and things you are sorry afterwards that you said, but people staying in the house and not to be got rid of at all. All June was lost to me in this way, and it was from first to last a radiant month of heat and beauty; but a garden where you meet the people you saw at breakfast, and will see again at lunch and dinner, is not a place to be happy in. Besides, they had a knack of finding out my favourite seats and lounging in them just when I longed to lounge myself; and they took books out of the library with them, and left them face downwards on the seats all night to get well drenched with dew, though they might have known that what is meat for roses is poison for books; and they gave me to understand that if they had had the arranging of the garden it would have been finished long ago – whereas I don't believe a garden ever is finished. They have all gone now, thank heaven, except one, so that I have a little breathing space before others begin to arrive. It seems that the place interests people, and that there is a sort of novelty in staying in such a deserted corner of the world, for they were in a perpetual state of mild amusement at being here at all.

Elizabeth von Arnim, 1898

Showing the garden

Come, Mrs Guffer, do come. I am longing for you to see the garden . . . Tea is not quite ready – and I'm so afraid you are going to run away the moment we've had our tea that I am determined you should have at least a *tiny* glimpse of the garden! I won't take you far . . . Happily it's very near . . . I always feel that I am most fortunate in having a part of my garden into which I can fairly *tumble* . . . Here we are already!

Oh, do you? . . . How very sweet of you!

As a matter of fact, you know I am rather sorry you should see the garden now, because alas! it is not looking its best . . . Oh, it doesn't *compare* to what it was last year . . . We've had a very poor season, I think . . . Oh, it's been very much too dry. . . . I think everyone has suffered . . .

Ruth Draper, 1960

Gardeners can be preposterous – full of ruthless cunning, guile, greed, conceit, self-pity. For these, and doubtless other reasons, many people obey the invitation to go round the owner's garden with them with the dread of boredom.

Elizabeth Jane Howard, 1991

Through England on a side-saddle

Thence to Ouborn [Woburn] and enter Bedfordshire thirteen mile; the Duke of Bedfords house we saw, which stands in a fine parke full of deer and wood, and some off the trees are kept cut in works and the shape of severall beasts; the house is an old building, low, there are very good stables and out offices, landry yard, etc.; the Gardens are fine, there is a large bowling-green with eight arbours kept cut neately, and seates in each, there is a seate up in a high tree that ascends from the green fifty steps, that commands the whole parke round to see the Deer hunted, as also a large prospect of the Country; there are three large Gardens, fine gravell walks and full of fruite – I eate a great quantety of the Red Coralina goosbery which is a large thin skin'd sweete goosebery – the walks are one above another with stone steps; in the square just by the dineing roome window is all sorts of pots of flowers and curious greens fine orange cittron and lemon trees and mirtles strip'd filleroy [phillyrea] and the fine aloes plant; on the side of this pass under an arch into a Cherry garden, in the midst of which stands a figure of stone resembling an old weeder woman used in the garden, and my Lord would have her Effigie which is done so like and her clothes so well that at first I tooke it to be a real living body; on the other side of the house is another large Garden severall gravell walks one above another, and on the flatts are fish ponds the whole length of the walke; above that in the next flat is two fish ponds, here are dwarfe trees spread of a great bigness.

Celia Fiennes, 1690

Italian villas and their gardens

Though it is an exaggeration to say that there are no flowers in Italian gardens, yet to enjoy and appreciate the Italian garden-craft one must always bear in mind that it is independent of floriculture.

The Italian garden does not exist for its flowers; its flowers exist for it: they are a late and infrequent adjunct to its beauties, a parenthetical grace counting only as one more touch in the general effect of enchantment. This is no doubt partly explained by the difficulty of cultivating any but spring flowers in so hot and dry a climate, and the result has been a wonderful development of the more permanent effects to be obtained from the three other factors in garden-composition – marble, water and perennial verdure – and the achievement, by their skilful blending, of a charm independent of the seasons.

It is hard to explain to the modern garden-lover, whose whole conception of the charm of gardens is formed of successive pictures of flower-loveliness, how this effect of enchantment can be produced by anything so dull and monotonous as a mere combination of clipped green and stone-work.

The traveller returning from Italy, with his eyes and imagination full of the ineffable Italian garden-magic, knows vaguely that the enchantment exists; that he has been under its spell, and that it is more potent, more enduring, more intoxicating to every sense than the most elaborate and glowing effects of modern horti-culture; but he may not have found the key to the mystery. Is it because the sky is bluer, because the vegetation is more luxuriant? Our midsummer skies are almost as deep, our foliage is as rich, and perhaps more varied; there are, indeed, not a few resemblances between the North American summer climate and that of Italy in spring and autumn.

Some of those who have fallen under the spell are inclined to ascribe the Italian garden-magic to the effect of time; but, wonder-working as this undoubtedly is, it leaves many beauties un-accounted for. To seek the answer one must go deeper: the garden must be studied in relation to the house, and both in relation to the landscape. The garden of the Middle Ages, the garden one sees in old missal illuminations and in early woodcuts, was a mere patch of ground within the castle precincts, where 'simples' were grown around a central well-head and fruit was espaliered against the walls. But in the rapid flowering of Italian civilisation the castle walls were soon thrown down, and the garden expanded, taking in the fish-pond, the bowling-green, the rose-arbour and the clipped walk. The Italian country house, especially in the centre and the south of Italy, was almost always built on a hillside, and one day the architect looked forth from the terrace of his villa, and saw that, in his survey of the garden, the enclosing landscape was naturally included: the two formed a part of the same composition.

The recognition of this fact was the first step in the development of the great garden-art of the Renaissance: the next was the architect's discovery of the means by which nature and art might be fused in his picture. He had now three problems to deal with: his garden must be adapted to the architectural lines of the house it adjoined; it must be adapted to the requirements of the inmates of the house, in the sense of providing shady walks, sunny bowling-greens, parterres and orchards, all conveniently accessible; and lastly it must be adapted to the landscape around it. At no time and in no country has this triple problem been so successfully dealt with as in the treatment of the Italian country house from the beginning of the sixteenth to the end of the eighteenth century; and in the blending of different elements, the subtle transition from the fixed and formal lines of art to the shifting and irregular lines of nature, and lastly in the essential convenience and livableness of the garden, lies the fundamental secret of the old garden-magic.

However much other factors may contribute to the total impression of charm, yet by eliminating them one after another, by *thinking away* the flowers, the sunlight, the rich tinting of time, one finds that, underlying all these, there is the deeper harmony of design which is independent of any adventitious effects. This does not imply that a plan of an Italian garden is as beautiful as the garden itself. The more permanent materials of which the latter is made – the stonework, the evergreen foliage, the effects of rushing or motionless water, above all the lines of the natural scenery – all form a part of the artist's design. But these things are as beautiful at one season as at another; and even these are but the accessories of the fundamental plan. The inherent beauty of the garden lies in the grouping of its parts – in the converging lines of its long ilex-walks, the alternation of sunny open spaces with cool wood-land shade, the proportion between terrace and bowling-green, or between the height of a wall and the width of a path. None of these details was negligible to the landscape-architect of the Renaissance: he considered the distribution of shade and sunlight, of straight lines of masonry and rippled lines of foliage, as carefully as he weighed the relation of his whole composition to the scene about it.

Then, again, any one who studies the old Italian gardens will be struck with the way in which the architect broadened and simplified his plan if it faced a grandiose landscape. Intricacy of detail, complicated groupings of terraces, fountains, labyrinths and porticoes, are found in sites where there is no great sweep of landscape attuning the eye to larger impressions. The farther north one goes, the less grand the landscape becomes and the more elaborate the garden. The great pleasure-grounds overlooking the Roman Campagna are laid out on severe and majestic lines: the parts are few; the total effect is one of breadth and simplicity.

It is because, in the modern revival of gardening, so little attention has been paid to these first principles of the art that the garden-lover should not content himself with a vague enjoyment of old Italian gardens, but should try to extract from them principles which may be applied at home. He should observe, for instance, that the old Italian garden was meant to be lived in – a use to which, at least in America, the modern garden is seldom put. He should note that, to this end, the grounds were as carefully and conveniently planned as the house, with broad paths (in which two or more could go abreast) leading from one division to another; with shade easily accessible from the house, as well as a sunny sheltered walk for winter; and with effective transitions from the dusk of wooded alleys to open flowery spaces or to the level sward of the bowling-green. He should remember that the terraces and formal gardens adjoined the house, that the ilex or laurel walks beyond were clipped into shape to effect a transition between the straight lines of masonry and the untrimmed growth of the woodland to which they led, and that each step away from architecture was a nearer approach to nature.

The cult of the Italian garden has spread from England to America, and there is a general feeling that, by placing a marble bench here and a sun-dial there, Italian 'effects' may be achieved. The results produced, even where much money and thought have been expended, are not altogether satisfactory; and some critics have thence inferred that the Italian garden is, so to speak, *untranslatable*, that it cannot be adequately rendered in another landscape and another age.

Certain effects, those which depend on architectural grandeur as well as those due to colouring and age, are no doubt unattainable; but there is, none the less, much to be learned from the old

Italian gardens, and the first lesson is that, if they are to be a real inspiration, they must be copied, not in the letter but in the spirit. That is, a marble sarcophagus and a dozen twisted columns will not make an Italian garden; but a piece of ground laid out and planted on the principles of the old garden-craft will be, not indeed an Italian garden in the literal sense, but, what is far better, *a garden as well adapted to its surroundings as were the models which inspired it.*

This is the secret to be learned from the villas of Italy; and no one who has looked at them with this object in view will be content to relapse into vague admiration of their loveliness. As Browning, in passing Cape St Vincent and Trafalgar Bay, cried out:

> 'Here and here did England help me: how can I help
>   England?' – say,

so the garden-lover, who longs to transfer something of the old garden-magic to his own patch of ground at home, will ask himself, in wandering under the umbrella-pines of the Villa Borghese, or through the box-parterres of the Villa Lante: What can I bring away from here? And the more he studies and compares, the more inevitably will the answer be: 'Not this or that amputated statue, or broken bas-relief, or fragmentary effect of any sort, but a sense of the informing spirit – an understanding of the gardener's purpose, and of the uses to which he meant his garden to be put.'

Edith Wharton, 1904

Mrs Wharton's garden

The garden of Mrs Wharton (the novelist) lies in the *enceinte* of the ruined castle above the town of Hyères. A steep road overhung by prickly pear and Judas trees leads to the house. A series of little gardens, sheltered and sunlit, are tucked away on terraces under the old walls and towers of grey stone. In some of these gardens are freesias and narcissus, in others róses; on one terrace are mandarins, and in a shady corner grow camellias, azaleas, and arums.

The glare of the stone walls is tempered by groups of giant carob trees, which give dense shade, and a very old Judas tree overhangs the courtyard with a great flush of rosy red.

Before the house is a wide stone terrace with just a couple of spreading plane trees for shade, and looking down upon the old town of Hyères, the plain and the sea beyond.

Lady Alice M. Martineau, 1924

The Commuter's wife

I want a purely American garden, which may be interpreted as anything and everything that will grow in our sparkling but capricious climate; also everything is to be in plenty – no single plants, but great masses and jungles of flowers without bare ground showing between . . .

'What *is* an American garden? I never heard of such a thing,' asked Mrs Jenks-Smith, the good-natured chatelaine of the new show place, The Bluffs . . . I told her that I used the term in relation to my bit of garden ground framed in the hillside woods, of which it had originally been a part; that it was to be itself, and not distorted into a feeble imitation of the classic gardens of other days and times . . .

'I know such things are very expensive,' she continued, with a sigh. 'You wouldn't believe what our Italian garden cost.'

Barbara Campbell, 1911

Royal advice to a Swedish gardener

I remember how, on my annual visit to a little place in the archi-
pelago of islands on which Stockholm with its suburbs is built,
I always tried to persuade the lady who was the owner of the place
to introduce a little more nature – employ a little less master-
gardening, if I may be allowed to use the expression. The existing
form of the garden was out of keeping with the surroundings, and
the charming situation was obscured instead of emphasised
. . . The owner herself was dissatisfied, would fain have it altered,
but did not quite know what was wrong, nor did she see how
to improve matters until her eyes were opened for what I call a
woodland garden . . . Some rocks behind the departed flower-bed,
with which it had harmonised but little, were now going to be of
great service in forming the finest of backgrounds imaginable.
Some moss-grown boulders were fetched from a secluded corner,
and by the aid of these the entire space between the rocks and the
path was very soon made to look like a continuous rockery.

Margaret, Crown Princess of Sweden, 1919

West Indian summer

I begged to be let off formal breakfasts, went out after my cup of
tea at sunrise as I did at home, and worked till noon. My first study
was of a slender tree-fern with leaves like lace-work, rising out of
a bank of creeping bracken which carpeted the ground and ran
up all the banks and trees, with a marvellous apple-green hue.
The native children used to take plunges into it as English children
do with haycocks, and it was so elastic that it rose up after them
as if nothing had happened. In the afternoon I could paint in the
garden, and had the benefit of the tea and gossip which went on
near me, sitting under a huge mango, the parson, his wife, and
people coming up on business from the plains with three or four
neighbours and idle officers from Newcastle. A brother of the

Bishop of Oxford with his pretty daughter stayed a while also at Craigton. Orchids were tied to the trees, and all sorts of lovely bushes were on the terraces, the *Amherstia nobilis*, 'Mahoo Yassa' tree, etc. etc., all wonders to be painted . . .

The view from the dining-room was like an opal: the sealine generally lost in a blue haze, the promontories of St. Augusta, and Port Royal with its long coral reef, stretching out into it all salmon-coloured, then the blue sea again, Kingston amid its gardens, and the great Vega all rich green, with one corner of purest emerald-green sugar-cane, the whole set between rich hillsides, with bananas and mangoes full of flowers, and the beautiful gold-brown star-apple tree taking the place in the landscape which the copper-beech does in England. The mahoo is the hardest and blackest wood in the island, and its velvety leaves and trumpet-flowers of copper and brass tints made a fine study: all the flowers seemed so big. The poinsettias were often a foot across, one passionflower covered two large trees, the dracænas were ten feet high, the gardenias loaded with sweet flowers. One day the captain started Agnes Wilberforce and myself on two horses with a groom for Newcastle, where he had arranged that Dr S. should meet us and show us the famous Fern Walk. It was a glorious day. We rode up the steep hills straight into the clouds, and found rain in the great village of barracks, but we went on in spite of it. The scarlet geraniums and zinnias of former soldiers' gardens had seeded themselves all about, and above them we came to patches of wild Alpinia, called by the English ginger and cardamom, with lovely waxy flowers smelling like their names. Great branches of *Oncidium* orchids were pushing their way through the bushes, and creepers in abundance, huge white cherokee roses, and quantities of begonias.

At last we turned into the forest at the top of the hill, and rode through the Fern Walk; it almost took away my breath with its lovely fairy-like beauty; the very mist which always seemed to hang among the tree and plants there made it the more lovely and mysterious. There were quantities of tree-ferns, and every other sort of fern, all growing piled on one another; trees with branches and stems quite covered with them, and with wild pines and orchids, many of the pines with rosy centres and flowers coming out of them. A close waxy pink ivy was running up everything as well as the creeping fern, and many lycopodiums, mosses, and lichens. It was like a scene in a pantomime, too good to be real, the tree-fern fronds crossing and recrossing each other like network. One saw dozens at one view, their slender stems draped and hidden by other ferns and creeping things. There were tall trees above, which seemed to have long fern-like leaves also hanging from them, when really it was only a large creeping fern which had found its way over them up to the very tops. They were most delicious to look at, and, my horse thought, to eat also, for he risked my life on a narrow ledge by turning his head to crop the leaves from the bank, when his hind-legs slipped over the precipice. I said 'Don't,' and the Doctor and Agnes laughed, while the good horse picked his legs up again and went on munching in a more sensible position.

Marianne North, 1892

Oh, to be in Pretoria

In South Africa I became conscious of an unpleasant failing. I suffered from envy. Maybe any other English garden-lover might feel it too, and would not blame me; but the pity of it is I know I shall never be able to lose it again entirely, as long as I live.

However happy I am in my Surrey garden, however my home-sick heart welcomed again the tender greys and greens of our inimitable isle, I suffer a pang from time to time as I remember how I have at last really seen things *grow*! When I recall the little geraniums, verbenas, asters, stocks, salvias, delphiniums, roses, lilies and countless other flowers which we proudly rear to adolescence and maturity here, and then look back on the abundant beauty of the same things in Africa, I feel that England is just sent to try us, and that it is small wonder Englishmen succeed as pioneers when they can find in Greater Britain overseas such suns and soil to work with . . .

With a true instinct for beauty the streets of Pretoria have been planted with Jackaranda trees, handsome, upstanding, covered in their season with sweet-scented flowers like blue wistaria. The intense sapphire of the African sky seems to have settled under one's feet as the flowers fall and lie massed, keeping their colour to the last; and at times the open veldt, too, will ape the sky when miles of those blue irises are out that they call tulips.

Marion Cran, 1922

When looking through old books or modern catalogues, one feels one has nothing in one's garden, but I must confess that visiting other people's gardens very often makes me feel I really have a very fair collection.

Mrs C. W. Earle, 1897

The Koraku-en or Arsenal Garden in Japan

It is now empty and deserted, and seems only filled with sadness, its groves recalling days gone by, when succeeding Daimyos entertained their friends in regal pomp, and the sound of revelry broke the silence of the woods; to-day only the incessant sound of metal hammering metal breaks the silence of the glades, and the sound of explosions from the Arsenal nearby might well rouse the dead. The garden covers a large extent of ground, and is an example of a scheme in which many separate scenes were skilfully worked together to form a perfect whole. Its fame dates from early in the seventeenth century, when the Daimyo of Mito, who was a great patron of landscape gardening, laid out the grounds. The fact that they are remarkable for many Chinese characteristics is not surprising, when we learn that the Shogun Iyemitsu took an interest in the work, and lent the aid of a great Chinese artist called Shunseu, who completed the scheme. A semi-circular stone bridge of Chinese design, called a Full-moon Bridge, spans a stretch of water in which, in the scorching heat of August mornings, the great buds of white lotus flowers will crack and slowly open, their giant leaves almost hiding the bridge; this important feature of the garden is called Seiko Kutsumi, after a famous lotus lake in China. The island in the lake is the Elysian Isle of Chinese fame, and formerly was connected with the shore by a long wooden bridge, which has long since disappeared; but the path wanders on, past the rocky shore, skirting the headland and high wooded promontory, through the dense gloom of a forest, and by the time I had made a complete tour of this garden I felt as though I had paid a flying visit to half Japan.

There was an avenue of cherry-trees to recall the avenues of Koganei; the river Tatsuda in miniature, its banks clothed with maples and other reddening trees, to give colour to the garden in autumn, when the setting sun will seem to light the torch and set all the trees ablaze; there also is the Oi-gawa or Rapid River with its wide pebble-strewn bed, down which a rapid-flowing stream is brought; then we are transported to scenes in China; and beyond, again, the wanderer is reminded of the scenery of Yatsuhashi, where one of the eight bridges crosses in zigzag fashion a marshy swamp which in the month of June is a mass of irises, great gorgeous blossoms of every conceivable shade of lilac and purple, completely hiding their foliage; then this little valley becomes a stream of colour and recalls the more extensive glories of Hori-kiri.

Perhaps most ingenious of all is that part of the garden where the cone of Fuji-yama appears, snow-capped in May, as it is densely planted with white azaleas. Many other scenes there were – tiny shrines built in imitation of great temples, cascades and waterfalls named after other celebrated falls, rare rocks, moss-grown lanterns, bridges of all designs; in fact, the garden seemed a perfect treasure-house, and I felt glad that this one garden has escaped the hand of the destroyer and is left entire, a masterpiece of conception and execution.

Florence du Cane, 1908

Brown study in Australia

I found my lap full of bottle-brush flowers, fluffed like the tail of an angry cat, crimson and cream-tipped, honey sweet; and of white bells like glorified heath; of wattle in white and cream and gold – downy as a duckling's breast; and long sprays of tea-plant, as decorative as Japanese almond and far more dainty. Tiny flat silken rosettes in pearly rose and white clustered close to the brown stem, and below them were last year's seeds, like rich brown buttons of an exhausting size compared to the pale frail flowers. There was also a handful of tiny brown blooms . . . called, I think, 'Baronia', or 'Veronia', at the sight of which every eye in the party took on that look of reverent sentiment which we in England accord to violets. And for the same reason I surmise, for the tiny unassuming flowers filled the air with a sweet and lingering fragrance.

Marion Cran, 1922

A garden for travellers

Is it possible to garden and to travel or are the two things contradictions in terms? If you talk to gardeners they always seem to be waiting. Expecting and hoping; watching in anguish or jubilation, forever urged on with greater ambitions. Can gardeners be otherwise? Can there be a kind of half gardening or must commitment be total? If gardening is the essence of continuation, of one thing flowing into another, a procession of followers that must be compounded of colour, habit and form then where does that leave travel? In almost total opposition. That is the true answer to my question. An impossibility. Leave a garden five days and disaster may occur which no amount of catching-up later can eradicate.

Yet a garden and travel is what we wanted. A traveller's garden. A time for cherishing and a time for wandering, and the only way was not to be ambitious. Not to want too much happening in the garden all the time, event after event; not to regret weeks and weeks of a merely green garden. It is hard. Our whole inclination is to buy more, propagate, divide and sow. Then other gardeners are such a danger, they are so generous. They offer such tempting plants and cuttings; they encourage you, persuade you and advise. But unless what they offer fits in to your garden *time* plan, you must resist in spite of the chance to extend your variety of flowers and shrubs. You really have to, if you know that the recurring travelling fever is going to break out in a month or two.

In 1980 we began our garden. Travel was our lodestar but a garden was our preoccupation. With about one and a half acres of undulating ground, a stream and lots of grey stone walls we had a great incentive to make a garden. We began by making a pond in the cattle-yard, dug out with a JCB to a depth of about two and a half feet (75 cm). Slowly ousting the rough grass and planting kingcups and iris, primulas and mimulus, the whole yard has grown into a densely planted chaos, where herb robert and lady's smock also thrive. We planted wild cherries, rowans, hazels as well as whitebeam, acers and *Malus* – about seventy trees under which in some places we have planted not only daffodils, squills and so on, but hundreds of species tulips some of which make pools of brilliant red, like spilled paint cast about under the bare-leaved trees in March and April. Later other tulips come up, *T. turkestanica* with its delicate, drooping creamy flowers so that the first year we saw them we thought that we had been sent the wrong order – they could not be tulips!

All this means there can be no travelling in the spring. We are trapped. We have to be here to see the bulbs; we have planted various crocus blending colour with colour so that subtle blues and mauves seep into each other and into warm creamy ones which soften the plantings of chrome yellow. Each year as we plant more bulbs, seduced by descriptions and catalogues, we just cannot turn our backs on them. We are caught indeed – we don't even open an atlas.

But in May there is a pause, or we say there is, though we know the garden is enticingly on the move and every bud is compelling, but we say there is a pause. Just long enough for a week or ten days for travel. On returning the garden is paramount, we are then moving inexorably into the rose season, for we have allowed roses and what goes with them to dominate us. Roses grown on barn walls, house walls, small stone out-buildings, garden walls and into trees; thickets of shrub roses grouped together into flowery scented mounds which make shadows, shapes and movement, and around which the grass paths have to be re-routed every year; roses growing with abandon over stumps or down banks; roses supporting clematis or muddled up with honeysuckle. Profusion and dishevelment and very heady smells, that is what the summer is about. Under and through the roses grow campanulas, pinkish verbascums and huge-headed mauve alliums.

Then we stop. This is the crucial moment. This is when we have to be indomitable. No wavering or longing for just a few herbaceous flowers, a compromise of beds, a weakness for an armful of delphiniums here and there (how I love them). Look at other people's gardens but don't hanker; enjoy their lovely summer borders, their dense beds of colour and bees, but no yearning. We close our minds to all the high summer possibilities. As our roses fade, their short three-week span declining, so must our acquisitive instinct for prolonging the summer flowering. This is difficult and requires stubborn single-mindedness, but the knowledge that once something is newly planted then you have to be there to watch its progress, this knowledge is the spur to confining the garden to certain periods and therefore to certain plants.

We find that after the first agonising, regretful moment of putting away the trowel and secateurs and heading south, miraculously we can forget our garden completely and anticipate and enjoy a different season. I realise what we lose and yet there are certain mountains in Greece where after the first end-of-summer rains there spring up wild flowers; where cyclamen magically appear overnight amongst the most hopelessly stony terrain; where sternbergias thickly cover the ground so densely that you cannot put a foot between. They grow along the edge of a deep ravine where once we saw a bustard perched among the flowers. Nightingales, goat bells and concealed *Ramonda serbica* growing in the shade of rocks – all this has made us forget the possibility of *Abelia grandiflora*, gentians or a blue mass of agapanthus. And there is one other bonus for travelling gardeners, a compensation that should not be underrated – coming home. If you never leave your garden then too you never know the anticipation and excitement of returning; of walking round to see what has come out (as well as the dread to find things wilting for water or in need of retying against the wall). For this return, having satiated our travelling malady, we have buddlejas underplanted with sedums, the large-headed pink ones and many late flowering clematis. The marvellous *viticellas*, the untimely and mysterious 'Duchess of Edinburgh' who always produces an abundance of buds far too late and *Clematis flammula* which covers the head of our *Malus floribunda* appearing like late autumn blossom.

So in trying to answer my first question, I think tentatively, that perhaps it is possible – to garden and to travel. But it certainly needs resolution. One exquisite *Eucryphia × nymansensis* wantonly planted in a moment of exuberance – and you are hooked. How can any gardener turn away from buds for their first year's flowering?

Mirabel Osler, 1986

Goodbye garden

Darling Clare,

I am overwhelmed with the deep melancholia which always attacks me when I am about to travel. I look round the garden as though I were seeing it for the last time. I feel like Bette Davis in *Dark Victory*, bravely planting hyacinths though blind and about to die of a tumour on the brain, both disabilities unnoticed by her husband. (Would Osbert have noticed? Probably not.)

As you know, I am leaving for Jordan tomorrow, with good companions, Petra in sight, they tell me the weather is perfect. I am going for a mere ten days and have been looking forward to it madly. But idiotic angst claws me.

I will not even be missing much here. I have seen the daffodils in their glorious prime, the *Scilla bithynica* is out, the primroses and *Anemone blanda* make yellow and blue carpets; all I am going to miss are the crown imperials, and they may hold until my return if the weather stays chilly. So what am I blithering about? Even if the cottage burns down, the garden will still be left, give or take a charred shrub or two. As soon as I am airborne I will feel elated. Pre-travel blues is, to me, like premenstrual tension (from which luckily I never suffered) to other women.

I must go and pack. Happy gardening, love to Calypso, Max, Charlie *et al*, from your mother on her way to the scaffold, i.e. Gatwick.

Anne Scott-James, 1990

KITCHEN GARDENERS

Perfume from Provence

HILAIRE IS tending his vines to-day. For months he has been alternately spraying the fruit with powdered sulphur and the leaves
with *sulfate de cuivre* to keep off *la maladie* which, owing to the
unwonted rain this summer, has attacked the vines in the valleys.
Ours have escaped, all but a scorching here and there from the
unprecedented August heat, and now Hilaire is tenderly tucking
great bunches of white Muscats into net-bags to protect them from
what he calls *méchantes abeilles* – which I call wasps.

A disastrous year for the crops of Provence, for the Clerk of the
Weather has gone mad and has sent us everything out of season.
But, as my fat peasant neighbour, Monsieur Pierre, remarks, what
else can you expect this year, the anniversary in date and day,
according to the Roman Catholic Calendar, of the murder of Our
Lord? Was not the President – *un brave homme* – assassinated? Are
there not floods, earthquakes, and other disasters all over the
world? *Que voulez-vous?* Certainly no more of this extraordinary
weather!

Even now, as Hilaire embags his grapes, lightning is tearing the
clouds into jagged strips and thunder crashes overhead. In a
moment rain will fall, and then, with the first drop, Hilaire will go
to ground. He hides himself under the garage which projects over
the lower terrace. Here he can chop up olive branches to add to
the winter store, and talk to the rabbits in their yard close by at the
same time; and here I often find him for a gossip.

'*Voilà le Directeur,*' he says to me, pointing to our old chinchilla
buck rabbit, whom he has separated from the lady rabbit and her
new-born family of eight, '*Bon travailleur! Maintenant – un peu de
repos*', and Hilaire taps his old nose significantly. He is about to
become Rabelaisian, and I hastily change the subject to vegetables,
which seem safer. I tell him that Monsieur is fond of *courgettes*
(things like little round or oval vegetable marrows) and that I want
a lot of them sown.

Does Madame want melons as well? asks Hilaire with seeming

irrelevance. Of course she does! What sane woman would not want the miracle of melons growing daily in the open air of her garden? Then the melons must be planted at least one *hectare* away from the *courgettes* so that they cannot see each other, affirms Hilaire. 'Si non, ils se marient,' explains Hilaire to a mystified Madame (this sex question cropping up again), and the melons will become *courgettes*. Why do not *courgettes* become melons? laments Madame. But it appears that in Nature with mixed alliances the plebeian type usually triumphs.

The rain has by this time ceased; there has not been enough to soak the soil sufficiently, and I see my evening clearly outlined before me. Hilaire fixes me with a firm eye and asks if he shall attach the hose for Madame, as everything in the garden wants watering. Madame sighs resignedly. In ten minutes she will be wound in the beastly embrace of a thirty-metre hose and cursing in its coils for the next two hours. And she had made such lovely plans to weed her precious rock-garden all by herself . . .

I think Hilaire finds watering with the hose a boring affair, and I cordially agree with him – it is. He has all the fun when he irrigates the garden in the old primitive way. In Portugal water is spilled upon the ground and the gardeners direct it in the way it should go by standing in it and wiggling their toes until little channels are made in the mud. Here in Provence we are more sophisticated. We make channels of cement, connected with the great stone water-tank above on the highest terrace, and then release the water. Hilaire loves doing this. He rushes up the stone stairways to the *bassin*, big enough for a swimming bath, takes out a huge plug, and in a minute a glorious torrent of water comes cascading and gurgling down the cement channels which border the vegetable beds on every terrace.

'La rivière, Madame!' shouts Hilaire joyously as he thunders down the steps from terrace to terrace in his heavy peasant boots in pursuit of the rushing water. It overflows its banks and floods down the shallow trenches dug for this purpose between lines of tomatoes, *salades*, and every kind of vegetable. When each channel is a miniature stream, Hilaire feverishly rakes the soil at its end into a little dam to close it, while the water permeates gently to the roots of the plants. It is a thrilling game, as he has to be very quick; for the volume of water is great, and as each trench fills and is dammed up, the main torrent rushes swiftly on and, if not directed into the prepared channels, would flood the terraces and endanger the walls . . .

But the vegetable and fruit garden is really Hilaire's kingdom where he reigns supreme, for we would not presume to make suggestions as to sowing in Provence. In England we did know something of the naughty little ways of vegetables, their likes and dislikes, their moods and caprices, but in Provence apparently they are more profligate, their appetites grosser, and their passions stronger.

I learned this first whilst watching Hilaire sowing peas and beans. He took each bean separately, wrapped it tenderly inside a ball of manure, and deposited it gently in a hole in the ground. Death to a fastidious English seed, but here in Provence they seem to like it! When all the balls were buried, Hilaire watered the ground copiously, and then, wiping his horny hands on his blue apron, informed me that in a few days Madame would see green leaves pricking through the ground and in a few weeks beanstalks mounting to the clouds. It sounded to me rather like a fairy-story I loved in my youth – but Hilaire was right.

He then proceeded to give me a lecture on the times and seasons for sowing. Everything, it seems, depends upon the moon. Beans and peas are amorous things, and must therefore be sown in the first quarter of the moon, for if they are sown while the lovely new moon is smiling down upon them, they spring towards her swiftly. During the last quarter, when her beauty is fading, they are less enthusiastic. Potatoes, carrots, and turnips, on the other hand, being, as I have always imagined, more phlegmatic in temperament, must be sown in the last quarter of the moon, who will drag their roots down for them as she sinks.

I shall never get used to the extraordinary growing powers of this climate and soil. I shall never cease to marvel when I find seeds planted on Monday pushing up leaves on Monday week. Hilaire set me to cut off *gourmandes* (suckers) from the tomatoes, and I filled two great baskets with them. I could hardly believe my eyes when a fortnight later he asked me to go over those tomatoes again, and I found as many *gourmandes* as before.

Lady Fortescue, 1947

Growing vegetables for
Gertrude Stein

In the spring of 1929 we became tenants of what had been the manor of Bilignin. We were enchanted with everything. But after careful examination of the two large vegetable gardens – the lower on a level with the terrace garden in front of the house, and the other on a considerably higher level and a distance from the court and portals – it was to my horror that I discovered the state they were in. Nothing but potatoes had been planted the year before. Poking about with a heavy stick, there seemed to be some resistance in a corner followed by a rippling movement. The rubbish and weeds would have to be cleaned out at once. In six days the seven men we mobilised in the village had accomplished this. In the corner where I had poked, a snake's nest and several snakes had been found. But so were raspberries and strawberries.

A plan was made for plots and paths. The French are adroit in weeding and gathering from paths a few inches in width. It was difficult for me to accommodate myself to them. A list of what vegetables and when they were to be planted had to be made. We had brought with us sacks of seeds of all the vegetables Gertrude Stein and I cared for and some with which we would experiment. To do the heavy work a boy from the hamlet had been found. After fertilisers had been turned into the ground and the topsoil raked to a powder, with a prayer the planting commenced. The seeds for early gathering had scarcely been disposed of when it was time to plant the slips bought from farmers' wives in the square at Belley at the Saturday-morning market. There were two horticulturists in Belley. But the slips we had from them were not all vigorous; we planted twice as many as we intended to grow.

The wind blew the seeds from the weeds in the uncultivated fields that surrounded the gardens. The topsoil was made of earth and heavy rains commenced to wash it away. These were the two disadvantages we should have to overcome. The weeds remained a tormenting, backbreaking experience all the summers we spent at Bilignin. After the autumn gathering was over, the topsoil would be renewed. Fortunately there was plenty of water. Only once was there a drought, when the ox carts brought water in barrels from the stream in the valley below. For watering we had bought three hundred feet of hose.

The work in the vegetables – Gertrude Stein was undertaking for the moment the care of the flowers and box hedges – was a full-time job and more. Later it became a joke, Gertrude Stein asking me what I saw when I closed my eyes, and I answered, weeds. That, she said, was not the answer, and so weeds were changed to strawberries. The small strawberries, called by the French wood strawberries, are not wild but cultivated. It took me an hour to gather a small basket for Gertrude Stein's breakfast, and later when there was a plantation of them in the upper garden our young guests were told that if they cared to eat them they should do the picking themselves.

The first gathering of the garden in May of salads, radishes and herbs made me feel like a mother about her baby – how could anything so beautiful be mine. And this emotion of wonder filled me for each vegetable as it was gathered every year. There is nothing that is comparable to it, as satisfactory or as thrilling, as gathering the vegetables one has grown.

Later when vegetables were ready to be picked it never occurred to us to question what way to cook them. Naturally the simplest, just to steam or boil them and serve them with the excellent country butter or cream that we had from a farmer almost within calling distance. Later still, when we had guests and the vegetables had lost the aura of a new-born miracle, sauces added variety.

Alice B. Toklas, 1954

Asparagus pea

This is not a pea at all, but a member of the Lotus family – and closely related to some of the more notorious lawn weeds, the trefoils. However, asparagus pea won't run amok and it's an absolute gem of a vegetable. With its pretty red flowers, pale green winged pods and neat bushy foliage, it looks good enough to grow in the flower garden or in pots on the patio. And the taste is superb. The pods, steamed whole and served with butter, have a hint of asparagus.

There are just two or three snags. The pods hide away deep down in the foliage and you need to do quite a lot of searching to find enough for a decent serving. Also, if you let them get more than one inch (2.5 cm) long they taste like boiled toe-nail clippings however carefully cooked. The whole pod becomes woody, so pick little and often.

Sue Phillips, 1990

French beans

I had resolved in so small a garden to spare no plot for cabbages or potatoes. No cabbage is beautiful except in a field, potatoes take too much space and care. I chose only the vegetables that have some charm of appearance, that would not strike too discordant a note in the quiet beauty of the garden.

I chose, for instance, dwarf French beans in preference to peas. Peas, too, take up a good deal of room, the pea-sticks are unsightly, and the last moments of the peas are distressing. The dwarf French bean is a tidy little plant, not nearly so picksome as peas, and it produced far bigger crops in the same space.

Not only this! The French bean has a flavour infinitely superior to its coarse brother, the Scarlet Runner, which extends its coarseness to some eighteen inches, and ends by cutting the diner's tongue like a knife! But the little French bean has a bland, smooth skin far removed from the unshaven male jowl of the Runner. There is, indeed, in comparison, almost a hint of shaving soap and Eau-de-Lubin about the French bean in its pale, delicate pod.

It is a delicious, mild and succulent little edible, and its brother, the climbing French bean, has the same smooth skin and suave flavour.

These beans seem to yield for ever; pick the pods while quite young, and you will find another crop in a day or so, and provided you hoe them lightly and regularly they seem to ask for little and give so much. The only manure mine had was a little hop manure forked into the ground in the autumn.

Muriel Stuart, 1936

Marrow on a mound

In view of the fact that all natural manure is so expensive why are such quantities of potential manure wasted in the majority of households? All vegetable and fruit refuse, tea leaves, coffee grounds, etc., from the kitchen, all carpet sweepings and dust from vacuum cleaners, all dead flowers, etc., should be added to the compost heap of weeds and green garden rubbish . . . With no trouble whatever beyond adding the rubbish every day to the pile the whole turns to ideal potting soil in ten months and if not wanted for this purpose makes a surface dressing second in value only to farm or stable manure. We grow a large number of Vegetable Marrows as we like to store them for the winter, so we put one rubbish heap in a sunny part and there is no disagreeable smell for the daily consignment of weeds is thrown over the refuse from the kitchen . . . On top of this we put two loads of top spit loam which not only makes the heap look neat but while the Vegetable Marrows are growing it is gradually rotting and by November the whole is an ideal surface dressing for beds – rich and crumbly . . .

Whilst Vegetable Marrows occupy one heap from early April to the end of October, another heap is 'growing' in another part of the garden.

Eleanour Sinclair Rohde, 1938

Parsnips

Nobody writes poems about parsnips. Nor do you find chefs clucking and fussing over them in expensive restaurants. Courgettes have all the fun, primped out in a hundred different ways. Parsnips rarely crawl out from their traditional berth, tucked under the Sunday roast . . . It was Jane Grigson who pointed out that the Russian for parsnip was *pasternak*. Would we feel the same way about *Dr Zhivago* if we knew it had been written by Boris Parsnip? It just shows how low the vegetable has sunk in our esteem.

For me, however, this has been the winter of the parsnip, thanks to a bumper crop, only improved by frosty weather. Cold intensifies the flavour of parsnips and converts some of their starch into sugar so that they are sweeter in cold winters than in mild ones.

The seed went in on 24 April. This is right at the end of the recommended time, but late sowings germinate faster than early ones and there is no particular advantage – unless you are a showman – in having early crops. The parsnip, though deeply comforting in winter, is not something you ever think of eating in summer.

The variety I used was 'White King' from Van Hage. Later, when the seedlings were well established, they were thinned out. The usual instruction is to leave 6–9 in/15–23 cm between each one. Mine are probably more like 4–6 in/10–15 cm apart, because I do not want monsters. Huge parsnips are difficult to dig up and peeling them is like painting the Forth Bridge. The thinning is important, though it seems wasteful, but it will be the only attention your parsnips need, apart from the general hoeing that goes on in vegetable beds to keep down weeds.

Situation is important. It needs to be open, and the soil on the dryish side when you sow. Seed has to be fresh. Some vegetable seed can be kept from year to year with no appreciable effect on germination rates. Not parsnip. Like most root vegetables, they do best in deep but light soil. Do not grow them in ground that has been very recently manured (unless, of course, you have your eye on the 'rudest root' class at your local horticultural show). Canker is their only enemy. This usually shows as reddish-brown, sometimes black, patches on the roots, especially at the shoulders. Sometimes it spreads through the whole of the parsnip, but usually the patches are small enough to be cut away when you are preparing the roots. There is no effective remedy, but fortunately many varieties are now bred to be resistant to the disease.

Anna Pavord, 1992

Sea-kale

About seventy years ago, Dr Lettsom, a celebrated physician and botanist of that day, happened to be travelling near Southampton, when he observed some plants pushing their way up through the sea-sand. Finding the shoots of these plants quite succulent, he inquired of some person in the neighbourhood if they were ever eaten, and was answered, that the country people had been in the habit of boiling these shoots and eating them as a vegetable from time immemorial. The doctor tasted them, and found them so good, that he took some seed to his friend Mr Curtis, the originator of the Botanical Magazine, who had then a nursery in Lambeth Marsh. Mr Curtis wrote a book about the plant, which brought it into notice, and he sold the seed in small packets at a high price: and thus, this long neglected British plant, which for so many years was only eaten by the poorest fishermen, became our highly prized and much esteemed sea-kale, which is now so great a favourite at the tables of the rich.

Sea-kale is raised either from seeds, or cuttings of the roots. In either case, when the plants are a year old, they are put into a bed thoroughly prepared as if for asparagus, and planted in the same manner. The first year the plants will require little care, except cutting down the flower-stems wherever they appear; but the second year they will be ready for forcing. This is performed by covering the plants first with river-sand; then turning what are called sea-kale pots over them, and lastly, covering the pots to the depth of fifteen or twenty inches with fresh stable dung, the heat from which will draw the shoots up, and make them succulent and fit to eat.

Mrs Jane Loudon, 1841

Potatoes

Our potato crop waits to be dug. As I fork up a root and scrape a potato with my fingernail the skin slips off. All around us work shouts to be done. We have no time now for quiet enjoyment of our garden, for the first frosts and the autumn rains will soon be upon us, checking our digging and planting.

We enjoy digging our potatoes. It is the big treasure hunt of the year, even more exciting than searching for the fruit in the tangle of straw round the strawberry plants. The excitement lies in the anticipation we feel each time we stick the fork into the ground. How many potatoes will there be beneath this plant? This anticipation never tires, even after rows of digging. Here is all the mystery of an unknown, invisible harvest. We can see the extent of our peas and beans, and we know that each green-leafed parsnip top will have a corresponding root below, but who can tell how many potatoes huddle beneath the plant that we see above the ground? As my fork brings up the cool, moist potatoes, I lay them out in the sun to dry. They look beautiful as they lie on the earth in creamy rows. The limp, fading haulms curve away from them by their side in regular lines. Minute, undeveloped potatoes cling to the tendril roots of the plants, smooth of skin and fresh of colour in contrast with the decay of the aged seed potato. A robin sits near us on the haft of a spade and sings his autumn song.

Clare Leighton, 1935

Vegetable beauty

I have often thought what a beautiful bit of summer gardening one could do, mainly planted with things usually grown in the kitchen garden only, and filling up spaces with quickly-grown flowering plants. For climbers there would be the Gourds and Marrows and Runner Beans; for splendour of port and beauty of foliage, Globe Artichokes and Sea-kale, one of the grandest of blue-leaved plants. Horse-radish also makes handsome tufts of its vigorous deep-green leaves, and Rhubarb is one of the grandest of large-leaved plants. Or if the garden were in shape a double square, the further portion being given to vegetables, why not have a bold planting of these grand things as a division between the two, and behind them a nine-feet-high foliage-screen of Jerusalem Artichoke. This Artichoke, closely allied to our perennial Sunflowers, is also a capital thing for a partition screen; a bed of it two or three feet wide is a complete protection through the summer and to the latest autumn.

Gertrude Jekyll, 1900

The Petit Potager

I've always been conscious of the fact that the entrance to our kitchen garden is – well – a bit of a mess. The gate is a typical farm inheritance, made of three-inch square (7.5 × 7.5 cm) iron mesh (the stuff used to reinforce concrete) and fastened with baler twine. The anti-rabbit fencing and windbreak netting both need to be repaired, the plastic covered greenhouse and ersatz polythene tunnels are a motley collection, and try as we might, bits of wire, corrugated iron, bamboo canes and ageing wheelbarrows gravitate towards what should be a neat row of workmanlike compost heaps near the gate.

Between the gate, the compost heaps and the first greenhouse is a smallish area, four yards by five (4 × 5 m). It occurred to me one day that I should make a herb garden there: it would make a pretty entrance to the garden, would be useful, and making it would be valuable experience. A friend drew me a lovely plan. But that's when it struck me that a plot that size is all the garden some people have ... and into my mind sprang the idea of the *petit potager*. Could I make a pretty miniature vegetable patch there, something decorative enough to liven the entrance to our garden, but suitable also for any urban or suburban front garden, where the longing to grow vegetables conflicts with the desire for 'something pretty in front'? ...

To say the *petit potager* was designed would be to exaggerate. It 'evolved' during the two rather wet and dreary seasons since its conception in the reluctant spring of 1985. It's essentially a rectangular area, the main axis lying in an east westerly direction. While the western ends are more or less squared off, the eastern ends are gently rounded, giving it an almost oval shape overall. It is divided into four matching but unequal sections with two paths, the longer running east west, the shorter north south. A simple arch straddles the main path at the centre.

Within these bare bones each section is subdivided into four – the dividing lines drawn with plants ...

I had wanted each segment to develop a character of its own, but what I hadn't anticipated was the character that would be stamped on the garden by the plants that just 'appeared'. These were self sown seedlings from previous years – borage, 'Pink Chiffon' poppies (quite legitimate as we use the poppy seed on buns and bread), calendulas, the old salad plant buck's horn plantain, and in the second season dill and nasturtium 'Alaska' as a result of their being sown in the first.

This surprise element often created dramatic effects that could never have been planned. But on the other hand, effects I visualised never materialised. In 1985, for example, the unifying circle was giant chives, and so successful had a patch of 'Hammond's Dwarf' runner beans been the previous year, I decided to encircle the chives with red and white-flowered dwarf runners. The idea was to create a lovely broad, even, band of red and white flowers, contrasting with the lush upright foliage of the chives. (The white-flowered beans, incidentally, were a new Hurst's variety I was trying out.) It never happened. By mid-summer both the chives and the beans had been engulfed by sprawling borage, calendula, dill, 'Dun' peas and ornamental kale – just a few bean flowers poking through bravely from time to time! I was learning lesson number one: desired effects can only be achieved by ruthless rooting out of all competition.

As with any gardening, ideas came as one worked. When weeding the dill patch one day I found an asparagus seedling, and thought how pretty a permanent clump of asparagus would be, or maybe just one plant. It would be pretty over a long period – one of the main criteria for a good *potager* plant ... Was it pretty? *I* think so, but then I was a little in love with it and perhaps blind to its faults. I loved the way its moods and character changed with the seasons and with the morning and evening light. Its colour cheered me every time I went into the kitchen garden.

But aware of my own bias, I was interested in the more detached reactions of visitors. Some were obviously delighted ... 'What a lovely idea' ... 'Fancy vegetables being so colourful' ... They instantly saw how the idea could be transformed to a small front garden. But others, I have to say, walked right by. I'd feel obliged to say casually, 'Oh by the way, this is my experimental "pretty bit" ... what do you think of it?' And I'd start to explain the underlying pattern. The inescapable truth is that its high points were interspersed with messy phases (the word messy appeared all too frequently in my notes!) ... and to the casual observer the messy phases were, at best, colourful chaos. Now I'm a sucker for colourful chaos, but it's not everybody's taste!

Let me share some of the high points. In the first year the north-westerly section looked dramatic, in an orderly way, throughout August and September. In the background sweet peas clambered colourfully up the arch (there wasn't time, that first year, to grow an edible crop of climbing beans). The central triangle was ablaze with the variegated leaves and brightly coloured flowers of nasturtium 'Alaska', mixed with a few plants of sparkling iceplant (*Mesembryanthemum crystallinum*), which we use in salads. The semicircle of mixed broad and curly leaved parsley made a strong contrasting green band behind them, and behind that were first dwarf runner beans, later chard. Further out was a semi-circle of the ornamental cabbage 'Cherry Sundae', twelve to fifteen inches in height (30–38 cm), the frilled and puckered green, white and purple leaves looking stunning, the colours becoming stronger as the season progressed. The section was rounded off neatly with an edge of the frilly green 'Lollo' lettuce.

By September the adjoining south-westerly segment was striking, largely because of the diagonal band of the calendula 'Neon' – its wonderful vibrant gold and bronze petals almost iridescent in sunlight. Soft, blue-green downy buds of borage threaded their way through the calendula. At the same time the dill was starting to run to seed, and it too looked brilliant when the sun caught it, contrasting with the red spires of seeding red 'Salad Bowl' lettuce, which I couldn't bear to pull up.

In spring the following year I found much satisfaction in the dense neat triangles of seedling crops – cress, glossy pak choi seedlings, salad rocket, red Salad Bowl lettuce, Mizuna mustard, clearly circled then with freshly planted giant chives, some already flowering, and enlivened too by the early pansy flowers at the foot of the arch.

By July the relatively prim orderliness of the early months had given way to a rampant blaze of colour, and I was writing enthusiastically: 'I love it now, the intermingling of orange calendula, the soft blue haze of borage, the odd poppy still pink though most of them forming seed heads and the very tall spikes of seeding dill – delicate, glistening greeny gold seed heads.' I did admit that 'you have to look for the vegetables. There has been lettuce around the edges all summer, and the 'Lollo' in a central triangle are developing. Also developing quietly is a triangle of fennel, the recently planted curly parsley, the 'Painted Lady' runner beans on the arch. Asparagus peas and dwarf runners are ready for harvesting.' A border of alternating red and green Salad Bowl was at its peak then: 'Marvellous rounded bushes, almost a foot high and two feet across, the frilly indented leaves merging with each other: a superb edge.'

The miserable summer probably accelerated the onset of the messy autumnal phase, but even so, in September the combination of the red and white 'Peacock' kales and the 'Lucullus' chard in the north-east section took some beating. The kales were planted in groups of four making very strong patches of colour with their stiff serrated leaves, the red with a light purple centre, the other leaves a contrasting blue green, and the whites creamy and green. As for the chard its huge, glossy, emerald green crinkly leaves radiated vegetable well-being! Again, the section with seeding dill, borage, fennel and kale, all contrasting foliage textures and different heights, had its glorious moments.

What I must do, to improve the overall impact of the *potager*, is to grow some unobtrusive backgrounds. Visually the greenhouse, fencing, compost heaps and water tanks constantly intrude. Perhaps this year I will plant screens of sunflowers, Jerusalem artichokes, climbing gourds or beans. Or should I make a second *potager* in the uncluttered setting of the front lawn?

Joy Larkcom, 1987

Open the gate and go round

I have a fancy to open the gate and go all round the kitchen garden quite prosaically. The other garden will seem still sweeter, after. Here, on the left, is a breadth of wonderful Lettuces, round and close like small round Cabbages with milk-white middles; and beyond, some taller and tied-up – more like salad. Near the Lettuces are tall ranks of Peas, hung all over with well-filled pods. I think I like these beautiful green Peas, growing here, as much as when served up in a dish for dinner. There seems always to be something attractive to Art of all kinds in pea pods; from the pods sculptured on the great bronze gates of the cathedral at Pisa, or the raised needlework of the sixteenth century, to the ornaments in the jewellers' shops of Paris or the portraits of Marrowfats or Telegraph Pea in the advertisement sheets of gardening papers. These last being really pictures, though not meant so. I remember once being shown a white satin spencer of Queen Elizabeth's, embroidered in butterflies and Green Pea pods half open to show the rows of peas within.

I think there is Beet-root, and a fine lot of young cabbages, beyond the Peas – in which no one can feel any particular interest; and oh! such a sweet patch of seedling Mrs Sinkins' white Pink. I wish that Pink did possess a more poetical name – Arethusa or Boule de Neige! but the thing is done, and to the end of time Mrs. Sinkins will be herself. Next comes a little square of Japanese Iris, the tall stems tipped with swelling buds whose grand unfolding I long to see. Rows of young Sage plants grow near, quite unlike sage-green, so called, in colour; and a nice little plantation of healthy-looking Fennel. That is for broiled mackerel: but there is to me another interest connected with Fennel that lies in a lurking hope, always unfulfilled, of finding upon it a caterpillar of the rare Papilio regina. Caterpillars of another sort are only too multitudinous on the Currants growing up the walls. The increase of them, and of the sawflies belonging to them, is not short of miraculous. One may stamp out whole families and clear the bushes, and next morning they will be beginning again. Yet invariably in the act of destroying there creeps in a sort of questioning, whether the caterpillars have not full as good a right to the Currants as we have; except indeed, that we and not they planted them. But the sawflies would seem to have at least a right to live – a greater right perhaps than we to have tarts; yet they are spared none the more for such-like uncomfortable reflections. On the south wall the fruit trees seem to be more or less flourishing. An old Nectarine is covered with fruit. Then comes Apricot tree No. 1, on which I find no Apricots; Nos. 2 and 3 the same, 4 dead, and 5 with 'a good few' on it. Then we come to Peaches: plenty of them. Then a beautiful dark-leaved Fig tree, and then the Cherries well fruited and well netted. And so on round the walls.

E. V. Boyle, 1889

To pass the hand among the leaves of the Fig tree, noting that they are a little harsh upon the upper surface and yet soft beneath; to be aware of their faint, dusky scent; to see the cracking of the coat of the fruit and the yellowing of the neck where it joins the branch – the two indications of ripeness – sometimes made clearer by the drop of honeyed moisture at the eye; then the handling of the fruit itself, which must needs be gentle because the tender coat is so readily bruised and torn; at the same time observing the slight greyish bloom and the colouring – low-toned transitions of purple and green; and finally to have the enjoyment of the luscious pulp, with the knowledge that it is one of the most wholesome and sustaining of fruit foods – surely all this is worthy garden service!

Gertrude Jekyll, 1911

FLOWER ARRANGERS

Triumphal arch

NO WAY of decorating a dinner-table, if oval or circular, can be prettier than ornamenting it with a handsome arch, which is, moreover, by no means difficult to arrange effectively. It should, however, be remembered that, as a rule, no tasteful or elegant floral arrangement can be put together without a little trouble. The size of the arch itself must, as a matter of course, be proportionate to the size of the table on which it is to be placed; and, the size having been determined, next comes the material of which the arch is to consist. This should be strong wire, stiff enough to keep its form without bending, and each end should be inserted in a piece of iron or lead in the form of a large flat weight, which forms the stand. These supports should each be planted in a circular zinc pan, and packed in with damp silver-sand to keep them firm. Means are thus provided for having a group of flowers at the base of each end of the arch, which, together with the zinc pans, should be painted green. The shade of green selected should be as near as possible that of the Ferns usually arranged round the edge. The next thing to be considered are the creepers with which the wire arch is to be covered. Of this class of plants there is such a variety (some hardy, others tender) that it would be impossible for me to enumerate all that are suitable for the purpose.

On the centre of the table, under the arch, a pot plant is often placed, but I like best to see a small stand of flowers in that position; it must, however, be small, or it will detract from the effect of the arch. For this purpose, a small-sized flat tazza, with a trumpet rising out of the centre is best. Were I about to arrange a table in this style, say in the month of June, I should select the following flowers: – Round the edge of the tazza I should arrange, lightly, fronds of Pteris serrulata, in the tazza itself some blooms, say two pink Cactuses, the same number of Water Lilies, a few sprays of pink and white Rhodanthe, and four fronds of Maiden-hair Fern. Down the trumpet I should twine a spray of Lygodium scandens, and in the trumpet itself I would put a plume of wild Grasses,

Rhodanthe, and a few fronds of Maiden-hair. The arch I should cover, with plants of Lygodium scandens, and in the pans I should arrange some of the flowers just named, with the addition of a few half-open Rose-buds, blue Forget-me-nots, or any other suitable flowers which may be at hand. Round the centre vase might be placed a few specimen glasses, each containing a Rose, bloom of Eucharis amazonica, &c., each backed by a Fern frond.

Annie Hassard, 1875

In mid-September a beautiful effect can be produced by placing clusters of scarlet geranium among trails of the wild clematis, known as 'Old Man's Beard'. When the seeds first begin to form, before the white, fluffy stage is reached, there is a soft, silvery lustre on the carpels, which tells extremely well by lamplight.

Mrs Ethel L. Chamberlain, 1892

The reds, pinks, and magentas I mix fearlessly and, if I possessed one, I should put them in a chalice of brilliant hard green malachite. There are qualities in the red of geraniums, and in the green of malachite, which have something to say to each other; together they make a note of shouting triumph quite indescribable, and quite outside one's usual ideas of colour combination.

Constance Spry, 1953

Doing (and not doing) the flowers

I love plants, and therefore flowers, but I cannot honestly say that I enjoy picking them. I find that the older I grow and the more dear my plants and garden become, the more reluctant I am to cut them. In a vase the flowers' lives are so fleeting, and if I let them stay on the plant they are likely to live on for days, even weeks.

My family are amused and tease me because I can walk around our well filled garden, even in spring, looking for flowers for the house, and although thousands of narcissi will be turning their faces towards me I will finish up in the lane picking cow parsley and wild arum leaves. It is also well known that I prefer to buy a bunch of mass-produced blooms about which my conscience does not trouble me than pick the individual blooms I have tended for weeks.

However, once I have cut a flower I have no sentiments about the way I use it. If I think that it would be improved by wiring, taping, shortening or any other artificial treatment, this I do, although my aim usually is to retain as much as possible of the natural beauty and character of the plant I have robbed . . .

Actually, going around the garden collecting throwaways for home arrangements is a pleasant way of getting through a few garden chores. So many plants should have the dead flowers removed if they are to give of their best, and quite often the newly exposed seed vessels have a jewel-like quality worth exploiting.

Gardeners can do quite a lot of useful work as they select flowers and materials for arrangement. You can prune, for example: the too low branch can be cut away piece by piece as required, the crossing twig can be removed, the spindly growth no good to the tree might have just the right line for an arrangement. Buds can be cut from the silver-leaved plants such as senecio and centaurea which grow much bushier for the treatment. Centres of other plants can be nipped out.

Those plants which give double service, producing flowers and some other part which is worth gathering or preserving, are a real boon to those who enjoy flower arrangement. I try to collect as many as I can.

Hostas of course come high on the list. These give even more than double value, for even when they are no longer green the tough curled and fluted leaves can be used in perpetuelle arrangements and the seed stems, filled and green or brown and empty, have great beauty. The hardy geraniums are not really good flowers for cutting, but they fill a garden with colour and they pay their dues in lovely leaves. I would not be without any of them. Even the wild herb robert is allowed to stay. *Geranium macrorrhizum* which scents the air even if it is lightly brushed, proffers lovely coloured leaves even in the dark days of winter. Bergenias, aquilegias, even paeonies have leaves sometimes most splendidly coloured. I find room for shrubs of all kinds, though some are visited more than others. Unexpectedly the golden privet has paid for its garden room time and time again. In summer the sharp yellow of its leaves looks well with analogous hues among dahlias or perhaps tagetes; roses as well seem to suit it. In winter it takes on purple tones that harmonise beautifully with winter flowers. I use it with red stems of dogwood and cypripediums, in purple glass or in copper, the hues of which are to be found also in the privet. Mahonia foliage is so long lasting. I gather it as I gather all shrub materials: as though I were stealing it and wished to leave no evidence of my crime. Even just two or three compound leaves are enough. The dark maples, 'Goldsworth Crimson' or 'Crimson King' have fine large leaves, important enough to be used on their own. There are many others, including berried kinds and of course species roses for their heps as well as their flowers. I always grow some annuals although I do not care very much for some of the improved forms; I like annuals to remain old favourites. Some, like nigella, have delightful seed boxes. The opium poppy is my mainstay. Its soft, glaucous buds, stems and seed heads look beautiful with anything. One way in which I use these poppies is to pull up the entire plant by the root, place it in water and allow it to develop indoors. It needs no arranging: its stems make their own lines . . .

We used to talk about 'doing the flowers' and there really is a difference between this and 'making a flower arrangement'. In one the needs of the flowers come first and in the other it is the desire, taste and talent of the individual which dictates the way they are employed.

I imagine that my own flowers are sometimes 'done' and sometimes 'arranged'. My husband appears to enjoy the results of 'doing', in my taking a handful of gaily coloured blooms and putting them into a vessel of water where he can bury his face in them, no more than that. And this is a lovely way of displaying all those flowers summer produces in such quantities; sweet peas, dahlias, marigolds, roses, anemones and poppies. I cut the last in bud just before they are ready to open, singe the stems, place in water and then leave to snake around in their own individual way . . .

Often my flower arrangement is virtually made while I am walking from the garden to the house after gathering my flowers. A handful of flowers, roughly similar, are arranged in a bunch, the stem length depending on the waiting container, the largest at the base and the smallest at the tip. The stems are then cut at the same level and the bunch stood on a pinholder ready fixed in the container. One needs only to pull the stems a little away from the vertical so that each flower has room to expand and each has its own living-room. If it is not hidden by the lowest bloom the pinholder is then disguised and the arrangement is completed.

Violet Stevenson, 1969

A bunch in the hand

One can hardly go wrong if a bunch of any one kind of flower is cut with long stalks and plenty of its own leafage, and especially if it is cut without carrying a basket. I cannot explain why it is, but have always observed that no intentional arrangement of flowers in the ordinary way gives an effect so good as that of a bunch held easily in the hand as flower by flower is cut, and put in water without fresh arrangement. The only glimmer of a reason I can see for it is that they are cut of uneven lengths, and that the natural way of carrying them in the hand is with the stalks fairly even, and that this gives just that freedom of top outline that is so much to be desired.

Gertrude Jekyll, 1900

Letter to John Ruskin

One of my delights in my poor father's life-time, when that acre of garden behind our little cottage was as closely set with flowers as a meadow is set with grass, was to arrange those flowers in jars, and I always found that the way to make a brilliant spot, a bit of colour that did your heart good, was to make the foundation white. Half-open roses amongst white pinks are delicious both to the scent and the sight. The Duke of Devonshire (almost the only great man whom I know, and who has always been so kind to me that I do not apologise for seeming to boast of his kindness, as I should of any other Duke), once brought me a nosegay composed in the same spirit – about a dozen forced moss-rose buds in the centre surrounded by some hundred flower-stalks of the lovely lily-of-the-valley, no leaves, and indeed I generally found that leaves of any sort, even the stemmage and stalkage of the lily, dimmed the colour. This bouquet was really ducal in fragrance and beauty, but my common pinks looked as well, perhaps better, with moss-roses or the dear old cottage rose, had a fine spicy odour and the great merit of coming at the same time and lasting for weeks, sometimes for months. Ask your own dear mother to try this next summer. I dare say that little common pink which grows like a weed is not choice enough for her garden, so you must come and fetch some roots from mine. By far the most gorgeous flower-jar that I ever made was of double white narcissus studded with choice ranunculuses, not hanging loose but packed tightly together. White hollyhocks too mixed with others of rich colour either in a tall jar with all their long spikes, for the bud of the hollyhock is beautiful and so is the peculiar green looking like a daisied lawn on a dewy morning – either in that form or the single blossoms laid closely together in a china dish are very bright and gay. So are dahlias, and dahlias look especially well arranged in a china bowl with a wire frame of the same sphere-like form, into which to insert the stalks. It makes a splendid globe of colour. In the autumn the magnolia grandiflora raising its sculpturesque beauty with a border of fuchsias and other gay flowers drooping round it is very graceful, and for a wild nosegay you will find the white water-lily surrounded by the purple willow-herb, the yellow loose-strife, the deep rose-colour of the ragged robin and the exquisite blue of the forget-me-not very imposing. I have seen people wondering that such an effect should be produced by wild flowers. But whether for scent or elegance, nothing can surpass a quantity of the meadow-sweet denuded of its leaves and left to the charm of its feathery lightness and its pearly, creamy tint. Forgive this blotted scrawl, dear friend.

Mary Russell Mitford, 1854

Altarpiece

One excellent way of arranging flowers in most rooms is to have a table, a kind of altar, especially dedicated to them. This does the flowers or plants much more justice that dotting them about the room. If, however, flowers or branches are arranged in vases in the Japanese style, the more they are isolated in prominent places that show them off, the better.

I am now staying with a friend who has no stove, only one greenhouse; and her flower-table, standing in the window, looks charming. At the back are two tall glass vases with Pampas grass in them, feathery and white, as we never can keep it in London; a small Eucalyptus-tree in a pot, cut back in summer and well shaped; a fine pot of Arums, just coming into flower; a small fern in front, and a bunch of paper-white Narcissus. These last, I fear, must have been grown elsewhere, as they could not be so early here without heat and very careful growing-on.

Mrs C. W. Earle, 1897

How to treat cut flowers

Perhaps the most important thing to remember when cutting flowers is that (a) you have performed a surgical operation on the plant, and (b) cut off its source of food supply. When fed by the roots, soil water enters the cells by means of osmosis and from thence is forced up to the topmost parts of the plant or tree. This root pressure as it is called exerts considerable force, as one can notice in spring by cutting a vine. So prolific is the flow of sap from below that it drips from the wound, or 'bleeds' as we term it. Once the flower stem is cut this pressure ceases and the method of obtaining water changes. Now the plant must *draw* up its nourishment – a very different procedure from receiving a pumped supply. Any mineral salts in solution the plant retains, but much of the water is passed out from pores (stoma) on the leaves, in the form of water vapour. Sir Edward Salisbury has stated that an Oak tree in full leaf takes in a ton of water a day. It certainly cannot accommodate such a quantity and so *has* to pass off the surplus in this way.

When a plant is cut the leaves continue to pass off water vapour, or transpire as we call it, but somewhat handicapped due to the slower rate of intake. That is why many cut flowers flag in vases. The stems just cannot manage everything – to take in water, look after the flowers and transpire all at the same time. Removal of some of the leaves therefore is only common-sense procedure. Placing wilted blooms in warm water is also sound practice, for this will rise more quickly than cold and so starts the flow into the stem.

Flowers for cutting should always be gathered in the cool part of the day – *never* when the sun has been shining on them for hours so that they wear a sleepy, half wilted air. Remove basal foliage with *all* blossoms and that from the stem as well with particularly large-leaved species. Next stand the blooms in deep water in a cool place for several hours, keeping the bowls in a dark place. Although tap water can be used I find soft or rain water better for some flowers, particularly *Iris Kaempferi* and the Calcifuges. Burning the ends of milky or mucilaginous sapped plants – like Poppies, Euphorbias and Dahlias prolongs life because it retains the vital juices. It is only necessary to hold the lighted taper for a few seconds to the cut end, or alternatively the tip should be immersed in boiling water for the same length of time. Plants which cast their petals can often be induced to hold them by this means, but the blossoms must be picked and treated whilst still in the bud stage.

Two or three pieces of lump charcoal dropped into a vase help to keep the water sweet, and I have found oil of peppermint useful with certain flowers for the same reason. Apart from imparting a pleasant mint fragrance to the room, it appears to accelerate transpiration – at any rate vases containing the oil needed topping up more frequently than control vases when tried out last season. One drop of oil is sufficient for half a pint of water . . .

Anemones are favourites for cutting purposes, but often defeat the arranger by refusing to open from buds when brought indoors. This is because an air bubble has risen into the cut end of the stem. To effect a remedy cut the end again and put the stems in a basin of warm water. Now cover the whole affair – basin and flowers – with a cover (cloche, meat cover, tin, etc.), and leave for an hour or two. On removing the cover you will find that every flower will have opened . . .

Lupins are a source of annoyance to many because of a tendency to bud dropping. They do this because the tops of the spikes are not receiving sufficient water. Remove most of the leaves, turn the stem upside down and fill its hollow centre with water. Now place a thumb over the end and invert the whole into a vase of tepid water. You thus effect a siphon which the warm water will start off, and the spikes should last seven to ten days. Delphiniums may be treated in the same way . . .

Alstroemerias for some odd reason seem to last longer when only an inch or two of water stands in the vase. Deeply immersed the stems soften. Place one or two pieces of charcoal in the vase. Nowadays the old *A. aurantiaca* is rather superseded by the more colourful Ligtu hybrids, but all are useful for cutting.

Most 'Daisy' flowers can be relied upon for cut flower work. Erigerons, Doronicums, Pyrethrums and Anthemis are the stand-bys in the garden. Always give them a long drink overnight before attempting arrangement . . .

Nothing looks more natural than Water-Lilies in a floating bowl, but alas most of the blooms close tightly about 4 p.m. They can be kept open by dropping a spot of paraffin wax at the base of each petal. This can be coloured with red ink or a vegetable dye to blend in with the colour of the flowers . . .

Red Hot Pokers are other good subjects for the summer and autumn, particularly the small-flowered *gracilis* forms and the variety 'Erecta'. This has the merit of never appearing untidy since the lower flowers do not wither when spent, but turn upwards to meet the younger blossoms.

Frances Perry, 1953

Snowdrops, sweet peas, mignonette

To save my time, I have Snowdrops, in small bunches of five or six, unequal heights, and tied once, loosely, with a worsted thread, and when popped into their place the thread is loosened, and the little bunch has more the character of a growing one, each flower separate. A tight bunch of Snowdrops is hideous . . .

Sweet Peas must be renewed the second day; they look best with their own green – nice tendrily pieces, which will last for several supplies of the flowers. We have them in distinct bunches of the three colours – White, Scarlet (so-called), and darkest Purple – in one glass, but if fresh they look well any way. Mignonette, unless forced, or consisting of late autumn sprigs, must be in a glass by itself and changed daily.

Frances Hope, 1881

Hellebores

Lent Hellebores, whose white and dusky red flowers are so precious in March and early April, live excellently in water if their stalks are freshly cut and slit up rather high. If this is not done they fade at once.

Gertrude Jekyll, 1900

Filling the vases

What there is to say about this might well be written in Catherine-wheels of fire – or emphasised and underlined by any known device that might make it register. It is the most difficult point of all to drive home. At this moment I feel the urge to be perhaps over-emphatic, for I am staying in a house where in every one of the large reception rooms there are two or three enormous vases of flowers, great branches of rhododendron and blossom, bowls of camellias, freesias, and other spring flowers, and every single one of them wants filling up. Anyone with half an eye for flowers can see the distress signals, and they will all be dead days before their time . . . As soon as the flowers are arranged the vases should be filled to the brim, care being taken to see that no overhanging leaf is so placed as to act as a siphon, a not uncommon source of trouble which can wreak considerable destruction on table-cloth or furniture. If the vase is a capacious one and not over-full of flowers, the water will probably not need replenishment till the next day, but shallow or over-full vases should be inspected a few hours after being arranged. Thereafter water should be added each day to fill up to the brim. In cold weather warm water may be used. It is neither necessary nor desirable to empty and refill the vases each day; the disturbance and handling involved is deleterious to the flowers, quite apart from the fact that it is far from easy to recapture the lines of a pleasing arrangement.

Beginners and young students are particularly negligent about this matter of filling up vases. They love arranging flowers and are perfectly happy to decorate every corner of the house, but filling up is another matter, and to me it is a sin not entirely out of the category of forgetting to fill up the drinking trough of a canary.

Constance Spry, 1953

They don't have to be vases

Containers can be found around the house and used for small arrangements. They don't have to be vases. They could be, perhaps, a pretty cup and saucer, a coffee cup, a small milk jug or even an old silver teapot or sauce-boat filled with spring flowers.

Glass is pretty especially when filled with gypsophila (Baby's Breath), sweet peas or white petunias. Custard glasses and brandy snifters are useful for this. And silver – a silver salt cellar could be a size between small and miniature, and silver sugar bowls or *sucriers* filled with a mixed summer bunch are ideal. Mugs and small jugs are, of course, useful and candlesticks with metal candle cups placed in the top are lovely for a summer evening party, or for Christmas with cascading red ribbons tied to a posy at the place of each guest. There are very many objects around the house that one has never thought to use . . .

Boxes, old tea caddies, biscuit boxes, anything which has a lid are particularly good for small arrangements because the lid gives background and so limits the number of flowers which you have to use. They are the most economical of flower containers as you have to fill only one side . . .

Copper looks lovely filled with pink, or with apricot and red flowers. A copper pot filled with marigolds or a brass measure arranged with nasturtiums can be beautiful . . .

For a low table, boxes are perfect containers, filled with bluebells (which must be cut on short stems or they will not last), or with wallflowers packed in tightly, also on short stems. It is the only method I can recommend for wallflowers, whose scent is, of course, superb. Later on, try filling the box with honeysuckle and a few short-stemmed and highly-scented sweet peas.

As I sit now on a dull winter's day just after the snow has gone, I am enjoying the perfume from a winter box consisting of a small spray of *Viburnum fragrans*, and the very first snowdrops, a few stems of erica, and winter jasmine which was brought into the house frozen and brown-looking and which opened out into lovely yellow sprays almost overnight. Always try to add a sprig of something sweet-scented in these little boxes.

Sheila McQueen, 1977

Florists' fashions

Many florists are graduates of commercial schools of floristry. All arrange flowers in the natural course of events, and a few are very good at it. In the biggest cities, there are gifted craftsmen who can create artistic bouquets of all sizes and for all purposes; many of them use unusual flowers as well as the old familiars. In the smaller cities, the flower stores turn out for the most part a standardised arrangement set in floral sponge and graded for price, so you can order by number a bouquet to suit your pocketbook. Yet even florists have their fads in arrangements and follow the trends of the year. Six years ago I was sick in a hospital in a city strange to me and my family. My loyal but distant friends rallied round and wired me flowers. These floral tributes arrived from as many as half a dozen stores in the city, but all of them were as like as two peas, for that year the florists of that city had discovered the flat-faced triangle set in a low container. Most of the triangles rose to a point in the exact centre; a few of them bore to the left or to the right, and most of them were made up of gladiolas or chrysanthemums, the florists' standbys. They were pretty, and they all gave me pleasure and saved the day for a lonely patient who had the added pleasure of wondering just how this particular stylised form had happened to hit this particular city that season – some teacher in a local school of floristry, perhaps? Fads also hit the amateurs. A show in New York one year had a vast preponderance of peaked, narrow arrangements rising high and thin, so strikingly so that when August and our village flower show rolled around I decided to make a parody arrangement and enter it. I constructed it to look as tall and narrow and ugly as possible. This was easy, because I happened to have a particularly hideous purple gladiola in my vegetable garden that year and a fine white specimen. Two sprays of purple and one of white with a leaf or two, all crowded together and rising high and thin, made an effect that amused me, but nobody recognised the thing as a parody and I deservedly received a solemn comment on my ill-considered prank.

Katharine S. White, 1958

Rebirths

I dedicate to them, these imprisoned flowers, a little of the pity that goes out to caged animals. Almost alive as they are, these die the more quickly for having travelled, having found a miserly, shifting, shallow soil. As the plant perishes one can guess at the life it had there and how tenaciously it held on to it. Its flagging, the pathetic inclination of its floral head, constitute a genuine syncope, accompanied by pallor, since the plant now reveals the whiter underside of petals and foliage. If it receives watery aid in time, it is restored in the most dramatic fashion. How many moments have I lost – if I can call them lost – with flowers as avid for moisture as the anemone, the tulip, the hyacinth, the wild orchid! Swooning with heat and thirst, their stalks, plunged into water, imbibe so much, so greedily, that the energetic movement of the flower, its return to the vertical, become visible, jerky at first and by fits and starts when the head is too rich and too heavy.

It is a pleasure sweet to a writer to witness the rebirth of a tulip in a crystal goblet. The ink dries on the pen while before me a creation, interrupted by a transient death, raises itself towards perfection and will attain it, shine for a day, perish the next . . . I can do better than watch the tulip regain its senses; I can hear the iris blossom. Its last protective silken layer rasps and splits down the length of an azure finger which uncoils at the proper time and, sitting by oneself in a small quiet room, one may start suddenly if one has forgotten that, on a nearby table, an iris has suddenly decided to blossom.

Colette, 1971

'Deaths of Flowers'

I would if I could choose
Age and die outwards as a tulip does;
Not as this iris drawing in, in-coiling
Its complex strange taut inflorescence, willing
Itself a bud again – though all achieved is
No more than a clenched sadness,

The tears of gum not flowing.
I would choose the tulip's reckless way of going;
Whose petals answer light, altering by fractions
From closed to wide, from one through many perfections,
Till wrecked, flamboyant, strayed beyond recall,
Like flakes of fire they piecemeal fall.

E. J. Scovell, 1991

Angelica for inspiration

When you are going away for a few days, leave a posy of sweet peas ('departure') and white clover ('think of me') to hold the fort till you get back. If your son or daughter is facing an important examination, encourage them with angelica ('inspiration') red clover ('industry') and pink cherry blossom ('education') . . .

Rosemary Verey, 1981

A recipe for pot-pourri

Thinking ahead for sweet scents in the house in winter, we begin to harvest rose petals, sweet-smelling herbs, or any fragrant flowers that become available. In gathering rose leaves I find it a good plan to spread them out for an hour or two on sheets to allow them to dry a little, and I then pack them into deep jars with salt, a handful of rough salt to every handful of roses. Sometimes the salt will draw out a thick brown juice from the petals, and unless mould appears this liquid is valuable, but it is as well to dry up the mixture with powdered orris-root. If, however, the petals remain reasonably dry, the orris-root may wait until the time comes for mixing the whole into *pot-pourri*.

We gather leaves of mint, thyme, lemon verbena, sweet geranium, and the flowers of lavender, white jasmine, Scotch marigolds, and sweet violets. All are dried a little before being put away in readiness for the final making into *pot-pourri*, which we do in October.

. . . Mix well together 1 oz each of ground cinnamon, all-spice, cloves, nutmeg, and powdered storax, and 4 oz of powdered orris-root. Add the juice and finely chopped rind of 3 lemons and the following liquids: ½ oz of oil of bergamot, ½ oz spirit of lavender, ½ oz oil of geranium, ½ oz essence of lemon. Mix together the powders, the liquids, and some of the salted rose-leaves in the bottom of one jar. You now have the nucleus of your *pot-pourri*. When the rose-leaves have soaked up some of the liquids stir them thoroughly and add the rest of your salted rose-leaves and pack down firmly in a jar, so that the whole mass becomes thoroughly impregnated with the oils. You may now add, without salting, any fresh rose-leaves that may come so late in the year, fresh violets, indeed any sweet-scented flower that you fancy. The following leaves also make an excellent addition: sweet bay-leaves cut up into shreds, sweet verbena, bergamot, mint, sweet balm, geranium leaves all dried and crumbled, and for colour, the dried petals of marigolds. The last-named add to the appearance of the *pot-pourri*, but have no perfume value. The flowers of lavender and the leaves of rosemary stripped from the stem are other good additions, and I also add thyme. When the whole mixture is complete and well mixed you may add a glass of brandy. If your *pot-pourri* should be too moist you may dry it by adding powdered orris-root; if too dry add some salt. During the time that the *pot-pourri* is being made, that is to say, from the time of mixing the first rose-leaves with the oils until the final leaves are put in, it should be kept tightly covered. This mixture will last for a long time, and freshly gathered materials may be added as they become available and need not be dried first. *Pot-pourri* is most effective in the house if it is not allowed to dry out, so you may add from time to time brandy, lemon-juice, and freshly salted petals.

Do not be tempted to add to this mixture any cheap, powerful perfumes or oils. I have known this done with the result that the *pot-pourri* smelt like a cheap, pseudo-oriental bazaar.

Constance Spry, 1953

VISIONARIES

HALF THE interest of a garden is the constant exercise of the imagination. You are always living three, or indeed six, months hence. I believe that people entirely devoid of imagination never can be really good gardeners. To be content with the present, and not striving about the future, is fatal.

Mrs C. W. Earle, 1897

Opportunity

It has been said that a new garden is not a garden at all. And when one considers the qualities inherent in an old garden, one grown old in the service of beauty and of human delight, its amenities of shelter and shade, its glowing flower-lit stretches, its gracious softness of contour; the sense of repose, of stability, of the preserving of reverenced memories that pervades it – when one considers these things, a new garden, crude, unproved, traditionless, would seem to have no points at all in its favour.

Much of my youthful life was spent in old gardens, blossomy inclosures with generations of bloom and sweetness behind them, eloquent of long years of happy human occupancy; and no one is more alive to their charm than I; but during the past twenty years it has fallen to my lot to make three gardens on wholly unimproved ground, and I am ready to testify that there is a deal to be said for a new garden – at least from the standpoint of the owner. It is the fair page, the fresh canvas – opportunity. It affords scope for the age-old joy of creating something – beauty we hope – out of raw materials and the stuff of our dreams.

In an established garden are luxuriant growth and a wealth of quiet interest; it surrounds us with peace and sweetness, gives us freely of itself but asks little of us in return. The new garden, on the contrary, grasps us by the arms and legs and drags us to its service, thrilling us by its need of us, at once challenging and imploring us to rescue it from its rawness, crudity, its outlaw state, and offers us by way of compensation – adventure.

Louise Beebe Wilder, 1924

'*I knew I need not hurry . . . '*

The right set of circumstances arising at just the right moment – as in many of one's major experiences – profoundly influenced my life, and turned me into a gardener absorbed by the craft, its history and the art it can become. When we came to live here in 1951 there was no time for gardening. The family were young and needed all my energies. After ten years my husband firmly suggested that I should try to take the garden in hand. He reminded me that I had grassed over most of his parents' borders to make wide open spaces for cricket, croquet and even ponies, always promising that one day the plants would be reinstated. Suddenly that day had come.

The garden already had many marvellous features – a beautiful house built in 1697 of honey-coloured Cotswold stone, surrounding walls ending in an amusing Gothic alcove, trees more than one hundred years old, yew hedges and yards of box planted in the nineteenth century; enough to make any gardener of experience and judgement jealous. Perhaps best of all was the soil which in places had been cultivated for generations. The assurance that people had lived and gardened here for so long was a tremendous incentive for me to add my contribution. But, curiously, I knew I need not hurry, and I still have this feeling. Good 'bones' are important, so it is wise to go slowly and get your plan right before launching into a vital project. Now I love thinking out and creating a new incident. Then I felt totally bewildered and unable to start.

How does one begin? In retrospect the important events seem incidental and fortuitous. As a 1960 Christmas present our eldest son gave me a subscription to the R.H.S. and our youngest daughter a large empty notebook labelled 'Your Gardening Book'. The vital impetus has always been my husband urging me on, expecting new borders to be made in a flash and imagining I would know how to do it. He laid a path with large pebbles picked up on the beaches in south Wales and planted the start of our lime walk. He had a lily pond made which later turned out to be the exact width of the classical 'temple' he was given and then had moved, stone by stone, from Fairford Park. He gave me Russell Page's *Education of a Gardener* and books by Vita Sackville-West. Between them all they made me determined to try to create something beautiful.

I became a compulsive visitor to the 'fortnightly' shows at Vincent Square and there found a wealth of gardening inspiration awaiting me. The early spring and autumn shows are still my favourites. Those first bulbs with their amazing delicacy are a recurrent miracle. Iris, crocus, anemones with their subtle clear colours are a delight to examine at close quarters, then to select for one's own garden. At my first autumn show though, I was bowled over by the beauty of the massed array of autumn colour. Obviously I had been living with my eyes half closed. But I soon discovered that many of the trees which turn brilliant autumn shades do not like our limestone soil. Gazing in admiration at *Sorbus* 'Embley' and *Vitis coignetiae* I asked the owner of the stand, rather tentatively, if either would thrive on our Cotswold limestone. To my delight he said they both would. Later I called at the nursery, Sherrard's of Newbury, and together we planned the first plantings of what we now call 'the wilderness'. I will always be grateful to Tim Sherrard for patiently helping me, for his advice and enthusiasm. We put in a number of long-term trees, a cedar, a tulip tree, catalpa, a wellingtonia, two metasequoias and a ginkgo. For spring there are flowering cherries and crabs. The most beautiful now in blossom are *Prunus* 'Ukon' and *P.* 'Tai Haku'. In autumn *Malus tschonoskii*, turns a fiery red. The whitebeams, *Sorbus aria* 'Lutescens' and *S.* 'Mitchellii' are remarkable in May when their grey leaf buds unfurl, and for autumn colour *S.* 'Embley' and *S. sargentiana* are outstanding.

A start had been made, which was a great relief, but still the main flower garden near the house had no plan. Luckily at this point – still 1962 – Russell Page's book was published. I was fascinated by his originality and certain important messages came through to me. There must be a starting point for a composition, and use must be made of the longest distances to create vistas, to lead the eye on and on. Each area of the garden must merge smoothly into the next, each have different moods and areas of light and shade. The garden must be designed to look inviting even in winter, when evergreens and shapes assume importance. Sweet smelling winter flowering shrubs should be near the house. An element of surprise is essential, and I must never forget that simplicity is often best. As for plants I must get to know them, so I can choose them to suit their sites as well as their neighbours.

My gardening notebook (now in volume IV) became a rag-bag of thoughts. There were names of trees and plants, new to me then and often entered three or four times before I finally recognised them. Visits to famous gardens and especially striking plant associations were noted. I saw mounds of purple sage with dark red tulips in one garden and with velvet-red Tuscany roses in another, apple green hart's tongue ferns between grey hostas. Those circular pools of grey and gold carpeting under old apple-trees at Powis Castle, rue and golden marjoram, lamium and creeping jenny – one day they would be adopted in our garden.

Rosemary Verey, 1980

A vision of wall-flowers

If I had plenty of suitable spaces and could spend more on my garden I would have special regions for many a good plant. As it is, I have to content myself with special gardens for Primroses and for Pæonies and for Michaelmas Daisies. And indeed I am truly thankful to be able to have these; but we garden-lovers are greedy folk, and always want to have more and more and more! I want to have a Rose-garden, and a Tulip-garden, and a Carnation-garden, and a Columbine-garden, and a Fern-garden, and several other kinds of special garden, but if I were able, the first I should make would be a Wall-flower garden.

It should be contrived either in connection with some old walls, or, failing these, with some walls or wall-like structures built on purpose. These walls would shock a builder, but would delight a good gardener, for they would present just those conditions most esteemed by wall-loving plants, of crumbling masonry built of half-formed or half-rotting stone, and of loose joints made to receive rather than to repel every drop of welcome rain. Wall-flowers are lime-loving plants, so the stones would be set in a loose bed of pounded mortar-rubbish, and there would be sloping banks, half wall half bank. I should, of course, take care that the lines of the garden should be in suitable relation to other near portions, a matter that could only be determined on the precise spot that might be available.

But for the planting, or rather the sowing of the main spaces, there would be little difficulty. I should first sow a packet of a good strain of blood-red single Wall-flower, spreading it over a large stretch of the space. Then a packet of a good yellow, either the Belvoir or the Bedfont, then the purple, and then one of the newer pale ones that have flowers of a colour between ivory-white and pale buff-yellow. I would keep the sowings in separate but informal drifts, each kind having its share, though not an equal share, of wall and bank and level. Some spaces nearest the eye should be filled with the small spreading Alpine Wall-flowers and their hybrids, but these are best secured from cuttings. The only ones I know of this class are *Cheiranthus alpinus*, whose colour is a beautiful clear lemon-yellow; *Cheiranthus mutabilis*, purple, changing to orange; and *Cheiranthus Marshalli*, the deep orange-coloured hybrid of *C. alpinus*. Seed of *C. alpinus* ought to be obtainable, though I have not tried to keep it. *C. Marshalli* never forms seed, and I have not seen it on *C. mutabilis*. A few other plants would be admitted to the Wall-flower garden, such as yellow Alyssum on sunny banks and Tiarella in cool or half-shady places, and in the wall-joints I would have in fair quantity the beautiful *Corydalis capnoides*, most delicate and lovely of the Fumitories. Leading to the Wall-flower garden I should like to have a way between narrow rock borders or dry walls. These should be planted with Aubrietias, varieties of *A. græca*, of full and light purple colour, double Cuckoo-flower in the two shades of colour, and a good quantity of the grey foliage and tender white bloom of *Cerastium tomentosum*, so common in gardens and yet so seldom well used; I would also have, but more sparingly, the all-pervading *Arabis albida*.

These plants, with the exception of the Cuckoo-flower, are among those most often found in gardens, but it is very rarely that they are used thoughtfully or intelligently, or in such a way as to produce the simple pictorial effect to which they so readily lend themselves. This planting of white and purple colouring I would back with plants or shrubs of dark foliage, and the path should be so directed into the Wall-flower garden, by passing through a turn or a tunnelled arch of Yew or some other dusky growth, that the one is not seen from the other; but so that the eye, attuned to the cold, fresh colouring of the white and purple, should be in the very best state to receive and enjoy the sumptuous splendour of the region beyond. I am not sure that the return journey would not present the more brilliant picture of the two, for I have often observed in passing from warm colouring to cold, that the eye receives a kind of delightful shock of surprise that colour can be so strong and so pure and so altogether satisfying . . .

I think I would also allow some bold patches of tall Tulips in the Wall-flower garden; orange and yellow and brown and purple, for one distinct departure from the form and habit of the main occupants of the garden would give value to both.

Gertrude Jekyll, 1900

The garden at dawn

June 16th – Yesterday morning I got up at three o'clock and stole through the echoing passages and strange dark rooms, undid with trembling hands the bolts of the door to the verandah, and passed out into a wonderful, unknown world. I stood for a few minutes motionless on the steps, almost frightened by the awful purity of nature when all the sin and ugliness is shut up and asleep, and there is nothing but the beauty left. It was quite light, yet a bright moon hung in the cloudless grey-blue sky; the flowers were all awake, saturating the air with scent; and a nightingale sat on a hornbeam quite close to me, in loud raptures at the coming of the sun. There in front of me was the sun-dial, there were the rose bushes, there was the bunch of pansies I had dropped the night before still lying on the path, but how strange and unfamiliar it all looked, and how holy – as though God must be walking there in the cool of the day.

I went down the path leading to the stream on the east side of the garden, brushing aside the rockets that were bending across it drowsy with dew, the larkspurs on either side of me rearing their spikes of heavenly blue against the steely blue of the sky, and the huge poppies like splashes of blood amongst the greys and blues and faint pearly whites of the innocent, new-born day. On the garden side of the stream there is a long row of silver birches, and on the other side a rye-field reaching across in powdery grey waves to the part of the sky where a solemn glow was already burning. I sat down on the twisted, half-fallen trunk of a birch and waited, my feet in the long grass and my slippers soaking in dew. Through the trees I could see the house with its closed shutters and drawn blinds, the people in it all missing, as I have missed day after day, the beauty of life at that hour. Just behind me the border of rockets and larkspurs came to an end, and, turning my head to watch a stealthy cat, my face brushed against a wet truss of blossom and got its first morning washing. It was wonderfully quiet, and the nightingale on the hornbeam had everything to itself as I sat motionless watching that glow in the east burning redder; wonderfully quiet, and so wonderfully beautiful because one associates daylight with people, and voices and bustle, and hurry-ings to and fro, and the dreariness of working to feed our bodies, and feeding our bodies that we may be able to work to feed them again; but here was the world wide awake and yet only for me, all the fresh pure air only for me, all the fragrance breathed only by me, not a living soul hearing the nightingale but me, the sun in a few moments coming up to warm only me, and nowhere a single hard word being spoken . . .

There were no clouds, and presently, while I watched, the sun came up quickly out of the rye, a great, bare, red ball, and the grey of the field turned yellow, and long shadows lay upon the grass, and the wet flowers flashed out diamonds . . .

I got up and turned my face away from the unbearable, in-different brightness. Myriads of small suns danced before my eyes as I went along the edge of the stream to the seat round the oak in my spring garden, where I sat a little, looking at the morning from there, drinking it in in long breaths, and determining to think of nothing but just be happy. What a smell of freshly mown grass there was, and how the little heaps into which it had been raked the evening before sparkled with dewdrops as the sun caught them. And over there, how hot the poppies were already beginning to look – blazing back boldly in the face of the sun, flashing back fire for fire. I crossed the wet grass to the hammock under the beech on the lawn, and lay in it a while trying to swing in time to the nightingale's tune; and then I walked round the ice-house to see how Goethe's corner looked at such an hour; and then I went down to the fir wood at the bottom of the garden where the light was slanting through green stems; and everywhere there was the same mystery, and emptiness, and wonder. When four o'clock drew near I set off home again, not desiring to meet gardeners and have my little hour of quiet talked about, still less my dressing-gown and slippers; so I picked a bunch of roses and hurried in, and just as I softly bolted the door, dreadfully afraid of being taken for a burglar, I heard the first water-cart of the day creaking round the corner. Fearfully I crept up to my room, and when I awoke at eight o'clock and saw the roses in a glass by my side, I remembered what had happened as though it had been years ago.

Elizabeth von Arnim, 1899

I have always wished for a sun-dial in the middle of my grass walks where they widen into a circle. Even in an unpretending modern garden I do not think a sun-dial is affected – or, at any rate, not very . . .

Mrs C. W. Earle, 1897

'Somewhere, in my childhood'

One of the most exquisite of Mrs. Browning's poems is *The Lost Bower*; it is endeared to me because it expresses so fully a childish bereavement of my own, for I have a lost garden. Somewhere, in my childhood, I saw this beautiful garden, filled with radiant blossoms, rich with fruit and berries, set with beehives, rabbit hutches, and a dovecote, and enclosed about with hedges; and through it ran a purling brook – a thing I ever longed for in my home garden. All one happy summer afternoon I played in it, and gathered from its beds and borders at will – and I have never seen it since. When I was still a child I used to ask to return to it, but no one seemed to understand; and when I was grown I asked where it was, describing it in every detail, and the only answer was that it was a dream, I had never seen and played in such a garden.

Mrs Alice Morse Earle, 1901

Lines from 'The Lost Bower'

> But that bower appeared a marvel
> In the wildness of the place!
> With such seeming art and travail,
> Finely fixed and fitted was
> Leaf to leaf, the dark-green ivy, to the summit from
> the base.
>
> And the ivy, veined and glossy,
> Was enwrought with eglantine;
> And the wild hop fibred closely,
> And the large-leaved columbine,
> Arch of door and window mullion, did right sylvanly
> entwine.
>
> Rose-trees, either side the door, were
> Growing lithe and growing tall;

Each one set a summer warder
For the keeping of the hall, –
With a red rose, and a white rose, leaning, nodding at
    the wall.

As I entered – mosses hushing
Stole all noises from my foot;
And a green elastic cushion,
Clasped within the linden's root,
Took me in a chair of silence, very rare and absolute.

Elizabeth Barrett Browning, 1850

A child's garden of seeds

At the age of five I was allotted some twelve square feet of soil for
a garden. This had been dug and raked to a fine tilth before being
handed over, and no Capability Brown ever experienced a greater
thrill than I in planning a new estate. The family had recently
visited an old property, where a small enclosure took my fancy to
the exclusion of all else, causing me to linger in what I ignorantly
thought had been described as a 'not-garden', although it looked
very much an 'is-garden' to me.

After this, nothing would do for my plot but to copy the novel
pattern on home ground as best I could. Laboriously I scratched
out a circle surrounded by squares and oblongs, making narrow
trenches in place of the original hedges. My elder brother sniffed
critically at the lopsided circle and crooked rectangles, saying the
plan reminded him of our bathroom linoleum. He was being bossy
on account of his thirteenth birthday and a first pair of long
trousers. Brother Ben, his junior by three years, was far kinder.
Bending over my plot, he evened up the circle by means of a trowel
tethered to a central stake, a practical home-made compass.

Next, there were seeds to be bought. In a shop stacked with bins
of chicken-feed and meal, our friend Miss Kirkby kept neat trays
of seed packets with pictures on them of how their contents
were supposed to turn out. I believed implicitly in the truth of this
gorgeousness. Before leaving home I had unlocked my savings box

and withdrawn the entire capital, thirteen copper pennies with the
face of King George the Fifth on them. Knowing that seeds cost
twopence a packet, I was able to work out that six would leave me
with one penny over. A sneaking idea that the nice shopkeeper
might let me have seven for thirteen pence was kept to myself.

Accompanied by Ben I walked, ran and skipped downhill to the
shop, among whose bins and sacks even the small squares of dog
biscuit looked tempting. Ben called me to order, and together
we studied the seed tray. First I picked out eschscholtzia, for I was
proud of knowing how to spell this alarming name, taught by my
gardening grandmother, and I always had enjoyed pulling little
dunce's caps off her plants. She also grew clarkia and godetia, so
I picked them out. Then I must have love-in-a-mist, and the strange
brownish plumes of mignonette for their lovely scent. A packet of
cornflowers swallowed up my shilling, and only one penny
remained for Shirley poppies and nasturtiums. I was close to tears
when Ben pulled a silver threepennybit from the pocket of his
shorts. 'Here you are,' he said. 'Oh, can you *really* spare it?' 'Of
course I can.' So the deal was done.

Joy of possession soon turned to dismay when I wondered how
to divide the supply evenly among the marked spaces without overcrowding the plants or leaving gaps between them. Somehow Ben
grasped the problem, and solved it with ease. Scrounging a roll of
kitchen paper, he spread a sheet on our playroom table and drew
with ruler and compasses a scale plan of my plot. Then he worked
out how best to distribute the contents of eight seed-packets, which
he carefully numbered. His calculations were beyond me, but my
nimble fingers were useful for setting groups of seed into hollows
in a paintbox palette. Next, Ben fashioned a collection of marker
sticks, numbered to match the packets.

After midday dinner we went out to copy Ben's plan on the
ground. It took us all the afternoon, by Ben's watch, but he said
the idea had worked out well, and his marker sticks were 'a good
wheeze'. He knew exactly where the different groups of my chosen
seeds had been sown. Now, of course, there would be many weeks
of waiting before they came into flower. I was quite ready for this,
having helped Granny to sow annuals when I was only four, last
year. Happily I went off to bed and fell asleep to the hooting
of owls under a bright moon. No hint of tomorrow's rude shock
disturbed my dreams.

It was Ben who broke the shattering news, after we had finished breakfast. Some animal, he said, *possibly* Bella our family cat, had used my plot overnight for its own purposes, scratching the grooved pattern all abroad and leaving our carefully sown seeds in a terrible mess which nobody could ever sort out. I was too shocked to go and look at the wreck of my poor garden. Granny, on a visit to us, having breakfasted in her own room, took charge of the situation. 'My dear child,' she said to me, 'don't give it another thought. Those annuals will look even better mixed up together, you'll see.' Something about her quiet face and the lace cap perched upon white hair reminded me of a marble monument in the church. She just had to be listened to and believed. 'Remember that patchwork quilt which you liked so much when you stayed with me? Well, you are going to have a patchwork garden, and I'm sure it will be quite lovely; much prettier and more natural than a stiff old knot-garden.'

As the season advanced and seedlings appeared, I did manage to thin out certain groups and make a few transplants into gaps left by Bella, but no trace of the original design remained. Everything grew well, and by the end of a warm July, with gentle refreshing showers, there was a grand display of blossom. On a Sunday morning I walked round the whole garden hand-in-hand with my father. Stopping at my little plot he exclaimed, 'This is the best show of the lot! It reminds me of a wild flowery meadow beside our rectory when I was a boy.' So I hadn't even made a wild garden, just a piece of meadowland. Because Father evidently preferred it that way, the plot pleased me, too. Looking back down the long tunnel of time, I can see now that my original misspelling wasn't far out, after all.

Dawn MacLeod, 1994

Up into a tree

For small suburban gardens, where it is not possible to achieve water amphitheatres or even terrace-walks, it will yet be possible to gain a different level in the garden by having recourse to another plan. A flight of wooden, rather ladder-like steps can lead up to a gallery surrounding a portion of the trunk of a tree. This, if the tree chances to be large and overshadowing, will give a very delightful retreat, in which the family can do their reading and writing. There is something that recalls the Swiss Family Robinson about it, and this feeling of a spice of adventure is all the more enjoyable.

Viscountess Wolseley, 1919

Sissinghurst – the Sleeping Beauty's castle

It is easy to write an article about somebody else's garden, but it is awkward (in the country phrase) to write about one's own. One hesitates to extol the successes, yet to lay the emphasis on the mistakes and failures would be to assume an apologetic humility which might well irritate the reader into exclaiming 'Then why write the article at all?'

I shall, therefore, take the line that it is possible, within twenty years, to create a reasonably presentable garden, acquiring a matured appearance and losing that look of new-ness which we associate with the narrow orange labels of nurserymen, fluttering from the wrist-slender stems of young trees. I hope that this may be an encouraging theme for those who now stand surveying a new site and wondering how long they must wait before they can accompany their friends without shame along the paths and can look up to, instead of over, the tops of the hedges.

True, the site at Sissinghurst was not a new one: it went back to the reign of Henry VIII. This was an advantage in many ways. It meant that some of the Tudor buildings remained as a background;

. . . it meant that some high Tudor walls of pink brick remained as the anatomy of the garden-to-be, and that two stretches of a much older moat remained to provide a black mirror of quiet water in the distance. It meant also that the soil had been cultivated for at least four hundred years, and it was not a bad soil to start with, being in the main what is geologically called Tunbridge Wells sand; a somewhat misleading name, since it was not sandy, but consisted of a top-spit of decently friable loam with a clay bottom, if we were so unwise as to turn up the sub-soil two spits deep.

These were the advantages, and I would not denigrate them. But in self-justification I must also draw attention to the disadvantages. The major nuisance was the truly appalling mess of rubbish to be cleared away before we could undertake any planting at all. The place had been in the market for several years since the death of the last owner, a farmer, who naturally had not regarded the sur-roundings of the old castle as a garden, but merely as a convenient dump for his rusty iron, or as allotments for his labourers, or as runs for their chickens. The amount of old bedsteads, old plough-shares, old Cabbage stalks, old broken-down earth closets, old matted wire, and mountains of sardine tins, all muddled up in a tangle of Bindweed, Nettles, and Ground-elder, should have sufficed to daunt anybody. Yet the place, when I first saw it on a summer day in 1930, caught instantly at my heart and my imagination. I fell in love; love at first sight. I saw what might be made of it. It was Sleeping Beauty's Castle; but a castle running away into sordidness and squalor; a garden crying out for rescue. It was easy to foresee, even then, what a struggle we should have to redeem it.

It took three years, with the help of one old man and his son, to clear most of the rubbish away. It is perhaps rather tiresome to grumble retrospectively over troubles long since surmounted, so I will just say that within three years we had got the place into some sort of order and could begin to plant hedges of Yew and Hornbeam where we wanted them. We planted the Yews very small, eighteen inches, and they have now grown so high and thick that visitors to the garden assume them to be several centuries old. I look back, now, with amusement, on those tiny Yews when they were first planted in 1933, one by one, separate, a row of little Christmas trees; when, in impatient despair, I could not imagine that ever within my own lifetime they could cohere into a dense thick hedge ten feet above my head. Yet so it is. I cannot see over, and I cannot push through. The Yew hedges have done well. They have been a success, and that without the help of manure, organic or inorganic.

The walls of course were a tremendous asset, and more or less determined the shape the garden would have to take. They conveniently broke up the site into separate enclosures . . . a careful study will reveal certain difficulties which had to be overcome if we wished to create satisfactory vistas and axes. The walls, in short, were not all at right angles to one another; the courtyard was not rectangular but coffin-shaped; the Tower was not opposite the main entrance; the moat walk, with its supporting wall, ran away on so queer a bias that the statue we placed on the bank behind the moat stood opposite both to the Tower and to the seat at the upper end of the moat walk. All this was disconcerting, and there were also minor crookednesses which had somehow to be camouflaged. I do not think that you would notice them from ground level now; though if you ascended the Tower and looked down, you might still give a sympathetic thought to the worried designer, with his immense sheets of ruled paper and his measuring-tapes and his indiarubbers, pushing his fingers through his rumpled hair, trying to get the puzzle to work out.

I could never have done it myself.

Fortunately, I had acquired, through marriage, the ideal collaborator. Harold Nicolson should have been a garden-architect in another life. He has a natural taste for symmetry, and an ingenuity for forcing focal points or long distance views where everything seemed against him, a capacity I totally lacked. After weeks of paper struggle he would come home to discover that I had stuck some tree or shrub bang in the middle of his projected path or gate-way. We did however agree entirely on what was to be the main principle of the garden: a combination of long axial walks, running north and south, east and west, usually with terminal points such as a statue or an archway or a pair of sentinel poplars, and the more intimate surprise of small geometrical gardens opening off them, rather as the rooms of an enormous house would open off the arterial corridors. There should be the strictest formality of design, with the maximum of informality in planting. This is what we aimed at, and is, I hope, what we have achieved.

The place lent itself happily to the informality side of the task. I had the easier job. The rosy walls might not run straight, but they cried out for a tumble of Roses and Honeysuckle, Figs and Vines. It was a romantic place, and, within the austerity of Harold Nicolson's straight lines, must be romantically treated. Very English, very Kentish with its distant prospect over woods and cornfields and hop-gardens and the North Downs, and the pointed oast-houses and the great barn, it yet had something foreign about it: a Norman manor-house perhaps; a faint echo of something slightly more southern, something that belonged to the *Contes de Perrault. La Belle au bois dormant* – I had been right in my first impression. That was why Figs and Vines and Roses looked so right, so inevitable. I planted them recklessly, and have never regretted it. But I think my deepest stab of pleasure came when I discovered that the country people gave the name of Rondel to a circular patch of turf surrounded by one of our Yew hedges. There was all poetry, all romance, in that name; it suggested Provence and the troubadours and the Courts of Love; but I think I liked it even better when I realised that they were using it as a term far more Kentishly familiar to them: the name they normally gave to the round floor for drying hops inside one of our Kentish oasts.

Similarly, they called a plantation of Nuts (Kent cobs and filberts) the *Nut-plat*. We adopted both names. They may sound affected to outsiders, but they are honestly native and natural and indigenous.

Of course, we made many mistakes. They were mostly due to ignorance. I knew very little about gardening in 1930. If only I had been better informed, I should have planted more flowering shrubs and flowering trees, which by now would have grown to their prime. As it was, I planted all the wrong things and planted them in the wrong places, too close together and unsuitably grouped and ignorantly chosen. If only one could go back twenty years and have it all over again!

It was a disappointment to inherit no plants of any value from an earlier century. We might reasonably have expected an ancient Mulberry or two; a Cedar; a Tulip tree; a group of Ilexes; some venerable Yews, possibly with some remains of topiary. There was nothing, except some deteriorating Apple trees in the orchard and the Nuts in the *Nut-plat*, which must have been set out in their five little avenues some seventy or eighty years ago. A few vague Daffodils and Snowdrops appeared in the spring, but that was all.

No, I am being ungrateful: we found a Rose, a *gallica*, running about like a weed; my friend, Mr Graham Thomas, to whom I gave a few roots, put it on the market as *gallica* var. 'Sissinghurst Castle,' but it is now thought to be *gallica* 'Tour des Maures.' This was a pleasant thing to find, but I wish there had been something more.

We started at scratch, or worse than scratch, which I suppose means the heavy handicap of weeds. These had enjoyed themselves so exuberantly during years of abandon in a propitious soil, that the moat wall was invisible and the presence of the *Nut-Plat* unsuspected until we began hacking our way through the jungle of brambles and briars which shrouded it. One of the ideas we had decided on from the first was that the garden with all its separate rooms and sub-sections must be a garden of seasonal features throughout the year; it was large enough to afford the space; we could have a spring garden, March to mid-May; and an early summer garden, May–July; and a late summer garden, July–August; and an autumn garden, September–October. Winter must take care of itself, with a few winter-flowering shrubs and some early bulbs.

I think it may be best if I now describe how we attempted to carry out this scheme.

The *Nut-plat* was the obvious place for the spring garden. Having noticed that the wild Primrose flourished particularly well in the neighbouring woods, I crammed the ground under the Nut trees with coloured Primroses and Polyanthus, on the assumption that where the wild flower will flourish, so also will the cultivated hybrids. This has been a success, not a failure; it really does look like a Persian carpet of many colours for six weeks and more, from early April till the second week in May in the broken light and shade of the Nuts. Harold Nicolson had perceived very quickly that this part of the garden should be devoted to the spring, so he ordained a double row of Limes, to make a pleached lime walk in years to come. We stuck them into what was then a rough piece of meadow, and left them to grow until we could deal with them, and could eventually make a broad paved path between them, and could under-plant them with a mass of low-growing spring-flowering things, sheets of the blue Anemones such as *blanda* and *apennina*, *Omphalodes Luciliae*, interspersed with large pools of Scillas, Chionodoxa, various Muscari, *Iris pumila*, *Tulipa dasystemon* and Erythronium, the Dog Tooth Violet. None of these might be very rare or choice, but in the aggregate they made up the effect we wanted to produce: a spring garden suggesting the foreground of Botticelli's Primavera . . .

The orchard supplemented the spring garden. It became full of bulbs and blossom.

The May–July garden is the Rondel garden, and depends chiefly upon Roses of the old-fashioned kind, of which there is now quite a collection . . . One must resign oneself to their short flowering period, and eke them out with other flowering shrubs in the long border under the wall. This in former days would almost automatically have become a herbaceous border, very garish in July and August, and far more pleasing no doubt to the general public, but to my mind the shrubs available to-day (many of which were of course unknown to our grandparents) are more interesting as well as more saving of labour. We have not, however, adhered rigidly to the exclusion of anything but Roses and shrubs: there are also many Irises, and Paeonies in a shady bed; a big group of *Eremurus robustus* against a background of Yew; Figs and Clematis and Roses on the wall; some Yuccas; and as many Pansies as I can get.

The white-and-grey garden . . . overlaps chronologically: it begins to look well in June, when the little avenue of Almond trees down the centre is draped with the lacy white festoons of *Rosa filipes* and the genuine old 'Garland' Rose, grown from cuttings taken from a very ancient climber at Knole, and when generous plantings of *Lilium regale* come up through the grey Artemisia and silvery *Cineraria maritima*; but it is perhaps at its best a little later on, when the great metallic-looking Onopordons have grown up, and clouds of *Gypsophila* 'Bristol Fairy' throw a veil round the pencils of a white Veronica, and a few belated white Delphiniums and white Eremuri persist. It is essentially a garden to sit in on a warm evening, because it looks so cool and unaffected by the long hot day. This bit of the garden is Sissinghurst's youngest child, a post-war child, and it has not yet been taught to do all that is required of it. Still, it promises well.

This brings us up to the end of August, the month which makes us most ashamed of our garden. By the middle of September it starts to recover itself a little, for a final spurt. There is a bright blue rectangular pool of *Gentiana sino-ornata*, which can give nothing but pleasure. Cyclamen come up everywhere. Some autumn trees begin to colour: *Parrotia persica*, Liquidambar, *Prunus Sargenti*, Cercidiphyllum, Disanthus and a long bank of Azaleas which I forgot to mention as a feature when in flower (and in scent) towards the end of May. The orchard takes on an autumnal beauty, comparable with its spring beauty, as the apples turn red and the leaves of the Cherries hang blood red above mauve chalices of Colchicum.

And then one says to oneself, 'There is nothing to look forward to until the Witch-hazel and the Winter-sweet break into flower and the tiny species Crocuses, and the little Irises, and spring comes again.'

One says also to oneself, 'Have I done the best I could by this responsibility which I took on?'

V. Sackville-West, 1953

Revelation

Our friend announced, 'There's a stile over here. We can climb over from the wood and into the field beyond. It's privately owned land but I know the owners. I don't think they'll mind.'

It was inexplicable, but when I climbed over that stile out of the wood, I knew that something felt very different. I have a memory of tall hedges rising before me, but at that moment I stood beside what I, from pure affection, would call a pond; it had a too essentially rural quality to be described as a lake. The more formal-looking hedges mingled so well with their rural cousins that I was doubtful whether they did indeed belong to some more formal setting, as my inner instinct lead me to believe.

I cannot now recall how I made my way through those formal hedges. A white-painted summer-house stood before a sheet of water which lay like a mirror on that still winter's day. Most vividly I recall something sheltering under the hedge, all encased in grey, which I deduced to be a statue, all wrapped up in its winter coat. Without knowing how, I then found myself transported to an orchard. It was like an orchard *ought* to be, I thought: it had an abundance of apple trees, but mixed with other fruit trees too, and there were signs of other life as well. Shrub roses, their green-, brown- and corky-coloured stems simply set in the grass as though they had chosen for themselves that very spot in which to grow. Some, like gentle fronds, I pictured with pale, delicate and fragile-petalled flowers; others, robustly guarding themselves with huge thorns, looked as though they bore larger, vivid, attention-seeking flowers. Climbing roses were entangled among some of the apple-tree branches, and caught a slight breeze which ruffled such leaves as had over-wintered, while the old apple-tree stood silent and unmoved.

The feeling within me that this orchard was ... special ... different ... increased. It was like hearing a great piece of music for the first time, which stirs those deep inner feelings, awakens one to greater sensitivity, and finally grips one in a total flood of its own power. There was an aura of timelessness, despite the fact that this was a living creation.

My husband and our friends had vanished, and I was far away, totally lost in what I had found, utterly consumed by the atmosphere. Even in the dullness of a dead February day it bore all the signs of love and care: some Prometheus had created this and brought it to life, and it radiated an aura that called forth those who would recognise the call, to taste, and to see.

Emerging from my reverie, I remembered that our friend had said he knew the owners; I rushed to catch the others, to ask. Like Alice in a dream, I ran along a narrow pathway between two tall yew hedges, and the need for me to know became in that moment a need beyond all others. The yew parted – the garden's spirit had carried me to its very heart, and there was no need to ask my burning question: a mellowed red-brick Elizabethan tower rose before me, the bastion of English gardening, to whose steps I had been taken, seemingly out of nowhere. It was Vita's tower at Sissinghurst Castle.

Jane Allsopp, 1994

No cure

When we left Alderley Grange seven years ago I was determined never again to be enslaved by a garden. The loss of a garden you have created and tended for thirteen years is a very traumatic experience. However the sadness was slightly mitigated by the knowledge that the not inconsiderable physical effort which it demanded was at an end. I was certain that I should be perfectly content with a sunless back garden in Bath. How wrong I was. Within a year it all began again. There is no cure for this obsession.

Alvilde Lees-Milne, 1983

My tomorrow garden

. . . If I had a garden. But it just so happens that I don't have a garden any more. There is nothing so terrible about not having a garden any more. The worrying thing would be if the future garden, whose reality is of no importance, were beyond my grasp. But it is not. A certain crackling noise the dry seeds make in their paper packet is enough to sow the very air around me with their flowers. The fennel's seeds are black, shiny like a mass of fleas, and even if you keep them a long time they still give off a smell of apricots when they're warmed, though they don't pass the scent on to their flowers. I shall sow the fennel seeds after the dream, after all my plans and memories, in the shape of what I have possessed and what I now anticipate, have taken root, have taken their places in my tomorrow garden. The hepaticas, I know, will certainly be blue, since I am always irritated these days by the ones that are that winy pink. They will be blue, and there will be enough of them to make an edging all around the basket ('all the baskets must be raised in the middle . . . ') that will display the dielytras hanging down in pennants, the weigelas, and the double deutzias. I shall have no pansies but those – with wide faces, beards, and moustaches – that look like Henry VIII; no saxifrages, unless, on some fine summer evening, when I politely offer them a lighted match, they will reply to my gesture with their little, harmless explosion of gas . . .

An arbor? Naturally I shall have an arbor. I'm not down to my last arbor yet. I must have a trellis for my purple dragon-tongued cobaeas to perch on, and for my cane melons . . . Cane melons? Why not a wickerwork marrow? Because the melon plant I am talking about hauls itself up the canes that are stuck up to support it, then runs between them like a green pea plant, marking every stage of its progress with little green and white melons that are very sweet and full of flavour. (See Mme Millet-Robinet on the subject.)

Then, if all those lovers of horticultural novelties have banished all the old prince's feathers from their gardens, I shall certainly take a few of them in myself, even if it's only so that I can call them by their old name: nun's scourge. They will go well with another feathery plant, silver coloured this time, the pampas grass, a good solid flower, though slightly stupid, which spends the winter to the left and right of the fireplace in trumpet shaped vases.

In summer, we shall turn up our noses at the pampas grass and stuff the vases with those suffocating white lilies, those lilies, more imperious than the orange blossom, more passionate than the tuberose, which climb up the staircase at midnight and come to find us in the very depths of our slumbers.

If it's a Breton garden – how I love this ideal flower bed of mine with its sumptuous border of 'ifs' – then there will be the daphne, that flower, so tiny and so timid, yet so immense too because of its fresh and noble fragrance, piercing and filling the Breton winter with its scent even in January. A bush of daphne in one of the showers that ride in with the tide from the west seems to have been watered with perfumes. If it is beside a lake, this garden of mine, I shall have, besides the load of shrubs that the late Old Gentleman always dragged about with him, some winter Japan allspice instead of the daphnes. The Japan allspice, which flowers in December, is about as bright and colourful as a small chip of cork. Its merit is unique and always reveals its whereabouts. Once, in the country-side outside Limoges where I did not know it was growing, I looked for it, stalked it, and found it, by following the traces of its fragrance through the icy air. Dull and grayish on its twig, but endowed with an immense power of attraction – when I think of the Japan allspice I think also of the nightingale. So I shall have some Japan allspice . . . Don't I have it already?

I shall have many other plants too, rose windows of verbena, pipes of birthwort, powder puffs of thrift, crosses of St Helena's cross, spikes of lupine, night-blooming bindweed, the marvel of Peru, nebulas of bent grass, and clouds of feathered pinks. Beggar's staff to aid the last steps of my journey; asters to fill my nights with stars. Harebells, a thousand harebells to ring at dawn just as the cock starts crowing; a dahlia pleated like a Clouet ruff, a foxglove in case a needy fox should visit me, and a rocket. Not, as you might think, a rocket to send into the sky, but a rocket to edge my flower bed with. Yes, to edge my flower bed with! And for that I need lobelias too, for the blue of the lobelia has no rival either in the sky or in the sea. As for honeysuckle, I shall choose the most delicate, the one that is wan with the burden of its own scent. Finally, I must have a magnolia, a good layer, one that will be covered all over with white eggs when Easter comes; and wistaria that will let its long flowers drip off it one by one till it turns the terrace into a lake of mauve. And some lady's slipper, enough to make shoes for everyone in the house. But no oleanders, if you please. They call the oleander the laurel rose, and I want only laurels and roses.

There is no guarantee that the flowers I have chosen would flatter the eye when assembled. Besides, there are others I can't call to mind at the moment. But there's no hurry. I shall dig them all into their storage trenches, some in my memory, the others in my imagination. There, thanks be to God, they can still find the humus, the slightly bitter water, the warmth and the gratitude which will perhaps keep them from dying.

Colette, 1966

To make a prairie it takes a clover and one bee,
One clover, and a bee,
And revery.
The revery alone will do,
If bees are few.

Emily Dickinson, 1858

Sources

ALLSOPP, Jane
  1994 'English, perennial, rustic, and alone', *Hortus*, No. 30
AMHERST, Alicia, *Hon.* (*afterwards Hon.* Mrs Evelyn Cecil)
  1895 *A History of Gardening in England*. London, Bernard Quaritch
  1902 *Children's Gardens*. London, Macmillan
ARNIM, Elizabeth, *Countess von*
  1898 *Elizabeth and her German Garden*. London, Macmillan (reprint Virago Press, 1985)
  1899 *The Solitary Summer*. London, Macmillan, (reprint Virago Press, 1993)
BOLAND, Maureen and Bridget
  1976 *Old Wives Lore for Gardeners*. London etc., Bodley Head
BOYLE, E. V., *Hon.*
  1889 *Days and Hours in a Garden*. London, Elliott Stock
BROWNING, Elizabeth Barrett
  1850 *Poems*. London, Chapman and Hall (and various later editions)
BUCHAN, Ursula
  1987 *The Pleasures of Gardening*. London, J. M. Dent and Sons
BURNETT, Frances Hodgson
  1911 *The Secret Garden*. London, William Heinemann (various reprints)
BURNEY, Fanny
  1794 *Diary and Letters*. London, Henry Colburn, 1854 (and later editions)
CAMPBELL, Barbara
  1911 *The Garden of a Commuter's Wife*. New York, Macmillan Co.
CANE, Florence du
  1908 *The Flowers and Gardens of Japan*. London, Adam & Charles
CHAMBERLAIN, *Mrs* Edith L. (with *Mrs* Fanny Douglas)
  1892 *The Gentlewoman's Book of Gardening*. London, Henry and Co.
CHATTO, Beth
  1980 'August', *A Gardener's Dozen*. BBC Enterprises
COATS, Alice M.
  1963 *Garden Shrubs and their Histories*. London, Vista Books

COLETTE
  1966 *Earthly Paradise*. London, Secker and Warburg
  1971 *Four Seasons*, trans. David le Vay. London, Peter Owen
COLVIN, Brenda
  1970 *Land and Landscape*. London, John Murray
CRAN, Marion
  1922 *The Garden of Experience*. London, Herbert Jenkins
CROWE, *Dame* Sylvia
  1951 *Garden Design*. London, Country Life (reprint Antique Collectors Club/Garden Art Press 1994)
DICKINSON, Emily
  1858 *Poems*, 3rd series. Boston, Roberts Bros., 1896 *or* Cambridge Mass. Harvard U.P., 1955
DRAPER, Ruth
  1955–6 *The Art of Ruth Draper: her dramas and characters*. With memoir by M. D. Zabec. London, O.U.P., 1960
EARLE, *Mrs* Alice Morse
  1901 *Old-Time Gardens*. New York, Macmillan Co.
EARLE, *Mrs* C. W.
  1897 *Pot-Pourri from a Surrey Garden*. London, Smith Elder and Co.
ELMHIRST, Dorothy
  1968 *Gardening Diary* (quoted by Reginald Snell: *From the Bare Stem*. Devon Books in association with the Dartington Press, 1989)
ELY, *Mrs* Helena Rutherfurd
  1903 *A Woman's Hardy Garden*. New York, Macmillan Co. (reprint Collier Books, 1990)
EWING, *Mrs* Juliana Horatia
  1886 *Mary's Meadow* and *Letters from a Little Garden*. London, SPCK
FARRAND, Beatrix
  1941 *Plant Book*. *Beatrix Farrand's Plant Book for Dumbarton Oaks, Washington*. Dumbarton Oaks Trustees for Harvard University, 1980
FIELD, Xenia
  1965 *Window-Box Gardening*. London, Studio Vista
FIENNES, Celia
  1690 *Through England on a Side Saddle in the Time of William and Mary*, ed. Christopher Morris. London, Cresset Press, 1947
FINNIS, Valerie
  1980 'November', *A Gardener's Dozen*. BBC Enterprises.
FISH, Margery
  1956 *We Made a Garden*. London, W.H.& L. Collingridge
  1958 *An All the Year Garden*. London, W.H.& L. Collingridge

FORTESCUE, Winifred, *Hon. Lady*

    1947 *Perfume from Provence*. London, William Blackwood and Sons (reprint Black Swan, Transworld, 1993)

FULLER, Margaret

    1980 'The Crossing House Garden', Wendy (sic) Fuller, *The Garden*, July 1980

GREER, Germaine

    1992 'News from Stump Cross', *The Oldie*, March 23, 1992

HASSARD, Annie

    1875 *Floral Decorations for the Dwelling House*. London, Macmillan Co.

HAVERGAL, Beatrix

    1939 'Market Gardening for Women' *and*

    1963 Letter to Alan Bloom (both quoted by Ursula Maddy: *Waterperry: a dream fulfilled*. Merlin Books, 1990)

HOBHOUSE, Penelope

    1976 *The Country Gardener*. Oxford, Phaidon

    1981 *The Smaller Garden*. London, Collins

    1985 *Colour in your Garden*. London, Collins

HOLDEN, Jean

    1992 'The Metropolitan Gardener: A Smaller Splash', *Hortus*, No. 21

HOLDEN, Molly

    1968 *To Make Me Grieve*. London, Chatto and Windus

    1975 *The Country Over*. London, Chatto and Windus

HOPE, Frances Jane

    1881 *Notes and Thoughts on Gardens and Woodlands*. London, Macmillan Co.

HOWARD, Elizabeth Jane

    1991 *Green Shades: an anthology of plants, gardens and gardeners*. London, Aurum Press

JACKSON, Marie E.

    1822 *The Florist's Manual*. London, Henry Colburn and Co.

JACKSON, Sheila

    1994 *Blooming Small*. London, Herbert Press

JEKYLL, Gertrude

    1899 *Wood and Garden*. London etc., Longmans, Green and Co. (reprint Antique Collectors Club, 1994)

    1900 *Home and Garden*. London, Longmans, Green and Co. (reprint Antique Collectors Club, 1982)

    1908 *Children and Gardens*. London, *Country Life* (reprint Antique Collectors Club, 1982)

    1911 *Colour Scheme in the Flower Garden*. London, George Newnes Ltd (reprint Antique Collectors Club, 1988)

JELLICOE, Susan (with Marjory Allen)

    1977 *Town Gardens to Live In*. London etc., Penguin Handbooks

JOHNSON, Louisa

    1843 *Every Lady her own Flower Gardener*. London, Wm. S. Orr & Co.

KEEN, Mary

    1987 *The Garden Border Book*. London, Viking/Penguin

    1991 *Colour Your Garden*. London, Conran Octopus

KENT, Elizabeth

    1831 *Flora Domestica*. London, Whittaker, Treacher & Co.

KING, *Mrs* Francis

    1915 *The Well-Considered Garden*. New York, Charles Scribner's Sons

    1927 *The Beginner's Garden*. New York, Charles Scribner's Sons

LARKCOM, Joy

    1987 'The Petit Potager', *The Garden*, January, February 1987

LEES-MILNE, Alvilde

    1983 'Essex House', *The Garden*, January 1983

LEIGHTON, Clare

    1935 *Four Hedges*. London, Victor Gollancz (reprint Sumach Press, 1991)

LE LIÈVRE Audrey

    1981 'The Adventurous Gardener in London', *The Garden*, October 1981

LINDSAY, Norah

    1931 'The Manor House – Sutton Courtenay', *Country Life*, May 16, 1931

LOUDON, *Mrs* Jane

    1841 *Practical Instructions in Gardening for Ladies*. London, John Murray

LUXBOROUGH, *Lady*

    1775 *Letters Written by the Late Rt. Hon. Lady Luxborough to William Shenstone*. London, J. Dodsley

LYCETT GREEN, Candida

    1987 'Mrs Rupert Lycett Green's Garden', *The New Englishwoman's Garden*, ed. Alvilde Lees-Milne and Rosemary Verey. London, Chatto and Windus

MacLEOD, Dawn

    1994 'An Essayist in the Garden: Looking Back', *Hortus*, No. 29

McQUEEN, Sheila

    1977 *Flower Arranging from your Garden*. London, Ward Lock

MALLIN, Hester

    1980 'A high-rise oasis', *The Garden*, February 1980

MARGARET, Crown Princess of Sweden
1919 'In Our Flower Garden', *The Girls Own Paper & Woman's Magazine*, 1921

MARTINEAU, A. M., *Lady*
1923 *The Herbaceous Garden*. London, Williams and Norgate
1924 *Gardening in Sunny Lands*. London, Richard Cobden-Sanderson

MERRITT, Anna Lea
1908 *An Artist's Garden*. London, George Allen & Sons

MEW, Charlotte
1929 *The Rambling Sailor*. London, The Poetry Bookshop

MITFORD, Mary Russell
1832 *Our Village*. London, Whittaker, Treacher & Co. (reprinted O.U.P., 1982)
1854 *Mary Russell Mitford Correspondence with Charles Boner and John Ruskin*, ed. Elizabeth Lee. London, T. Fisher Unwin, 1914

MORRELL, Ottoline, *Lady*
1918 *Ottoline at Garsington*, ed. R. Gathorne-Hardy. London, Faber and Faber, 1974

MURE, Cecily
1968 'Adaptation to environment – the making of a small town garden', *R.H.S. Journal*, March 1968

MURRAY, Kathleen
1913 *My Garden in the Wilderness*. Calcutta & Simla, Thacker Spink & Co.

NORTH, Marianne
1892 *Recollections of a Happy Life*. London, Macmillan Co. (another edition, ed. Susan Morgan, University Press of Virginia, 1993)

OSLER, Mirabel
1986 'A Garden for Travellers', *The Garden*, June 1986

PAVORD, Anna
1992 *Gardening Companion*. London, Chatto and Windus

PAYNE, Joan
1987 'The Hon. Mrs Michael Payne's Garden', *The New Englishwoman's Garden*, ed. Alvilde Lees-Milne and Rosemary Verey. London, Chatto and Windus

PERÉNYI, Eleanor
1981 *Green Thoughts*. London, Allen Lane (reprint Pimlico, 1994)

PERRY, Frances
1953 'Hardy Flowers for Cutting', *R.H.S. Journal*, October, 1953

PHILLIPS, Sue
1990 'Edible Oddities', *The Garden*, February 1990

PITTER, Ruth
 1966 *Collected Poems.* London, Enitharmon Press, 1990
PLATH, Sylvia
 1962 *Letters Home.* London, Faber and Faber, 1975
PRATT, Anne
 1889 *The Flowering Plants, Grasses, Sedges and Ferns of Great Britain.* London, Frederick Warne and Co.
ROHDE, Eleanour Sinclair
 1938 *Vegetable Cultivation and Cookery.* London, The Garden Book Club
ROTHSCHILD, Miriam (with Clive Farrell)
 1983 *The Butterfly Gardener.* London, Michael Joseph
SACKVILLE-WEST, Vita, *Hon.*
 1953 'The Garden at Sissinghurst Castle', *R.H.S. Journal*, November 1953
 1958 *Even More for Your Garden.* London, Michael Joseph
SCHWERDT, Pamela and Sibylle Kreutzberger
 1978 'Behind the scenes at Sissinghurst', *The Garden*, October 1978
SCOTT-JAMES, Anne
 1971 *Down to Earth.* London, Michael Joseph
 1990 *Gardening Letters to my Daughter.* London, Michael Joseph
SCOVELL, E. J.
 1991 *Selected Poems.* Manchester, Carcanet Press
SETON, Frances Eveleen, *Lady*
 1927 *My Town Garden.* London, Nisbet & Co.
SMITH, Stevie
 1975 *The Collected Poems of Stevie Smith.* London, Allen Lane (reprint Penguin, 1989)
SPRY, Constance
 1953 *A Constance Spry Anthology.* London, J. M. Dent & Sons
STEEN, Nancy
 1966 *The Charm of Old Roses.* London, Herbert Jenkins
STEVENSON, Violet
 1969 'Flower Arrangements from the Garden', *R.H.S Journal*, June 1969
STUART, Muriel
 1936 *Fool's Garden.* London, Jonathan Cape
TARLING, Thomasina
 1988 'The enclosed garden', *The Garden*, March 1988
TAYLOR, Jane
 1989 'Plants that smell of other things', *Hortus*, No. 11
TOKLAS, Alice B.
 1984 *The Alice B. Toklas Cook Book.* London, Michael Joseph

UNDERWOOD, *Mrs* Desmond (Pamela)

1975 'Silver Leaves Among the Green', *The Garden*, July 1975

VEREY, Rosemary

1980 'Barnsley House', *The Englishwoman's Garden*, ed. Alvilde Lees-Milne and Rosemary Verey. London, Chatto and Windus

1981 *The Scented Garden*. London, Michael Joseph

WALLING, Edna

1948 *A Gardener's Log*. Melbourne, Geoffrey Cumberlege and O.U.P.

WHARTON, Edith

1904 *Italian Villas and their Gardens*. London etc., John Lane and Bodley Head (reprint Da Capo Press, 1976)

WHITE, Katharine S.

1958 *Onward and Upward in the Garden*. New York, Farrar Straus & Giroux (reprint 1980)

WILDER, Louise Beebe

1924 *Adventures in my Garden and Rock Garden*. New York, Doubleday, Page & Co. (reprint Dover Publications, 1976)

WILLIAMS, *Mrs* Leslie

1901 *A Garden in the Suburbs*. London, John Lane and Bodley Head

WILLMOTT, Ellen

1910 *The Genus Rosa*. London, John Murray

WOLSELEY, Frances, *Viscountess*

1919 *Gardens, Their Form and Design*. London, Edward Arnold

WORDSWORTH, Dorothy

1802 *The Grasmere Journal*, ed. Helen Darbishire, O.U.P., 1958 (reprint ed. P. Woof, O.U.P., 1993)

Acknowledgements

My greatest thanks are due to Dr Brent Elliott and his assistants, Gillian Goudge and Jennifer Vine, at the Royal Horticultural Society's incomparable Lindley Library. Every book and periodical I asked for was rapidly produced, as well as several that I did not know I wanted until they showed them to me. Grateful thanks, too, to Ian Hodgson, editor of the Royal Horticultural Society's Journal, *The Garden*, and to David Wheeler, editor of *Hortus*, for kindly allowing me to reproduce articles from their periodicals. I have a particular debt of gratitude to all those authors who responded so generously to my requests to reprint extracts from their work.

Permission to quote copyright material is gratefully acknowledged to the following: Aitken, Stone and Wylie for the extract from 'News from Stump Cross' by Germaine Greer; Aurum Press for the extract from *Green Shades*, © Elizabeth Jane Howard 1991; BBC Enterprises Ltd. for extracts reproduced from 'August' by Beth Chatto and 'November' by Valerie Finnis from the book *A Gardener's Dozen*; the authors' estate for the extract from *Old Wives Lore for Gardeners* by Maureen and Bridget Boland; Lesley Ann Boyd-Carpenter for extracts from *We Made a Garden* and *An All the Year Garden* by Margery Fish; Ursula Buchan for the extract from her *The Pleasures of Gardening*; Carcanet Press Ltd. for 'Deaths of Flowers' from *Selected Poems* by E.J. Scovell, 1991; Cassell plc for the extract from *Complete Flower Arranging* by Sheila McQueen; Chatto & Windus for extracts from *Gardening Companion* by Anna Pavord; Conran Octopus and the author for extracts from *Colour Your Garden*, © Mary Keen; Curtis Brown for extracts from *Even More for Your Garden*, by Vita Sackville-West, © 1958 Vita Sackville-West, reproduced by permission of Curtis Brown, London on behalf of the author's estate; the Dartington Hall Trust for extracts from Dorothy Elmhirst's Garden Notebooks as quoted in *From the Bare Stem* by Reginald Snell; Doubleday, a division of Bantam Doubleday Dell Publishing Group, Inc., for the extract from *The Art of Ruth Draper* by Morton Dauwen Zabec, © Doubleday 1960; Faber and Faber Ltd. and HarperCollins Publishers, Inc. for the excerpt from *Letters Home by Sylvia Plath, Correspondence 1950–1963* ed. Aurelia Schober Plath, © 1975 Aurelia Schober Plath; the Trustees for Harvard University, Dumbarton Oaks, for the extract from *Beatrix Farrand's Plant Book for Dumbarton Oaks*, ed. D.K.McGuire; Farrar, Straus & Giroux, Inc. for the excerpt from 'More about the Arrangers' from *Onward and Upward in the Garden* by Katherine S. White, © 1979 by E.B.White as executor of the estate of Katherine S. White; Margaret Fuller for exerpts from 'The Crossing House Garden', *The Garden*, 1980; Adrian M. Goodman, executor of the estate of the late Mrs Julian Vinogradoff, for the extract from *Ottoline at Garsington* by Robert Gathorne-Hardy; the Herbert Press Limited for extracts from *Blooming Small* by Sheila Jackson; David Higham Associates for the extract 'Circles of Soil' from *Down to Earth* by Anne Scott-James; Penelope Hobhouse for extracts from *Colour in Your Garden* and *The Smaller Garden*; Alan Holden for 'Giant Decorative Dahlia' from *To Make Me Grieve*, and 'Clover' and 'Rose of Sharon' from *The Country Over* by Molly Holden, © Alan Holden; Michael Joseph and HarperCollins Publishers Inc. for the exerpt from *The Alice B. Toklas Cook Book* by Alice B. Toklas, © 1954 Alice B. Toklas, copyright renewed 1982 Edward M. Burns; Michael Joseph for the extracts from *The Butterfly Gardener* by Miriam Rothschild and Clive Farrell, © Lane Charitable Trust for Conservation, 1983; Michael Joseph for the extract from *Gardening Letters to my Daughter* by Anne Scott-James, © Anne Scott-James, 1990; Mary Keen for an extract from *The Garden Border Book*, © Mary Keen; The Landscape Institute for the extract from *Land and Landscape* by Brenda Colvin, © The Landscape Institute; Joy Larkcom for extracts from 'The Petit Potager', *The Garden*, 1987; James Lees-Milne for the extract from 'Essex House' by Alvilde Lees-Milne in *The Garden*, 1983; Audrey le Lièvre for the extract from 'The Adventurous Gardener in London', *The Garden*, 1981; Candida Lycett Green for the quotation from her essay in *The Englishwoman's Garden*; James MacGibbon for permission to reprint 'I love . . . ' from *The Collected Poems of Stevie Smith* (Penguin 20th Century Classics), © James MacGibbon 1971; Hester Mallin for the extract from 'A high-rise oasis', *The Garden*, 1980; Marshall Editions for the extract from *The Scented Garden* by Rosemary Verey, © 1981 Rosemary Verey; The Medici Society Limited, London, for the extract from *Vegetable Cultivation and Cookery* by Eleanour Sinclair Rohde; the Orion Publishing Group Ltd for the extract from *A Constance Spry Anthology*, published by J.M. Dent and Sons; Mirabel Osler for 'A Garden for Travellers', *The Garden*, 1986; Peter Owen Publishers, London, for the extract from *Four Seasons* by Colette; Packard Publishing Ltd. for the extract from *Garden Design* by Sylvia Crowe; Joan Payne for the extract from her essay in *The Englishwoman's Garden*; Penguin Books Ltd. for extracts from *Town Gardens to Live In* by Susan Jellicoe and Marjory Allen; Penguin Books Ltd. and Random House, New York, for extracts from *Green Thoughts* by Eleanor Perényi, © 1981 Eleanor Perényi; Phaidon Press Ltd. for the extract reprinted from *The Country Gardener* by Penelope Hobhouse, © 1976 Phaidon Press Ltd.; Sue Phillips for the extract from 'Edible Oddities', *The Garden*, 1990; Random House, UK Ltd. on behalf of the author's estate for extracts from *Four Hedges* by Clare Leighton; Reed Consumer Books for the extract from *Earthly Paradise* by Colette, published by Martin Secker and Warburg Ltd.; Pamela Schwerdt for the extract from 'Behind the scenes at Sissinghurst' by Pamela Schwerdt and Sibylle Kreutzberger, *The Garden*, 1978; Simon & Schuster for the extract from *Garden Shrubs and their Histories* by Alice M. Coats; Scribner, an imprint of Simon and Schuster, Inc. for the extract from *The Beginner's Garden* by Mrs Francis King, © 1927 Charles Scribner's Sons, and *The Well-Considered Garden* by Mrs Francis King, © 1915 Charles Scribner's Sons; the Society of Authors for the extract from *Perfume from Provence* by Lady Fortescue, © 1935 Lady Fortescue; the author's estate for the extracts from *Fool's Garden* by Muriel Stuart; Thomasina Tarling for the quotation from 'The enclosed garden', *The Garden*, 1988; Rosemary Verey for the extract from her essay in *The Englishwoman's Garden*.

Every effort has been made to trace copyright holders in all the copyright material in this book. The editor regrets any oversight and suggests that the publisher be contacted in any such event.

Biographical Notes

JANE ALLSOPP was a student at Pershore College of Horticulture and is now an inspector for *The Good Gardens Guide*. She lives in Ludlow and has written about Housman and Shropshire in *The Land of Lost Content* (1995).

ALICIA AMHERST *Hon.* (1865–1941) was born in Norfolk and published her admired *History of Gardening in England* when she was barely thirty. Thereafter she married Evelyn Cecil (later Lord Rockley), travelled widely with him, helped to rescue the Chelsea Physic Garden from extinction, wrote five more gardening books, (including one on children's gardens), and contributed articles to periodicals.

ELIZABETH VON ARNIM *Countess* (1866–1941) was born in New Zealand, studied the piano at the Royal College of Music, London, and married Count von Arnim when she was twenty-four. She wrote her best-selling books about the gardens of his estate at Nassenheide in her early thirties. She later wrote a series of novels of which one, *Vera*, described her unhappy second marriage to Lord Russell.

MAUREEN and BRIDGET BOLAND, two sisters with a shared love of gardening, first had a London backyard, then a garden in Hampshire. Before retirement, Maureen worked in various London bookshops, Bridget was a playwright, screenwriter and novelist.

E.V. BOYLE *Hon.* (1825–1916), writer and illustrator, was the wife of a parish rector who was the younger son of the Earl of Cork. She re-created the garden at Huntercome Manor, Bucks., introducing many old-fashioned flowers, and first described the result in the *Gardener's Chronicle*. Later her articles were gathered together and published as *Days and Hours in a Garden* which was reprinted seven times. She went on to write three other books about gardens.

ELIZABETH BARRETT BROWNING (1806–1861) spent her childhood at Hope End in Herefordshire and the last fifteen years of her life in Florence; the usual image of her as an invalid in Wimpole Street is misleading. Her garden poem *The Lost Bower* recounts a quest for the primal garden of Eden.

URSULA BUCHAN turned to gardening (temporarily as she thought) after gaining a modern history degree at Cambridge. She trained at Wisley and at Kew, and has now become a full-time garden journalist and author. She has published seven books to date and is the gardening columnist for the *Sunday Telegraph* and the *Spectator*.

FRANCES HODGSON BURNETT (1849–1924) was a prolific author of adult and children's fiction. She made her name with *Little Lord Fauntleroy* (1886), but *The Secret Garden* is her classic work.

FANNY BURNEY (1752–1840) was a fine letter-writer as well as novelist. She reported to her father, with amusement, the struggles of her aristocratic French husband (General d'Arblay) in their garden.

BARBARA CAMPBELL (1859–1934) was the pseudonym of Mabel Osgood Wright, whose country home, 'Waldstein', near Fairfield, Connecticut, was the subject of her semi-autobiographical works, in which the other characters are her father, her English husband, her neighbours and her staff. After *The Garden of a Commuter's Wife* she wrote *The Garden, You and I* (1906) in letter form.

FLORENCE DU CANE and her sister, Ella, were Edwardian travellers who left London for Japan, Madeira and the Canary Islands. Between 1908 and 1911 they produced handsome books on the places they visited, Florence writing the text and Ella providing the illustrations.

MRS EDITH L. CHAMBERLAIN's volume on gardening for gentle-women was part of a series called *The Victorian Library for Gentlewomen* under the patronage of Queen Victoria. It took its place among volumes on hygiene, sports and embroidery.

BETH CHATTO (1923–) trained as a teacher before marrying Andrew Chatto, a fruit farmer who studied the natural associations of plants. Inspired by him, and by the painter and plantsman Cedric Morris, she began her now celebrated garden round White Barn House at Elmstead Market in 1960, and soon afterwards opened her nursery for unusual plants. She had no formal horticultural education, but hers became one of the most renowned nurseries in Britain and beyond, and her displays at the Chelsea Flower Show have won her gold medals. She has written standard works on dry and damp gardens and was awarded the Victoria Medal of Honour in 1988.

ALICE M. COATS (1905–1978) was a leading plant historian who started life as an artist specialising in lino-prints and trained at the Slade School. Crippling arthritis obliged her to change direction, and she wrote her two standard works on the histories of garden shrubs and garden flowers.

COLETTE (1873–1954), one of the foremost French authors of her day, grew up in her mother Sido's garden in Burgundy. Throughout the rest of her life, in Paris and elsewhere, the passionate love of flowers she inherited from Sido remained.

BRENDA COLVIN (1897–1981) grew up in India and studied horticulture at Swanley College. Under the influence of Madeline Agar she quickly discovered that landscape architecture was her real interest. By 1922 she had founded her own practice and was becoming noted in particular for her skilled compositions using architectural plants. From its inception onwards she was closely identified with the Institute of Landscape Architects, becoming its President in 1951. She was awarded a C.B.E. in 1973, and privately published a collection of poems in 1977.

MARION CRAN (1879–1942) was born in South Africa, trained as a nurse in Dublin, and raised her family in a cottage in Surrey woodland. With her third husband she bought a fourteenth-century house in Kent and made her own garden there. She was Vice-President of the National Gardens Guild, travelled extensively, was a pioneer broadcaster, and wrote poetry, journalism, and at least twelve garden books.

SYLVIA CROWE Dame (1901–) graduated from Swanley College into a garden job with Cutbush of Barnet. She soon became a garden designer and thereafter worked with Sir Geoffrey Jellicoe on Mablethorpe in Lincolnshire, and with Sir Frederick Gibberd on Harlow New Town, as well as becoming the first consultant to the Forestry Commission. She also designed gardens for Oxford Colleges, was president of the Institute of Landscape Architects, and was made a Dame Commander of the British Empire in 1973.

EMILY DICKINSON (1830–1886) was born in Amherst, Massachusetts, and spent most of her adult life as a semi-recluse, refusing to leave her home. Only seven of her 2000 short and oddly-punctuated poems were published during her lifetime.

RUTH DRAPER (1884–1956) was an American diseuse, famous throughout the English-speaking world for the ironic dramatic monologues she wrote and performed.

MRS ALICE MORSE EARLE (1853–1911) was a historian of colonial America. She produced a wide-ranging series of books in which gardening took its place amongst a variety of subjects such as costume, home life, punishments, child life, stage-coaches and taverns.

MRS C.W. EARLE (Theresa) (1836–1925) see Introduction.

DOROTHY ELMHIRST (1887–1968) was born in Washington D.C. of a prestigious and very wealthy family. When she married her second husband, Leonard Elmhirst, she was able to subsidise his dream of an experimental co-educational school at Dartington, and later to finance the making of a thirty-eight acre garden round the medieval hall, first employing Beatrix Farrand and, after the war, Percy Cane. From 1940 onwards she became increasingly absorbed by the garden and kept a gardening diary for the last twenty-five years of her life.

MRS HELENA RUTHERFORD ELY (–1920) was an influential American garden writer at the turn of the century, who wrote her first book after her children had grown up. She was a founding member of the Garden Club of America.

MRS JULIANA HORATIA EWING (1841–1885) wrote much-loved children's books, often in serial form in *Aunt Judy's Magazine* which her mother had founded. She was an admirer of Parkinson and was ahead of her time in founding a Parkinson Society (1884), whose aim was 'to search out and cultivate old garden flowers'.

BEATRIX FARRAND (1872–1959) was a niece of Edith Wharton. She had no formal education but studied painting in Paris as a young girl, before setting up as a landscape gardener in New York. Ultimately she became one of the most celebrated of American garden designers, some of her finest work being done at the universities of Princeton, Yale, and Harvard's Dumbarton Oaks.

XENIA FIELD (1894–) was a labour politician (Junior Whip on the London County Council), a playwright, short-story writer and Justice of the Peace, as well as a gardener and rosarian. Her book on window-boxes inspired some florists to start window-box businesses, and led to her new career as gardening editor of the *Daily Mirror*.

CELIA FIENNES (1662–1741) rode on horseback through every county of England between 1685 and 1703, and her journal of this time provided a comprehensive, if idiosyncratic, survey of the whole country.

VALERIE FINNIS is a distinguished gardener and photographer. For almost thirty years she worked at Waterperry Horticultural School where she became famous for her flair as a plantswoman and her specialised knowledge of alpines. In 1970 she married Sir David Scott and worked with him in the garden of the Dower House at Boughton House. She was awarded the Victoria Medal of Honour in 1976, and set up the Merlin Trust, in memory of Sir David's only son, to help young gardeners.

MARGERY FISH (1892–1969) was a journalist on the *Daily Mail* who took up gardening in late-middle age when she and her husband, a former *Daily Mail* editor, bought East Lambrook Manor in Somerset. Inspired by her neighbour, Mrs Clive of Brympton d'Evercy, she began to collect forgotten cottage garden plants and later popularised them in her writings and lectures.

LADY FORTESCUE (Winifred) *Hon.* (1888–1951) made her name with *Perfume from Provence* and wrote five more books in rapid succession from her adopted home, Alpes Maritimes. Earlier in her career she had been an actress, then had lived at Windsor Castle where her husband was librarian and archivist.

MARGARET FULLER (1936–) has been a passionate gardener since early childhood. She married at sixteen and has raised three sons, but otherwise her life has been filled with creating the Crossing House Garden at Shepreth, and briefly helping in the garden of her botanist/gardener friends and neighbours, Faith Raven and her late husband John.

GERMAINE GREER (1939–) was educated at the universities of Melbourne, Sydney and Cambridge and is now special lecturer and unofficial fellow at Newnham College. She is a noted and provocative writer, essayist, feminist and journalist as well as teacher. She has made two gardens, one in Italy, the other at Stump Cross, Cambridgeshire.

ANNIE HASSARD was a dedicated professional flower arranger of the nineteenth century. She won many prizes in the table-decoration competitions which were a regular feature of Victorian flower shows.

BEATRIX HAVERGAL (1901–1980) founded the Waterperry Horticultural School which turns out highly-skilled women gardeners. She was an outstanding lecturer with huge enthusiasm and drive, but did not like writing, believing that theory must be combined with practical work. She sought to balance the school's books with the help of a stall in Oxford's covered market, and was renowned for mounting Waterperry's gold-medal exhibits of Royal Sovereign strawberries at Chelsea Shows. She was awarded the Victoria Medal of Honour in 1966.

PENELOPE HOBHOUSE (1929–) distinguished garden writer, historian and consultant, restored the nine-acre garden at Hadspen House in Somerset before taking charge of the National Trust Garden at Tintinhall House, where she and her second husband lived and worked for many years. She has a BA in Economics from Cambridge, is a council member of the Garden History Society and travels worldwide, lecturing and designing. She is now making her own garden in Dorset.

JEAN HOLDEN's interest in gardening started when she began to bring up a family, hoping that her two urban children might get close to nature in her allotment. Her writing includes horticulture, humour and poetry, and in 1991 she won the Badoit/Guild of Food Writers Award.

MOLLY HOLDEN (1927–1981) published three books of poetry in her lifetime. She was confined to a wheelchair with multiple sclerosis at the age of thirty-seven, but she went on describing the views through her windows till she could no longer hold a pen. She lived with her husband and two children in a house on the outskirts of Bromsgrove, Worcestershire.

FRANCES JANE HOPE (?–1880) gardened at Wardie Lodge, Edinburgh, and under her care the large garden there became celebrated – particularly for hellebores and for the inclusion of decorative vegetables in the flower garden. She was an early and authoritative contributor to gardening periodicals.

ELIZABETH JANE HOWARD (1923–) the well-known novelist, has also written plays, reviews, a film script, and garden columns, and has made her own gardens in London and the country.

MARIE E. JACKSON (Maria Jacson) (1755–1829) was a well-connected pre-Victorian writer whose title pages read 'by a Lady'. Her first subject was botany: she wrote *Botanical Dialogues Designed for the Use of Schools* in 1797, and *Botanical Lectures* in 1804; but her lifelong enthusiasm for plants and gardens finally gave her confidence to write her *Florist's Manual*, complete with diagrams, in 1822.

SHEILA JACKSON is an authority on costume design as well as a book illustrator. She took up gardening seriously thirty years ago when she acquired a very small London garden beside a railway line.

GERTRUDE JEKYLL (1843–1932) *see* Introduction.

SUSAN JELLICOE (1903–86) designed the planting in all her husband's (Sir Geoffrey Jellicoe's) work, from Hemel Hempstead Water Gardens in 1954, to Sutton Place in 1980. She also wrote with him *The Landscape of Man* (1975). She had no formal training and claimed that Brenda Colvin taught her all she knew.

LOUISA JOHNSON, writer and painter, published her little pocket book, *Every Lady Her Own Flower Gardener*, in 1843. It went into nine editions in ten years. Aimed at 'the economical and industrious only', it sought to help those who liked flowers but could not take 'more than common pains' to grow them. It was followed by *Every Lady's Guide to her own Greenhouse* in 1851.

MARY KEEN *Lady*, made a beautiful garden round her family's Queen Anne house in Berkshire, and subsequently became a designer and consultant (responsible for the newly planted gardens at Glyndeborne) as well as a member of the National Trust Gardens advisory panel, a well-known journalist and author of several garden books. With her four children now grown up, she is making a new garden near Cirencester.

ELIZABETH KENT (?–1861) was the blue-stocking sister-in-law of Leigh Hunt, who helped her to choose quotations for her first book, *Flora Domestica*. She alternately minded the Hunts' babies and helped entertain literary visitors to the household. She was a friend of Shelley, and encouraged John Clare to write poetry. Her botanical knowledge was admired by J. C. Loudon.

MRS FRANCIS KING (Louisa Yeomans) (1863–1948) grew up in New Jersey and was a devote admirer of Gertrude Jekyll who corresponded with her and supplied an introduction to her first book. She became a widely-read gardening writer and helped to found the Garden Club of America.

JOY LARKCOM graduated BSc in horticulture, London, in 1957, and after working as a teacher and a journalist, embarked on a year-long 'Grand Vegetable Tour' round Europe with her family in a caravan. Subsequent travels in China, Japan, Taiwan and the USA have made her a leading authority on rare vegetables. She has been awarded the RHS Veitch Memorial Medal, and Gardening Writer of the Year Award, 1992.

ALVILDE LEES-MILNE (1909–1994) was a friend of Vita Sackville-West and learnt much from her at Sissinghurst during the 1950s. In the sixties she and her husband, James Lees-Milne, bought Alderley Grange in Gloucestershire where she created a garden out of a wilderness. She again recreated a garden when the Lees-Milnes moved to Essex House, Badminton, in 1975, and advised on various gardens in France.

CLARE LEIGHTON (1901–1989) was a vigorous and striking wood engraver who studied at the Slade and exhibited at the Royal Academy and abroad. She illustrated many classics as well as her own four books. She gardened on a slope of the Chilterns, emigrated to America in 1939, became an American citizen in 1946, and lectured at Duke University.

AUDREY LE LIÈVRE *Dr*, comes from a Guernsey family and spends as much time there as she can. Her work includes biography, plant histories and travel writings. She is the author of *Miss Willmott of Warley Place* (1980).

NORAH LINDSAY (1866–1948) was one of the first 'amateur-professional' garden designers, moving in high society and showing the influence of Gertrude Jekyll in her plantings. Her daughter, Nancy, became a noted plantswoman.

MRS JANE LOUDON (1807–1858) acted as amanuensis and travelling companion to her husband, John Claudius Loudon, and began to write popular botanical books to pay off the debts incurred by his *Arboretum*. She soon proved that there was a female audience for gardening books, and her *Instructions in Gardening for Ladies* (1840) became a best-seller. With prodigious professionalism and energy she wrote or edited a score of books.

LADY LUXBOROUGH (Henrietta) (1699–1756) was banished to her husband's derelict estate at Barrells, Warwickshire, as a punishment for supposed infidelity. There, at the age of almost fifty, she energetically embarked on creating a 'landskip' garden complete with pavilion, aviary and ha-ha, having as her friendly consultant William Shenstone, famous for his romantic garden-making at The Leasowes.

CANDIDA LYCETT GREEN (1942–) has raised five children, made gardens and written about them, worked on television documentaries and, in 1994, edited the first volume of her father John Betjeman's letters.

DAWN MACLEOD worked with Mairi Sawyer in the great Highland gardens of Inverewe after World War Two, and is a garden writer and regular contributor to *Hortus*. Her *Down To Earth Women* was published in 1982.

SHEILA MCQUEEN was for many years chief demonstrator and decorator for the Constance Spry organisation. She lectured worldwide, arranged the flowers at Royal weddings, and was awarded the Victoria Medal of Honour.

HESTER MALLIN has lived in the East End of London all her life. An authority on inner-city gardening, she has lectured in the Middle East and on board ocean-going liners. She began the highrise garden she describes in 1974, but in 1980 she moved it all to the twenty-second floor of another tower block in Bow.

MARGARET, CROWN PRINCESS OF SWEDEN (1882–1920), born Princess Margaret of Connaught, grand-daughter of Queen Victoria, became much respected in her adopted country as an authority on the welfare of women and children. She originally wrote her gardening articles in Swedish, believing that the Swedes were behind the English in gardening expertise, and her two gardening books were illustrated with her own water-colours.

ALICE M. MARTINEAU *Lady* (1866–1956) designed a garden in Athens for the King and Queen of the Hellenes in 1921, and advised Queen Marie of Rumania on the royal gardens of Bucharest. She wrote a book of advice on Riviera gardens, with a foreword by Edith Wharton, travelled widely in America and championed the use of Californian plants.

ANNA LEA MERRITT (1844–1930) was a largely self-taught artist whose most famous painting, *Love Locked Out*, was purchased by the Chantrey Bequest. Born in Philadelphia she married the art critic Henry Merritt and lived for some years at Andover in Hampshire.

CHARLOTTE MEW (1869–1928) spent most of her life in Bloomsbury. She was reserved and underrated, and only published one volume of poetry during her lifetime. Her second volume, *The Rambling Sailor*, appeared postumously.

MARY RUSSELL MITFORD (1787–1855) wrote partly to earn money to support her spendthrift father. The famous series of sketches called *Our Village* was based on Three Mile Cross, near Reading, where she and Dr Mitford lived for thirty years.

OTTOLINE MORRELL *Lady* (1873–1938), hostess and patron of the arts, entertained the literary elite of her day at Garsington Manor, which she and her husband, Philip Morrell, bought in 1915 and where, for twelve years, she created an inspired Italianate garden.

CECILY MURE worked a transformation on her tiny Kensington garden through the originality and intensity of her planting. She was a skilled embroideress who was well into her fifties when she began to experiment with plants.

KATHLEEN MURRAY loved the Scottish Highlands as a child, but spent most of her married life in India. She wrote about her two gardens in Behar, and later published *Beloved Marian: The Social History of Mr and Mrs Warren Hastings* (1938).

MARIANNE NORTH (1830–1890) travelled the world, first with her father and later by herself, and made over 800 paintings of plants, now housed in the North Gallery of the Royal Botanic Gardens, Kew. She wrote two volumes of autobiography about her 'happy life'.

MIRABEL OSLER is a writer with an individual voice. She championed 'chaos' in her first book, describing the exuberant country garden she and her husband made in Shropshire. Now in her small town garden in Ludlow, she is experimenting with formality, inspired by the gallic tradition she encountered when researching her book *The Secret Gardens of France*.

ANNA PAVORD was once a television director but is now the well-known gardening correspondent of the *Independent*, where she has worked since the paper's launch in 1986. She has published several successful books and presented garden programmes on Channel Four television.

JOAN PAYNE *Hon.* is a dedicated gardener who has been improving the garden round her Berkshire house for twenty years, using her husband's structural ideas in her own rich plantings.

ELEANOR PERÉNYI was born in Washington D.C. When she married Baron Zsigmond Perényi she moved to his estate in Hungary. Subsequently she bought a New England house with less than an acre of land and has gardened there for over forty years. She has worked as a journalist on various magazines, and written a book on Liszt.

FRANCES PERRY (1907–1993) studied at Swanley College and married into the well-known Perry family of nurserymen and horticulturalists. Under their influence she wrote her standard work, *Water Gardening*, and soon become an authority on many subjects and the author of many books. She was horticultural adviser to Middlesex County Council for many years, principal of a college for adult education, and followed Vita Sackville-West as garden columnist of the *Observer*. She was awarded the Victoria Medal of Honour in 1971.

SUE PHILLIPS is a qualified horticulturalist who is also an author, journalist and, as a member of the renowned former *Gardener's Question Time* team, a well-known broadcaster. She has co-owned and managed a small nursery.

RUTH PITTER (1897–1992) was a botanist, ornithologist and gardener as well as a poet who published eight volumes of work over half a century. In 1955 she became the first woman to receive the Queen's Gold Medal for poetry. Her five-acre garden was near Aylesbury.

SYLVIA PLATH (1932–1963), poet and novelist, was born in Massachusetts. After her marriage to Ted Hughes she lived for a time in Devon, where bee-keeping provided the basis for some of her most powerful poems. Twelve years after her tragic death, her mother published her *Letters Home*.

ANNE PRATT (1806–1993), botanical author and illustrator, was a self-educated naturalist whose many books combined accuracy with accessibility and gave generations of Victorian children a grounding in botany.

ELEANOUR SINCLAIR ROHDE (1881–1950) was an Oxford history graduate who researched early medieval gardens and re-popularised herb growing. She divided her time between the British Museum and her parents' garden at Reigate where she studied traditional plants and compiled specialist seed lists. She was a prolific writer, and served as president of the Society of Women Journalists.

MIRIAM ROTHSCHILD Hon. (1908–) is a scientist, an FRS who has written many contributions to scientific journals and who is a world authority on fleas. She has made her garden at Ashton Wold a haven for wild-flowers and has had an important influence on wild-flower gardening. Her recreation in Who's Who is listed as 'watching butterflies'.

VITA SACKVILLE-WEST Hon. (1892–1962), poet, novelist and gardener, expressed her feelings about Sissinghurst in her long poem The Garden, but it was her weekly column in the Observer, continued for twenty-five years, which made her a household name amongst gardeners. Though she was a gifted and successful creative writer, her greatest creation is the already legendary garden she made at Sissinghurst.

PAMELA SCHWERDT and SIBYLLE KREUTZBERGER studied and taught at Waterperry Horticultural School before taking charge of the garden at Sissinghurst. They remained there all their working life, thus fulfilling Vita's hopes for the garden.

ANNE SCOTT-JAMES (1913–), was a classical scholar who became a distinguished journalist and editor in the field of current affairs as well as fashion. But her hobby, gardening, has gradually taken over, both in a series of garden articles and in various well-received books, including a history of Sissinghurst. She collaborated with her second husband, Osbert Lancaster, on The Pleasure Garden.

E.J. SCOVELL (1907–) was born in Sheffield and worked as an ecological field assistant with her husband, Charles Elton, in the rain forests of Brazil and Panama. Her first volume of poems was published in 1944, and since then close-up studies of the flowers in her Oxford garden have inspired some of her poems.

LADY SETON (Frances Eveleen) grew up at Miltown Castle, Charville. After World War One she gardened with a 'trench tool' in Kensington, and when her husband, Sir Malcolm Seton, died, she lived in Hampstead where she made a very small garden and wrote her only book.

STEVIE SMITH (1902–1971), poet and novelist, lived for most of her life with her aunt in Palmer's Green, London. Her witty, quasi-naive poems have a devoted following.

CONSTANCE SPRY (1886–1960) revolutionised flower arranging, but for the first half of her life flowers were only a hobby. She was trained as a health lecturer, and became the principal of Homerton and South Hackney Day Continuation School. In 1928, with her second husband's encouragement, she began to arrange flowers professionally, and her fame spread: she opened 'Flower Decorations' in South Audley Street, lectured, demonstrated, wrote books and founded the first flower-arranging school.

NANCY STEEN was a New Zealander who became an authority on old roses before they were fashionable. She began to make a garden in the Aukland suburb of Remuera in 1944, collecting for it roses that she found by the roadside or on wasteland. Her garden became a showpiece and, with her husband, she toured overseas, giving illustrated lectures.

VIOLET STEVENSON grew up in Somerset and after school worked in a nursery, a seedshop and as a florist. She became an internationally renowned flower arranger, as well as horticulturalist, writer and journalist. With her husband, the author Leslie Johns, she created a large garden in the Cotswolds out of a cabbage patch.

MURIEL STUART made her first garden with the help of her little son round a new house on the outskirts of London. The book she wrote about it won high praise and she wrote a second book, *Gardener's Nightcap* (1938). She also published several volumes of poetry.

THOMASINA TARLING ran the garden department at the General Trading Company for fifteen years. She then started the Covent Garden branch of Clifton Nurseries before launching, with a partner, her own firm, Gardening Angels, which specialised in town gardens, roof terraces and awkward spaces. She has made four gardens of her own.

JANE TAYLOR has written twelve gardening books and numerous articles, as well as running her own nursery garden, working for the National Trust at Coleton, Devon, and acting as Deputy Secretary of the NCCPG. She has held various national collections herself.

ALICE B. TOKLAS (1877–1967) was born in San Francisco but spent most of her life in France where, from 1907 onwards, she was Gertrude Stein's friend, companion and secretary. Gertrude Stein wrote her 'autobiography' for her, but her cookbook is her own

MRS DESMOND UNDERWOOD (Pamela) had originally grown carnations for the cut-flower trade, and first took cuttings of silver-leaved plants from her neighbour, Beth Chatto. Her Ramparts Nursery subsequently became famous for its prize-winning displays of pinks surrounded by grey and silver leaves, and she was awarded the Victoria Medal of Honour in 1977.

ROSEMARY VEREY only began gardening when her four children were grown up, but is now one of the leading names in British horticulture, not only because of the garden she has made round Barnsley House, but because of her lectures and her many books.

EDNA WALLING (1896–1973) was born in England but spent all her gardening life in Australia, studying horticulture at Burnley College, and working first as a jobbing gardener. She had an original ecological approach to planting which she explained in her writings, and she became a garden designer much sought-after by the rich and fashionable.

EDITH WHARTON (1862–1937), novelist and short-story writer, was born in New York but spent most of her life in France, where her two gardens, one near Paris and the other on the Riviera, were among the chief joys of her life.

KATHERINE S. WHITE (1892–) worked on the *New Yorker* from its inception in 1925, and was associate editor for thirty-four years. She edited *The Sub-Treasury of American Humour* with her second husband in 1941. Her Maine garden was her hobby: she liked to 'fix flowers'.

LOUISE BEEBE WILDER (1878–1938) spent her childhood in Baltimore, and became one of America's most popular garden writers, as well as an expert on rock gardens and the author of at least eight books which combined autobiography with expertise.

MRS LESLIE WILLIAMS (Margaret) was an enthusiastic amateur gardener in Edwardian England who followed her book on gardens with two books on domestic pets: *The cat, its care and management* (1908), and *Darling dogs* (1912).

ELLEN WILLMOTT (1858–1934) *see* Introduction.

VISCOUNTESS WOLSELEY (Frances) (1872–1936) *see* Introduction.

DOROTHY WORDSWORTH (1771–1855) lived with her brother William all her adult life. Her *Grasmere Journal*, covering the years when they lived and gardened at Dove Cottage, was undertaken to 'give William pleasure', and it seems obvious that he drew on its precise observation before writing his famous poem *Daffodils*.

Author Index

THE VIRAGO BOOK OF
LOVE AND LOSS

Edited by Georgina Hammick

Elizabeth Bowen, Janette Turner Hospital, Doris Lessing, Shena Mackay, Alice Munro, Grace Paley, Dorothy Parker and Sylvia Townsend Warner are among the writers whose considerable talents feature in this memorable exploration of love and loss. Here is the subterfuge and yearning of an illicit relationship, the intolerable oppression of summer in the face of a loved one's death and a mother who obscures her loneliness with irascible complaints to her son. Alongside stories of love's frailties are those shadowed by lost opportunities, lingering regrets and the bruising of age. This seductive collection brings together some of the foremost writers of this century. Whether devastating or poignant, or glistening with wry humour, these stories reach into the corners of the heart.

THE VIRAGO BOOK OF
WOMEN TRAVELLERS

Edited by Mary Morris
with Larry O'Connor

'An excellent collection'
– *Sunday Times*

'A volume in which rich and unexpected seams of
precious minerals await discovery'
– *Guardian*

'From the acerbic wit of Freya Stark to the raw courage
of Dervla Murphy, over three hundred years of the best
and bravest women's travel writing is gathered here in
a collection of stunning journeys we can all take – on
the page and in the imagination'
– *The List*

OF WOMEN AND ANGELS
The Virago Book of Women and Spirituality

Sarah Anderson

This anthology looks at spirituality in its broadest sense and includes extracts from fiction and poetry as well as writings by women known for their search for spiritual fulfilment, women whose inner journeys were often very different from those of men. Crossing all religious boundaries, disciplines and ages, this represents not just Christianity, Judaism, Buddhism, Hinduism, Sufism but also women who do not conform to any mainstream orthodox religion. Some of the writers included are: Simone Well, St Teresa of Avila, Julian of Norwich, Emily Brontë, Iris Murdoch, Lady Mary Herbert, Kathleen Raine, Alice Walker, Hildegard of Bingen, Rabiah Balhki, Emily Dickinson, Nangsa Obum, Virginia Woolf and many more.

THE VIRAGO BOOK OF
WICKED VERSE

Edited by Jill Dawson

This wonderfully sharp and witty collection of poems feisty,
bawdy, erotic, irreverent, is an illuminating comment on
women's ability to transform poetry into a medium of
subersiveness. There are jibes at hypocrisy and prejudice,
plenty of sexiness and sauciness, and a riotous turning of the
'Lady Poet' image on its head. With poets spanning continents
and centuries, this anthology demonstrates lavishly the myriad
ways in which women can be 'wicked' by their definition
and wilfully so!

**Poems by: Aphra Behn, Wendy Cope, Emily Dickinson,
Carol Ann Duffy, Suniti Namjoshi, Grace Nichols,
Vicki Raymond, Ntozake Shange, Izumi Shikibu,
Anna Wickham and many more**

THE VIRAGO/OXFAM DIARY 1996: WOMEN AND LAND

Edited by Troth Wells

'In the 1950s Miss Nora Johnston of Manor Farm, Surrey, started a milking programme "Music while you Milk" with the aid of a portable instrument of her own design, in an effort to prove that happy cows produce more.' From the humorous to the serious, the first Virago diary is packed full of interesting facts and poetry centred around women and the land, accompanied by stunning black and white photographs. The stylish 1996 Diary features women and the land from land girls in the Second World War to canal builders in India, from Gertrude Jekyll to milkmaids in Croatia. A percentage of the proceeds of every copy sold goes to Oxfam.

Books by post:

☐	The Virago Book of Love and Loss	Georgina Hammick (ed)	£6.99
☐	The Virago Book of Women Travellers	Mary Morris (ed)	£8.99
☐	The Virago Book of Love Poetry	Wendy Mulford (ed)	£7.99
☐	Virago/Oxfam Diary: Women and Land	Troth Wells (ed)	£6.99

Virago now offers an exciting range of quality titles by both established and new authors which can be ordered from the following address:

Little, Brown and Company (UK),
P.O. Box 11,
Falmouth,
Cornwall TR10 9EN.

Alternatively you may fax your order to the above address.
Fax No. 01326 317444.

Payments can be made as follows: cheque, postal order (payable to Little, Brown and Company) or by credit cards, Visa/Access. Do not send cash or currency. UK customers and B.F.P.O. please allow £1.00 for postage and packing for the first book, plus 50p for the second book, plus 30p for each additional book up to a maximum charge of £3.00 (7 books plus).

Overseas customers including Ireland, please allow £2.00 for the first book plus £1.00 for the second book, plus 50p for each additional book.

NAME (Block Letters) ....

....

ADDRESS ....

....

....

☐ I enclose my remittance for ....

☐ I wish to pay by Access/Visa Card

Number ☐☐☐☐☐☐☐☐☐☐☐☐☐☐☐☐

Card Expiry Date ☐☐☐☐